Praise for the author's previous book
The Five Dharma Types

"The author demonstrates a deep understanding of his subject. He writes clearly and eloquently, offering a spiritually inspired, and ultimately practical, guidebook for personal fulfillment."

PUBLISHERS WEEKLY

". . . this book is enthralling and should appeal to many students of Vedic tradition and yoga."

LIBRARY JOURNAL

"Simon Chokoisky's *The Five Dharma Types* is a beautiful book. Reading it carefully will give you insight into your dharma and help you heal your life."

DR. VASANT LAD, AUTHOR OF
AYURVEDA: THE SCIENCE OF SELF-HEALING AND
FOUNDER OF THE AYURVEDIC INSTITUTE

"This work has opened doors of insight and perception, allowing me to see our species in a fresh and hopeful light. I hope people will read this book more than once, and slowly."

ROBIN GILE, COAUTHOR OF
THE COMPLETE IDIOT'S GUIDE TO PALMISTRY

Gambler's Dharma

SPORTS BETTING
WITH
VEDIC ASTROLOGY

SIMON CHOKOISKY

Destiny Books
Rochester, Vermont • Toronto, Canada

Destiny Books
One Park Street
Rochester, Vermont 05767
www.DestinyBooks.com

Destiny Books is a division of Inner Traditions International

Library of Congress Cataloging-in-Publication Data
Names: Chokoisky, Simon, author.
Title: Gambler's Dharma : sports betting with Vedic astrology / Simon Chokoisky.
Description: Rochester, Vermont : Destiny Books, 2017. | Includes index.
Identifiers: LCCN 2016041348 (print) |
    ISBN 9781620555651 (pbk.) | ISBN 9781620555668 (e-book)
Subjects: LCSH: Hindu astrology. | Sports betting—Miscellanea.
Classification: LCC BF1714.H5 C525 2017 |
    DDC 133.5/9445—dc23
LC record available at https://lccn.loc.gov/2016041348

Printed and bound in the United States by P.A. Hutchison Company

10 9 8 7 6 5 4 3 2 1

Vedic astrology charts were created using Parashara's Light (Vedic Astrology Software), used with permission from GeoVision Software, Inc., P.O. Box 2152, Fairfield, Iowa, 52556, www.parashara.com

Text design and layout by Virginia Scott Bowman
This book was typeset in Garamond Premier Pro, Gill Sans, and Myriad Pro with Parma Petit, Garamond Premier Pro, and Gill Sans used as display typefaces

Cover image courtesy of IngImage

To send correspondence to the author of this book, mail a first-class letter to the author c/o Inner Traditions • Bear & Company, One Park Street, Rochester, VT 05767, and we will forward the communication, or contact the author directly at **spirittype.com**.

For Mantriji

Contents

Acknowledgments

Deepest gratitude to my first Jyotisha teacher, Hart de Fouw, a modern *rishi* in the true sense of that word.

Wonder and gratitude to Mantriji, who pushed, prodded, and propelled me to write a book on Jyotisha. This probably isn't what you expected; I hope you like it nonetheless.

Thanks to all the Vedic astrologers who wittingly or not advanced my knowledge of the science: to Charlotte Benson, my first counselor and astrologer, a cynosure who showed me what was possible; and to Christina Collins, who inspired chapter 7.

Thanks to my mom for supporting this Educator/Outsider's dream, without needing to understand it.

Finally, thanks to my wife, Ventzi, who, despite knowing that books on Vedic astrology don't sell like Harry Potter, still supported me, knowing perhaps that in Jyotisha, and the Vedic vidya of which it is part, is the real living magic.

Preface

*It doesn't matter how beautiful your theory is, it doesn't matter
how smart you are. If it doesn't agree with experiment, it's wrong.*
RICHARD P. FEYNMAN

This is the most expensive book I have ever written.

Don't get me wrong, every author puts in time and energy, agonizing over jots and tittles, colons and semicolons, in order to satisfy editors and make their books fit for public consumption. But above and beyond the rigors of writing, the book you are now holding cost me tens of thousands of dollars to produce because its principles were fired and tested by yours truly in the real-life world of sports betting.* This is for two reasons: first, to prove that predictions about a given event were done *before the fact,* not in hindsight, which is always a few rows lower on the eye chart than foresight; and second, to demonstrate that Jyotisha—a.k.a. Vedic astrology—can deliver real-world results in the most mundane of arenas. Sports betting, or as some prefer to call it, sports investing, offers black and white outcomes. If statements like "You are a generous, nice, and spiritual person, that will be $150, please" are the kind of astrology you're used to, this book may be a shock to your system.

By using only the beginner's techniques included in chapter 3, I turned $75 into over $24,000 in just over a month, though admittedly I had grace and beginner's luck on my side, the importance of which is examined here as well. So, why was this book so expensive if I won so much money? Because I

---

*Documentation of the author's results can be found online at www.spirittype.com
/winnings.

also spent it testing new techniques and theories—sometimes with disastrous results. In the final analysis, however, I am grateful to say that I remain "in the black," and that during my foray into the gambler's dharma I made far more than I lost, and all because of Vedic astrology and its arsenal of predictive techniques.

The truth is, I'm not a great astrologer. I know precious little about predicting earthquakes or forecasting elections. Though I can read and write Sanskrit and the Devanagari script, I'm too lazy to study the classics. Because of this I've had to tweak what I know to make it work in the field of sports investing, or invent techniques to fill in what's missing.

I've done my best to write this book to make it accessible for both novices and more advanced astrologers, with simpler ideas at the beginning, progressing to more advanced techniques later on. Astrology takes lifetimes to master, but that shouldn't deter beginners from studying. If it didn't offer sweet results even to neophytes, astrology would have become extinct long ago. In fact, sometimes all you need to pick a winner is a name chart and a good ephemeris, as we'll learn later.

Note that the techniques in this book are designed for one-on-one competitions between teams or individuals. This covers soccer, football, baseball, boxing, basketball, cricket, rugby, martial arts, and the spitting contest between you and your neighbor's kid (as long as one of you is the favorite). It does *not* cover events with multiple contestants, such as horse racing, sailing, or golf.

Another requirement is an exact start time for the event in question. Everything that is born, that has a life span and an ending, is a space-time event. This includes contests as well as human beings. And just as your natal chart describes your success or failure in life, so can a contest horoscope show the success or failure of a team as measured by victory, defeat, or draw.

My ultimate aim in writing this book is to show that by mastering some or all of these techniques, you may eventually translate them into other areas of life, such as natal and horary astrology. After all, sport is a proving ground for new techniques, and the real race is beyond its enclosures. Therefore, throughout this book I occasionally suggest ways to use the vehicles provided here to navigate in other realms, hopefully furthering their utility to humankind.

Finally, whether you are a seasoned astrologer or a newbie, you may have a learning curve when it comes to understanding the shorthand of sports handicapping, the lingo of underdogs and favorites, and how to understand who's who and what's what. But don't fret—all is explained in the coming chapters.

Jyotish or Jyotisha?
The Original Vedic Astrology

Okay, what's the deal? Some write it one way, others the other. Which is it? More importantly, *what* is it?

The Sanskrit word *Jyotisha* can be translated as "lord of light" (referring to the astrologers and the planets themselves), "lore of light" (referring to the science), and "light on life" (referring to the process of applying the science to the world). It includes the study of astronomy, astrology, and the science of timekeeping. In modern Hindi, a language that likes to curtail the final *a* in such words, it becomes *Jyotish,* much as the name Rama becomes simply Ram. Easy, right? Not so easy, then, is what we call an astrologer. In Sanskrit there are many ways to name an astrologer, which bears on astrology's importance in Indian (Vedic) society. Some of these are:

> *Daivajna,* a knower of fate and the divine
>
> *Kalajna,* a knower of time
>
> *Samvatsara,* the compiler of the year, or almanac maker
>
> *Nakshatra suchaka,* messenger of the stars
>
> *Jyotisha, Jyotishi,* a lord of light, or one who understands the lords of light
>   (yes, that word means both *astrologer* and *astrology**

But for now we'll stick to simple English whenever possible. You can refer to the glossary at the back of this book to familiarize yourself with the Sanskrit terminology involved in chart readings.

---

*You may have noticed that all of these are masculine nouns. What, then, do we call female astrologers? If you want to use Sanskrit terms, you would make the last *a* sound in *daivajna* or *kalajna* long. As a Sanskrit joke goes, what stands between a man and a woman is often the length of a vowel. Alternately, you may use the more specific term *jyotishini.*

This book represents the culmination of two years of research, over the course of which I was blessed to meet astrologers who generously shared their insights. I also met those who, for whatever reason, refused to share the techniques they used. This attitude of holding on to secrets, uncommonly common among astrologers, ultimately diminishes the Jyotisha tradition and the astrologers who practice it, because as stewards of a royal science we have an obligation not only to advance our own understanding but, by putting forth our research, to promote the science itself.

It is not specific techniques but one's skill and insight that make an astrologer special. During the twentieth century some of the finest researchers were also the greatest teachers of Jyotisha; Dr. B. V. Raman, K. S. Krishnamurti, and Sheshadri Iyer not only developed new techniques of prediction, they wrote books to share their knowledge. Rather than being diminished by this, they grew in stature, by pumping the next generation of astrologers with the fuel needed to take the vehicle of Vedic astrology higher.

One hundred years ago astrologers had never heard of terms like *sublords* and *ruling planets;* we have K. S. Krishnamurti to thank for bringing these to light. *Yogis* and *avayogis,* terms now commonly used in modern Jyotisha, were little known outside of southern India before Sheshadri Iyer came along to elucidate them. New techniques constantly refresh the Jyotisha tradition and enliven discussion, though, again, it is not techniques that make an astrologer great, but rather the skill and insight that he or she has developed to *use* the available techniques.

I have seen masters read horoscopes from the back of napkins and make astounding predictions. I have also seen less skilled astrologers—myself among them—wrapped up in reams of data and printouts still fail to predict their way out of a bag. In the same way there are doctors who, despite the best technology and drugs, fail to accurately diagnose and treat disease, while others, using only a person's pulse and a few herbs, are able to create wholeness and healing for their patients.

Jyotisha is a living, breathing tradition. It takes rigorous study, self-sacrifice, and spiritual cultivation to become worthy of having it live inside you. It also takes generosity—the generosity of passing on to the next generation the fruits of your dedication. The following, then, is my attempt to add a drop of lore into the ocean that others have filled with rivers of their wisdom.

Author's Note

Note on calculations: I use the Rahu/Ketu mean node in all charts, though there is room for research and discussion here, as there is in much of astrology's rich menu of techniques.

Caution: This book should not be construed as an endorsement of gambling, which is illegal throughout most of the world, potentially addictive, and spiritually and psychologically difficult to digest. The techniques in this book were tested in part with sports wagering in order to prove their usefulness in this and other applications, such as planning a trip or a marriage. Please use discretion when applying them and understand that no technique works 100 percent of the time.

1

A Gambler's Dharma

The ABCs of Reading a Vedic Chart

*D*harma means "the right path" or "your rightful purpose." A gambler's dharma, narrowly defined, can mean that for a period of time—a month, a year, or even a lifetime—a person's rightful purpose involves speculation. This is a rare and often dangerous path reserved for a few. A wider definition, however, tells us that anyone who risks something to be themselves, to share their purpose with the world, is a type of gambler. Anyone who carves out new roads, sometimes butting up against painful dead ends, sometimes clearing the way to an undiscovered country, gambles with their comfort, livelihood, or reputation. But a person driven by purpose will go to the ends of the earth to share it. It is astrology's job to help people find their purpose.

> A snapshot of the heavens at the moment a baby is born, a question is asked, or a match is played can reveal how that life, question, or competition will play out.

To do this, astrology uses a map of the sky drawn for a particular space-time event to judge its potential. A snapshot of the heavens at the moment a baby is born, a question is asked, or a match is played can reveal how that life, question, or competition will play out. Every birth conceals the fruit of its life, every question contains the seed of its answer, every battle's outcome is known from the moment of its inception. This is the core precept of astrology as I understand it.

This space-time map is commonly represented in Western astrology by a circle, as seen in the chart on page 2.

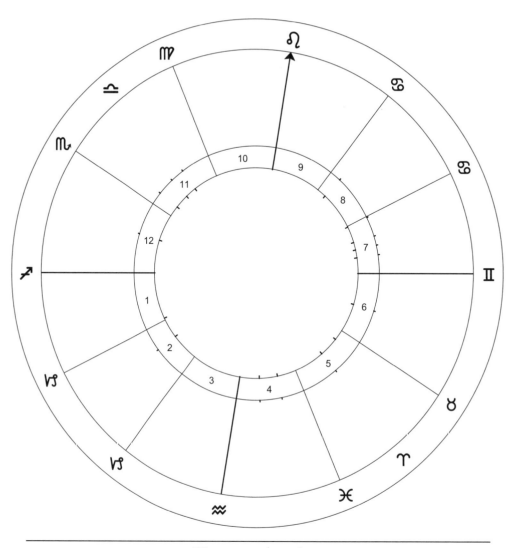

Western astrology chart

Vedic astrology, on the other hand, employs the square charts found throughout this book. While the Western depiction is perhaps a closer representation of the heavens, there are a number of reasons why we opt for the square shape in Vedic astrology.

Vedic astrology is a *vidya*—an inspired, living body of knowledge that is part of a family of vidyas that includes ayurveda, vastu shastra, tantra, mantra, and others that comprise the Vedic lineage. In depicting the sky as a square, Jyotisha perhaps borrows from its sister science vastu shastra, which says that square shapes are inherently more stable than their curvilinear counterparts. In vastu shastra, squares and rectangles indicate stability and durability, humankind's way of carving out a piece of permanence in an impermanent world, while curvilinear shapes connote movement, restlessness, and change, depicting nature herself unfettered by human touch. You can verify this yourself the next time you're in an airplane: the square shapes you spot from high above indicate human dwelling and cultivation sites, while nature is inherently curvy. That is also why settled human civilizations tend to favor squarish plots and dwellings, while nomadic tribes prefer to live in circular enclosures like yurts and teepees, which mirror the evanescent and ever-changing flow of nature. So if you want stability and permanence, it's hip to be square. If you want never-ending change and excitement, prefer the circle.

The square's affinity to permanency and order is perhaps why Vedic astrology appears to some as more fated and predictive, while Western astrology's circle is more psychological. The predictive tendency of Vedic astrology is evidenced in this book, where we attempt to fix the outcome of an event before it has even begun.

We will use two variants of the square chart—the North (below) and South (page 5) Indian variants.

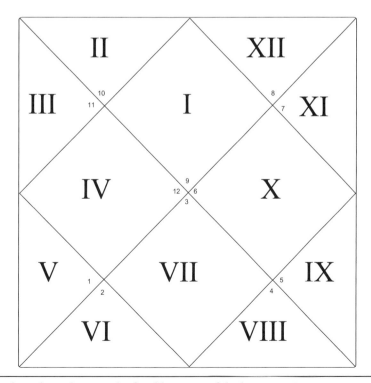

North Indian chart showing the fixed location of the houses in Roman numerals. Note that the Arabic numerals represent the signs, which change position from chart to chart.

In the North Indian chart, the houses are represented by Roman numerals. (These Roman numerals are for explanatory purposes only and are not included in horoscope depictions in this book; it's assumed that you already know the houses before looking at the charts.) These houses are fixed, meaning that the rhomboid represented by Roman numeral I is always the 1st house, while VII is always the 7th house. The remaining houses are numbered accordingly. What changes in this type of chart is the signs. These are indicated by the tiny Arabic numerals as follows:

1 = Aries
2 = Taurus
3 = Gemini
4 = Cancer
5 = Leo
6 = Virgo
7 = Libra
8 = Scorpio
9 = Sagittarius
10 = Capricorn
11 = Aquarius
12 = Pisces

Thus in North Indian charts, the first house remains fixed, while the *sign* on the first house varies, from 1 (Aries) to 12 (Pisces), depending upon the time, date, and place of an event.

The opposite is true in the South Indian chart, wherein the *signs* remain fixed while the houses change. Thus the square that indicates Ari (Aries) is always Aries, while its adjacent squares are Pisces (to the left) and Taurus (to the right). The ascendant (or lagna, or 1st house) is indicated by Asc. The houses proceed in clockwise order from the ascendant (though again, these are not usually marked; it's assumed that once you know the ascendant, you can count out the houses successively). I've added the houses in the chart on page 5 so you can follow.

Both the North Indian chart on page 3 and the South Indian chart on page 5 indicate a Sagittarius ascendant. Both formats require some practice to get used to. In fact, it is not uncommon for astrologers with expertise in one chart style to have trouble reading the other. In this book, both the North and the South formats are

(IV) Pis	(V) Ari	(VI) Tau	(VII) Gem
(III) Aqu			(VIII) Can
(II) Cap			(IX) Leo
(I) *Asc* Sag	(XII) Sco	(XI) Libr	(X) Virg

South Indian chart with "Asc" representing the ascendant (or lagna, or 1st house), which changes from chart to chart. Here the houses are shown by Roman numerals moving clockwise from "Asc."

depicted. Depending on where you learn Vedic astrology (and from whom), you will likely favor one or the other.

The Houses

Each house, called a *bhava* in Sanskrit, depicts a part of the human experience. Here is a summary of those house meanings:

> House 1: self/body
> House 2: sustenance
> House 3: effort
> House 4: home/mother/education

House 5: children
House 6: service/strife
House 7: partnership
House 8: death
House 9: father/grace
House 10: profession
House 11: easy money
House 12: loss

These meanings are shared across both Western and Vedic astrology. Of course, there are more detailed significations for each house. In fact, anything and everything that exists has to be represented by one or more of the twelve bhavas: toenail fungus, particle physics, and great-grandmothers all have their houses, while other matters may span multiple bhavas. Consider the liver, one of the body's largest organs, which takes up both the 5th and 6th houses. Consider also victory and defeat, which we examine in this book. One of the basic tenets of Vedic astrology states that houses 3, 6, 10, and 11, called *upachaya bhavas,* or "houses of accumulation," tend to bring victory over enemies when occupied by malefic planets.

Malefic and Benefic Planets

Planet	Malefic/Benefic
Sun	Malefic
Moon	Benefic
Mars	Malefic
Rahu	Malefic
Jupiter	Benefic
Saturn	Malefic
Mercury	Benefic
Ketu	Malefic
Venus	Benefic

Which are the malefic planets? Consider Saturn, Mars, Rahu, Ketu, and the Sun malefic for our purposes. What are Rahu and Ketu? These are not actual celestial bodies but rather mathematical points that indicate where eclipses occur; in English they are called the north (Rahu) and south (Ketu) nodes of the moon. Vedic astrology uses the term *graha,* Sanskrit for "grabber," to indicate the various celestial players that act in a horoscope and in our shared human dramas. The Greeks used the term *planetes,* meaning "wanderer," in a similar way. Therefore, etymologically and in this book, a planet may refer to any of the sky wanderers shaping our experience, be they a star, the Moon, a dwarf planet, an asteroid, a shadow planet, or some other celestial influencer.

If this is confusing, it's probably best to put this book down for a bit and first take a primer course in Vedic astrology. There are plenty of good resources on the subject.* If, on the other hand, this all sounds reasonable to you, then by all means let us proceed to learn the art and science of contest prediction and its financial cohort, sports betting, sometimes called *sports investing* or even *sports whispering,* depending on the crowd you walk with.

Basic Terminology Used in This Book

Ayanamsha: Ayanamsha refers to the offset between the sidereal and the tropical zodiacs. The sidereal zodiac refers to the actual constellations in the sky (*sidereal* means "relating to the stars") and is primarily used by Vedic astrologers. The tropical zodiac was adopted during the Hellenistic period and refers to the seasons and not to the constellations. It is primarily used by Western astrologers. The offset between these is currently 24 degrees. This means that if you are a Scorpio Sun sign in Western astrology, your Sun would be 24 degrees back in Vedic astrology and most likely fall in the constellation of Libra.

There are several offsets, or ayanamshas, used by Vedic astrologers. In this book I use the Krishnamurti ayanamsha (developed by twentieth-century astrologer K. S. Krishnamurti), as it is key to the sublord technique described in chapter 6. For the remaining charts and techniques, the Lahiri ayanamsha, which is standard across most of Jyotisha, works just fine.

Cusp: A cusp is a juncture between one house, or bhava, and another. Like the property line that separates your house from your neighbor's, a cusp defines and separates two separate plots in space as well as the meanings that go with them. House cusps are indicated in degrees and minutes. A cusp at 9°23' means that

---

*Hart de Fouw and Robert Svoboda's *Light on Life,* and James Kelleher's *Path of Light,* vols. 1 and 2, are excellent texts for both beginners and advanced Jyotishis alike.

9 degrees and 23 minutes of arc (out of the 30 degrees possible for any given sign) is the demarcation point between one house and another. (Note that in the charts throughout this book this is noted as degrees:minutes or degrees:minutes:seconds, i.e. 25:53 or 08:45:52, as this is the chosen notation of the astrology software used in this book.)

The most important cusps in astrology are the 1st, 10th, 7th, and 4th. The 1st house cusp indicates the exact degree and minute position of the the *lagna,* or ascendant. Planets on one side of this are visible in the sky; on the other side they lie below the horizon and are thus invisible.

Opposite the ascendant, exactly 180 degrees away, is the 7th house cusp, also called the descendant. These two, the ascendant and the descendant, are the most important points in the horoscope, especially for contest prediction, as they represent the favorite (the ascendant) and underdog (the descendant) teams.

> **These two, the ascendant and the descendant, are the most important points in the horoscope, especially for contest prediction, as they represent the favorite (the ascendant) and underdog (the descendant) teams.**

Lagna: From the Sanskrit root *lag,* which means "to tie down," the lagna refers to the sign rising on the eastern horizon at the time and place an event occurs (it is also called the rising sign or ascendant). Such an event may be a person's birth or the start of a ballgame.

Lord: The lord refers to the planetary ruler of a sign or house. Suppose Taurus was the ascendant (or rising sign, 1st house cusp, or lagna). Since Venus rules Taurus, Venus by extension becomes the lord of the 1st house. In this example, Mars would therefore rule the 7th house, since Taurus and Scorpio are opposite each other, and Scorpio is ruled by Mars.

LT: Local time refers to the time given for a match at the location where it is played. Thus 19:07:45 LT means 7 minutes, 45 seconds past 7 p.m. clock time.

Nakshatra: Unique to Vedic astrology, nakshatras are asterisms—small constellations—that predate the twelve commonly known signs of the zodiac. Originally numbering twenty-eight, there are currently twenty-seven nakshatras used in Vedic astrology, each with specific marker stars (see *tara,* below).

Navamsha: A harmonic division of the main chart, or *rashi,* the navamsha, or "ninth division," divides each sign into nine equal segments according to a specific scheme, thus totaling 108 navamshas over the entire twelve signs of the zodiac.

Orb: This refers to the degrees on either side of a cusp within which a planet exerts influence. For contest prediction we use a 2°30' orb, as explained in the chapters that follow. For example, if the lagna degree is 15, and a planet is at 16°39' it falls within the 2°30' orb of that cusp, thereby influencing it for good or ill, according to that planet's nature.

Rashi: From the Sanskrit word for "heap," *rashi* is usually translated as "sign" in English, though it is more accurately the collection of meanings attributed to a sign. Secondarily, the term *rashi* refers to the main horoscope, as distinguished from the navamsha, the harmonic ninth-division chart.

Sublord: Specific to Krishnamurti Paddhati (Krishnamurti's method), the sublord, frequently shortened to *sub,* refers to the planet ruling the nakshatra subdivision of a particular cusp or planet.

Tara: A yogatara, or tara for short, is a marker star of a nakshatra. For example, Spica is the yogatara of Chitra nakshatra.

Abbreviations of Planets

In the charts in this book the planets are abbreviated as follows:

Ce: Ceres	Ch: Chiron	Gk: Gulika	Ke: Ketu
Ju: Jupiter	Ma: Mars	Me: Mercury	Mo: Moon
Ne: Neptune	Pl: Pluto	Ra: Rahu	Sa: Saturn
Su: Sun	Uk: Upaketu	Ur: Uranus	Ve: Venus

R: Retrograde planets (*grahas*) receive an *R* next to their names—i.e., CeR = Ceres retrograde.

2

Dharmo Rakshati

The Dharma and Grace of Prediction

Dharma eva hato hanti / Dharmo rakshati rakshitah
(Dharma harms when harmed / Dharma protects when protected)
From the Mahabharata

Science cannot solve the ultimate mystery of nature. And that
is because, in the last analysis, we ourselves are . . . part of the
mystery we are trying to solve.
Max Planck

As introduced in the epigraph above, this chapter is about encouraging dharma to play nice.

In the words of my Jyotisha mentor, "An astrologer's job is to put themselves out of business," meaning that when done well, astrology helps us understand ourselves so thoroughly that we no longer need guidance from an astrologer. Similarly, it is a doctor's job to seed durable health and teach their patients self-care so they don't need to see the doctor again. This is called *dharma,* and spreading dharma is the goal of any Vedic science.

In ancient India, various traditions evolved to help us find our dharma, the natural law of our being, by following which we minimize undesirable karma (pain and suffering) while optimizing harmonious life experience. Ayurveda helps us align with the dharma of the body; vastu shastra, the traditional Indian science of architecture, sheds light on our relationship to our surroundings; the dharma types guide us to our life's true purpose; yoga, tantra, and Vedanta align us with our spiritual essence; and Jyotisha, or Vedic astrology, "the eye of the Veda," helps us make sense of the cosmos and how we relate to it. Knowing Vedanta won't heal your toenail fungus; knowing ayurveda won't directly teach you how to become enlightened. Each applies to a specific level of dharma, and as the saying goes, it's important to keep your cooks, spouse, king, gods, and planets happy. Honor the five levels of dharma, and life will run more smoothly. Or, if you're married, just keep your spouse happy and hope for the best.

> In ancient India, various traditions evolved to help us find our dharma, the natural law of our being, by following which we minimize undesirable karma (pain and suffering) while optimizing harmonious life experience.

TABLE 2.1. THE FIVE LEVELS OF DHARMA AND THEIR ACCOMPANYING SCIENCES

LEVEL OF DHARMA	SCIENCE	AREA(S) AFFECTED
Physical	Ayurveda	From the skin in: how to care for and relate to your **body**
Environmental	Vastu shastra	From your skin to the limit of your environment, and ultimately the skin of the planet, the atmosphere: how to care for and relate to your **physical environment**
Social	Dharma types	Nonphysical environment: how to care for and relate to your **society**
Spiritual	Yoga, Vedanta, tantra, and other spiritual disciplines	Ethics and morals, nonphysical local environment: how to care for and relate to your **spiritual self**
Cosmic	Jyotisha	Outer space, from the skin of the planet outward: how to understand your karma and relate to the **planets, stars, and cosmos**

It has been my experience that the techniques in this book work, but whether they work in the crucible of your own experience depends on, among other things, how well you are living your dharma and whether or not that dharma is aligned for speculation. Having a bad day? Not following your purpose? If your stars are mis-aligned for accurate predictions, then the system you use, no matter how powerful, will produce limited success. This has been my own experience, for as my dharma type, the Educator, indicates, it was not in my dharma to entertain speculation over the long term.

In the minds of our forebears, science was both objective and subjective, and the scientist was always considered part of the experiment, influencing its outcome by his or her presence and intention. This idea is not foreign to modern science, as witnessed by the current reproducibility problem, which occurs when one group of scientists tries to reproduce the results obtained by another:

> The gold standard for science is reproducibility. Ideally, research results are only worthy of attention, publication, and citation if independent researchers can replicate them using a particular study's techniques and materials. But for much of the scientific literature, results aren't reproducible at all.[*]

> Replication is essential to science because it validates key discoveries and helps scientists make progress in their fields of research. But it turns out many study findings are nearly impossible to emulate.[†]

> In studying complex entities, especially animals and human beings, the complexity of the system and of the techniques can all too easily lead to results that seem robust in the lab, and valid to editors and referees of journals, but which do not stand the test of further studies.[‡]

Astrology suffers from the same reproducibility issues. Though astrological techniques abound, no one technique has yet solved the problem of how to read a horoscope. Books on astrology, like those on diet, offer contrary views. Have you ever wondered why diet books constantly top bestseller lists? After all, if one way of eating worked, shouldn't that be *it,* the Holy Grail of diets? When human beings are involved the answer is that it's not that simple—some diets work for some people and not for others; similarly, some Vedic astrology

---

[*]"Science's Reproducibility Problem," www.the-scientist.com/?articles.view/articleNo/33719 /title /Science-s-Reproducibility-Problem/.

[†]"Science's Reproducibility Problem: 100 Psych Studies Were Tested and Only Half Held Up," www.newsweek.com/reproducibility-science-psychology-studies-366744.

[‡]"Challenges in Irreproducible Research," www.nature.com/news/reproducibility-1.17552. For more on the reproducibility problem, see "Putting Scientific Research to the Test," www .sciencefriday.com/segment/08/28/2015/putting-scientific-research-to-the-test.html.

techniques seem to work for their proponents, but not so much when others try to use them. What's more, they may be effective sometimes and not other times, just like diet. Salad and rice cakes might be great in the summer, but try eating them exclusively in the winter and you've got a recipe for disaster. Why? Ask your ayurvedic physician, but it all boils down to this: Everything in nature has a dharma. Live with dharma and you will thrive; fail to do so and you will suffer. Consider cheese-making...

The Dharma Types

Did you know that up to 60 percent of bacteria in high-quality cheese comes from the environment, and, specifically, the cheese-maker's hands?* What's more, if he or she is upset or sick, the totality of bugs living on the person's inner and outer skin, called the *microbiome,* will be off—that is, the cheese-maker will have more bad bugs and less good bugs in his or her gut (inner skin) and on his or her hands (outer skin), thereby affecting the quality of the cheese. Sound crazy? Maybe. But it's supported by centuries of cheese-maker and food-preparer know-how. Cook when you're sad, and everyone at the table will cry with you. Do it when you're frisky, and, well, you get the picture. Similarly, when living your dharma, you affect the environment in a more harmonious way than when you live against it. How do you know your dharma? It helps to know your dharma type.†

The Charaka Samhita, a seminal ayurvedic text, suggests that ayurveda be practiced in distinct ways by each of the four castes. This is in line with the Bhagavad Gita and other treatises on dharma that outline different livelihoods for each caste. I have adapted this to our five dharma types and their practice of astrology below. In case you're not familiar with what a dharma type is, consider it your operating system, the software of your soul, which allows you to hook directly into your purpose on this planet. Unlike the castes, which corrupt the essence of these archetypes, your dharma type is neither hereditary nor hierarchical. No one type

---

*"How to Make Cheese Using the Microbes on Your Feet," www.dailydot.com/geek/foot-bacteria-cheese-project/; and "A Yummy Cheese-y Love Story," http://lifespa.com/a-yummy-cheese-y-love-story/.
†In my book *The 5 Dharma Types: Vedic Wisdom for Discovering Your Purpose and Destiny,* I go into detail about the dharma types and their duties.

is better than another, though they all have unique gifts to share. In the context of Vedic astrology, the following are the types and their gifts:

Educators should use Vedic astrology to give spiritual and worldly counsel, for teaching, and for furthering research and human wisdom. It is not to be practiced for money, whenever possible, though charity is accepted. Philosophy, counsel, and education are their specialties.

Warriors should use Vedic astrology to solve problems and offer solutions to people in crisis, but they too should not do it exclusively for the money. Reward is a side effect of their practice, and medical, legal, and mundane (political) subjects are their specialty.

Merchants should use Vedic astrology to help others become prosperous and successful. In the process, they should make money and devote a portion of their income to charity (see chapter 9, "The Spiritual Side of Betting," for more on this). Remedial measures, rituals, relationships, and financial astrology are their specialties, as is *muhurta,* or electional astrology, which concerns itself with finding the most prosperous time to start a business or a marriage, since this often involves promoting the prosperity of a given situation.

Laborers should use Vedic astrology as a form of devotion and service. They can help others with health and family problems, and they can accept money. Children, health, veterinary, and mundane astrology are some of their specialties.

Outsiders* can practice any form or branch of the science and are often best at blending different systems into something new. The Outsider's dharma is innovation; accordingly, Outsiders often mix disparate techniques to create their own methods.

To find your dharma type and life cycle, take the simple test at www.spirittype.com. As far as money is concerned, suffice it to say that certain dharma types have

---

*Though never designating a fifth caste, the standard Indian caste system nevertheless makes ample reference to "outsiders" and "untouchables," effectively naming a fifth dharma type. One of the names for these outsiders is *mleccha,* coming from the root *mlich,* which means "to mumble," and it refers specifically to anyone who does not speak Sanskrit. By that definition, we are all Outsiders.

prohibitions on working exclusively for money, while others are allowed to frolic in it since it is part of their purpose—their dharma—to do so. Since this book deals with winning and investment, let's take a look at each dharma type's relationship to money and speculation.

TABLE 2.2. DHARMA TYPES AND THEIR RELATIONSHIP TO MONEY

DHARMA TYPE	RELATIONSHIP TO MONEY	RELATIONSHIP TO SPECULATION
Educators	Money is a side effect of giving your talents to society and should not be the primary aim of work	Educators think they can outsmart the system
Warriors		Warriors see the system as a challenge to be mastered
Merchants	Money is a valid reason to work, as it is a tool to help you share your dharma with the world	Naturally luckier than other types, Merchants understand gaming and risk, and how to leverage money
Laborers		Laborers have an aversion to gambling and investment as it is not "real" work; when they invest, they take a long view to prosperity
Outsiders	Since Outsiders often "play" another type, this depends on the type they are emulating	Since Outsiders often "play" another type, this depends on the type they are emulating

Whether in markets or in sports investing, Educators think they can outsmart the system by using data, forecasts, and planning. What they're missing is that working for money without a commensurate contribution to society, by teaching and enlightening others, goes against their dharma, and going against your dharma is the *dumbest* thing you can do because in the end nature always makes you pay. For my part, as an Educator I was blessed to witness the effects of these techniques and get the hint from nature when it was time to move on from betting. Well, okay, it took a *lot* of hints. Whatever the life cycle or personal situation, gambling is never a good long-term strategy for Educators.

> **Going against your dharma is the *dumbest* thing you can do because in the end nature always makes you pay.**

Warriors think they can beat the system with their problem-solving ability and sheer force of determination. This may work in the short term, but the long-term attrition of the money game usually wears them down and ultimately breaks their will and focus. The United States didn't win the Cold War with weapons, they did it with money. As a Merchant country, the United States spent rather than shot its way past the Warrior Soviets, driving them to essentially surrender—something the Romans, another Merchant empire, were also masterful at doing. Though the Romans lost many battles, they won the wars. Gambling is a Merchant game; for their long-term sanity, Warriors should stay away.

Gambling is ideally suited to Merchant types because they understand how money works better than anyone. However, they need to be careful not to hoard wealth. Much better for their health and sanity is mobilizing their winnings to give opportunities to others, by financing, sheltering, clothing, educating, and otherwise empowering people to help themselves. Charity is the Merchant's antidote to loneliness and despair. They must use it, and often.

> **Gambling is ideally suited to Merchant types because they understand how money works better than anyone.**

Laborers don't mind working for money as long as they are providing a service to earn it. Their investment strategy for that money is long term, and they do better betting less frequently on sure bets, games, or investments they're certain they can win. Laborers have the best gut instincts of any dharma type because their intelligence relates to the enteric nervous system, which lets them viscerally *feel* when a team is going to win or lose, without necessarily being able to explain why.

Outsiders, whose dharma is to innovate and rebel, don't mind bending the rules to make money in new and unusual ways. But because they are also chameleons, their attitudes toward money may range from extremely conservative to utterly liberal, depending on the type they are emulating—that is, whether they're playing an Educator, Laborer, Warrior, or Merchant.

Baseball in America

"I had a friend who was a big baseball player / back in high school / He could throw that speedball by you / make you look like a fool boy!"

These, the opening lyrics of Bruce Springsteen's "Glory Days," are appropriated here to illustrate the role baseball plays at the heart of the American ethic. In my book *The 5 Dharma Types*, I review the dharma type of each sport and find that American football is for Warriors, European football is a Merchant game, and baseball was and very much remains a Laborer pastime.

One way to judge how well a person or a country is following its dharma is to look at its pastimes. Merchants disintegrate when they take on Warrior qualities. For the United States, as for the Roman empire, a move toward violent sports like American football (as with the spectacles of the Roman Coliseum) marks a devolution, a disintegration of values ending in self-destruction. Much better for Merchant peoples and countries like the United States is to move toward their point of evolution, which is the Laborer type. This includes embracing Laborer activities like cooking, picnics, variety shows, and baseball. What was once America's game during the height of our country's international popularity has faded behind football, basketball, hockey, and other more violence-prone prime-time moneymakers. Nonetheless, baseball's popularity is making a comeback, and to honor this former national pastime I've included a good deal of baseball charts in this book.

Other Influences: Dasha and Bhukti

In addition to the primary influence of your basic dharma type, you move through life cycles that affect how your type expresses itself.

Think of it like this: The chart is a map of your life, indicating potentials that may come to fruition at different times. Just as a woman may have the potential to give birth, that potential is not active when she's three years old or when she's ninety-three. There is a window—in this case between menarche and menopause—when certain potentials become active. So it is with the natal chart. Each potential is indicated by a planet. When you run the period of a planet, that is called its *dasha*. Since these dashas are long, ranging from six to twenty years in length, they are further broken down into proportional subdivisions called *bhuktis*. These two divisions help give more precise predictions. It is one thing to say "You will get married during your twenty-year Venus period." It is quite another to say "You will marry during your one-year Venus-Sun period."

Dasha comes from the Sanskrit root *damsh,* "to bite," and *bhukti* from the root *bhuj,* "to eat, enjoy, or experience." In a sense, your dasha and bhukti are the periods in which you are served up that portion of your karma that is ready to be experienced. If it's desirable, you can enjoy it in full; if it's undesirable, you still have to bite and eat it, though the enjoyment is up to you. It's all a matter of timing. For example, as an Educator, it's not your dharma to work exclusively for profit; however, if you happen to be in a Merchant period, that might be just what you need to do, at least for a while. Or you may be a Laborer dharma type who moves into an Outsider period. As a result, you decide to go from the safe and steady mutual fund to more risky and exotic investments. Depending on your horoscope, these may work out famously—or not.

When to Bet: "How Will I Know?"

Knowing when to predict, and for some people, when to invest in sports outcomes, requires insight and maturity. If a client asks, "Will my team win? Oh, and does this haircut work for me? And by the way, I just met this guy online, do you think he's the one?" these are probably not questions worth bothering the astrology muse about. After all, if the client cannot clearly elucidate his or her question, how can you, the astrologer, be expected to extract the answer? The seed of the answer lies in the question: clarity of purpose is primary. But if a mother asks "Will this team win? My son said he would commit suicide if they don't," that may be well worth looking at the chart to ease her mind.

In such cases, good intentions and sound judgment can take you a long way. But if you're using astrology to gain insight to wager on sports yourself, or if you are advising others who will be using the information to profit themselves, extra care is necessary. When involving yourself or others with the karma of money, it is important to be very clear about your intentions. Are you predicting for altruistic or for selfish reasons? Knowing the difference can help you understand when to predict and when to lie low.

In Sanskrit, verbs fall into one of two categories: *for your benefit* or *for the benefit of others*—that is, they are conjugated differently based on whether you are doing something for yourself or for another person. For example, the verb *to get* is a selfish verb, as are the verbs *to be born, to die,* and *to think,* though some verbs, like *to cook,* can be both, depending on whether you're cooking for yourself or for others. Sanskrit verbs, like the human actions they describe, can be complicated! Similarly, when you make predictions for your own benefit, it is wise to follow a different protocol than when predicting for altruistic reasons.

When practicing Jyotisha for the benefit of others, there are fewer restrictions on when and how to share your wisdom. Here are a few:

- Don't make predictions during major *sandhis* (junctures in time and space), such as sunrise and sunset, eclipses, or solar *sankranti* (the sidereal solar ingress, roughly around the fifteenth of every month), or, for that matter, while standing at the Four Corners area of the United States, where Colorado, Utah, Arizona, and New Mexico meet at one point. Standing on a street corner like a doomsday prophet is not good either, since it's a major sandhi—plus, such prophets rarely get any respect.

- Don't do Jyotisha in moving vehicles like cars or airplanes. Traveling is a juncture between two points; think about all the lines and borders you're crossing while moving about. I know it's tempting during a five- or even a fifteen-hour flight to make some predictions, but resist the urge. Cozy up and watch the in-flight movie instead.

- These sandhi rules apply across the board to other Vedic sciences. For example, ayurveda warns that sex during sandhis, especially eclipses, is deleterious to health, both your own and that of any baby born from such a union. In short, avoid sandhis for any auspicious undertaking, except spiritual practice.

- Finally, do not undertake Jyotisha for *nastikas,* "nonbelievers," the kind of people who only ask questions to test your knowledge. The ancient Indian sage Parashara, who wrote many important Vedic texts, warns that indulging such folks is not good for Jyotisha or for your reputation. This rule also means that you shouldn't predict for anyone who doesn't have a real desire to know. Dilettantes are for the ball. Jyotisha is for the dedicated—and the desperate.

These are the general rules when practicing astrology for others. Here, then, are some additional rules when doing it for yourself, whether to gamble or to otherwise make yourself rich.

- Don't do it. Okay, if you must, consider the following points *in addition to the rules enumerated above*. Yes, selfish verbs are more complex than selfless ones. That's why gurus like to say, "Serve others, and leave the rest to God." That's because when serving yourself, things get more precarious, karmically speaking.
- Do not wager when the moon is transiting your 8th house.
- Do not wager when the moon is in the 1st, 3rd, 5th, or 7th nakshatra from your own, especially if the moon also falls in the 6th, 8th, or 12th house of your horoscope. For example, if your moon at birth was in Punarvasu nakshatra (ruled by Jupiter in the Vimshottari dasha scheme), then you should avoid days when the transiting moon moves through nakshatras owned by Jupiter, Mercury, Venus, and the Moon, as these are the 1st, 3rd, 5th, and 7th from the birth star, particularly if these are also otherwise afflicted. And if this makes no sense to you yet, don't worry—it's a slightly more advanced technique that you don't need to know to benefit from the rest of this book. A full explanation of the method is found in appendix 3, page 206.
- Do not wager when planets are *kutila,* or stationary. Stationary planets appear stuck in planetary purgatory, or celestial limbo. Moving neither forward nor backward, they live in a temporary sandhi, making gambling or predicting during such times critically unreliable. Things act in reverse when planets are kutila, and usually reliable techniques can backfire. I can't tell you how many bets I lost before I figured this out. Don't be like me. You can find when planets appear stationary by consulting a good astrology software or ephemeris.

Another way to assess whether you have the karma to engage in speculation is to see if the yogas in your horoscope support this or indicate the opposite— loss and self-destruction. Most Vedic astrologers are familiar with the wealth- and status-conferring combinations, called *dhana* and *raja* yogas, but fewer know the yogas that break these, like the *daridra* yogas (poverty-inducing combinations). Here, for your reference, are some from the granddaddy of Jyotisha, sage Parashara:

- 1st house lord in the 12th, and 12th house lord in the 1st, while conjunct or aspected by a *maraka* planet (maraka planets are the lords of houses 2 and 7)

- 1st house lord in the 8th, and 8th house lord in the 1st, while conjunct or aspected by a maraka planet
- 1st house lord in the 8th, and 1st house lord or Moon with Ketu
- 1st house lord in the 6th, 8th, or 12th, with a malefic, while the 2nd house lord is in an enemy sign or debilitated
- 1st house lord conjoined with the 6th, 8th, or 12th house lord or with Saturn, without the aspect of a benefic
- 1st house lord and the D9 1st house lord (navamsha lagna ruler) conjunct or aspected by a maraka planet*

The Importance of Grace and Intuition

Even knowing all this, the difference between correct and incorrect predictions often comes down to grace. Grace and skill are the two wings of the Jyotir Vidya. Skill is developed through study and practice, while grace is invited by sincerely doing your dharma. Without one or the other, your predictions will fall flat. Because it can be impossible to keep track of all eventualities, it is important to have the second wing (grace) help you when your first wing (skill) has failed. An old saying goes, "It's better to be lucky than good." This means that being steered away from the bad days and toward the good days is an act of Providence (or your own desirable karma), especially when you forget or overlook one of these major factors, as everyone does at some point or another. Sometimes it takes that gut feeling, that inner voice that tells you, *No, today is not a good day, despite what the chart says.*

Scientifically minded folks tend to sneer at the word *intuition,* as it represents an unquantifiable "sixth sense," something hard to fit into a purely scientific paradigm. However, the Vedic view is that the mind *is* in fact a sixth sense, collecting information from the other five senses and synthesizing it into a holistic whole.

> **Science is understanding nature by taking apart its components; intuition is understanding nature by putting them together, synthesizing information to form a holistic conclusion.**

The Online Etymology Dictionary (www.etymonline.com) defines *intuition* as "insight, direct or immediate cognition, spiritual perception," while *science* comes

---

*From the Brihat Parashara Hora Shastra, chapter 42, "Combinations for Penury."

from a root that means "to split apart, dissect." Thus, science is understanding nature by taking apart its components; intuition is understanding nature by putting them together, synthesizing information to form a holistic conclusion.

Many charts will show good points for both teams. Some may be very close calls. This is where intuition born of grace and experience—that feeling that comes from having seen thousands of combinations and being open to your own inner knowing—can make the difference. Psychologists who study skill acquisition note that at the highest level, mastery becomes an unconscious part of us, a "feeling" about the right move at the right time. Ancient traditions refined this basic reality of human skill and performance and expressed it as "the muse."

K. S. Krishnamurti

K. S. Krishnamurti (1908–1972) is considered by some to have been a reincarnation of Varahamihira, the great fifth-century sage who authored the Brihat Samhita and other important treatises. This is in part because Krishnamurti, like Varahamihira, sought to modernize Jyotisha's principles to make them relevant to his time. His focus on precise calculations and scientific observation revolutionized Jyotisha prediction. He was famous for routinely and precisely predicting mundane events like the arrival of trains (which are notoriously late in India) and when the electricity would return, as well as the more standard life events that made him a favorite of both industrialists and the indigent. Like Varahamihira, he was scientific in his approach and rejected anything that didn't work in the light of empirical observation. He is controversial in India for bringing the Western Placidus house system to bear upon the Vedic horoscope, a practice he incorporated into his Krishnamurti Paddhati (Krishnamurti Method), or KP for short.

Krishnamurti further revolutionized Vedic astrology by dividing nakshatras into subdivisions, each ruled by its own sublord. In essence, he took a method already used for dividing *time,* the dasha amd bhukti described earlier, and used it to divide *space,* i.e., the zodiac. He traveled widely, teaching his method for free throughout India, and published his research and innovations in publications called the KP Readers,* which to this day are the main source of authentic instruction from K. S. Krishnamurti.

---

*Available for purchase online at www.scribd.com.

The ancient Greeks, Romans, and Egyptians, as well as Vedic peoples, acknowledged the presence of a muse (Ishta devata in Sanskrit) that is the external manifestation of a body of knowledge or an inspirational deity that gives access to this knowledge. In Vedic astrology this muse is known as the Jyotir Vidya, and she is considered the living, breathing embodiment of Jyotisha. The muse is an embodiment of the skill mastery we wish to cultivate, who whispers in our ear when we are open to hearing. The muse may also express her- or himself as a feeling in the stomach, a slight discomfort for a negative outcome, a sense of certainty or ease for a positive one. For a player or performer it can create confidence. Michael Jordan once said that when he was "in the zone," the basket looked ten feet wide, and there was no doubt about making the shot. Bobby Fischer once said that at any given time there are billions of possible combinations on the chessboard, but only one right move. Finding that right move depends on your connection to an Ishta devata.

Intuition in Action

Once, a friend asked for a game pick. I gave him my thoughts on a chart that looked like a slam dunk, an easy winner. As it turns out, that team got demolished by the opposition. As I returned to look at the chart, I couldn't find anything to indicate such a heavy shellacking by the other team. Scratching my head, I thought, *Something isn't right here, this can't be . . .* At that moment I noticed the date: it was the wrong day! I had pulled the chart for the following morning instead of this morning. When I called my friend, he told me that something about my pick didn't feel right. He told me, "When I looked at the logos for the two teams, one stood out, growing bigger and brighter, as if it was telling me 'I'm going to win!' But since it wasn't the logo for the team you gave me I brushed it aside and went ahead with your selection. I should have listened to my gut."

Even though my pick was technically good, my friend's intuition correctly indicated that it was the wrong choice. Intuition is the capacity to see beyond the tyranny of the five senses, to understand what those senses have failed to grasp. It prevents us from making blunders like this one.

Karma Chameleon:
Fixed, Mixed, and Take Your Pick

Helping us arrive at the right move, or in our case the correct prediction, is our ability to understand karma. Everything that is born in space and time has a karmic signature, and in theory that signature is open to being read using the techniques in this book. That means that two games with the same chart and therefore the same karmic signature should produce identical results. For example, here's a chart for two different games played in different cities at different times on the same day:

Chicago Cubs vs. Minnesota Twins, 13:11 LT, June 20, 2015, Minneapolis, Minnesota, *and* Los Angeles Angels vs. Oakland Athletics, 13:07 LT, June 20, 2015, Oakland, California

Though the two games appear to have been played only minutes apart, the caption shows local time (abbreviated LT), and the cities where these games were played—Minneapolis and Oakland—are in fact two time zones apart, which means that when it was 13:07 in Oakland, the Minnesota game was already two-thirds finished. (The home team is always to the *right* of the vs. (versus) in the caption.) The two games have almost exact ascendant degrees, and by extension, identical planetary positions. In both games, the favorite team won. In both games, the score was 4 to 1.

Eerie? Yes. Does this happen all the time? Well, often enough to make us believe that Jyotisha works. But sometimes even minute differences in a chart can have game-changing effects, which we'll explore in chapters 5 and 6. The games above had a certain level of karmic fixity or a "fated" quality. But don't count out free will just yet. Even in these matchups, the runs were scored at different times, and the game had a different complexion than one would expect if *everything* were predestined. Free will plays a part; the question in judging charts is, how much?

The easiest charts to read are those in which karma appears relatively fixed. That means that despite the best efforts of players to the contrary, a certain result is likely. Most charts, however, especially as you begin to study, will show good and bad for both sides. But the more practiced you become, the more you will discern where free will is at play and where games are relatively fated. These are the games you count on as a sports investor.

> **Free will plays a part; the question in judging charts is, how much?**

To judge a natal chart properly, the rule of three is useful to remember:

1. If something happens once, it could be a coincidence.
2. If something happens twice, it could be a pattern.
3. If something happens three or more times, it *is* a pattern.

One swallow does not a summer make (unless it's a really big swallow—i.e., one technique alone, when it is outstanding, *can* indicate success or failure). But when several indications point to an outcome—say, marital discord—you can more safely predict divorce in a person's life. Similarly, when a team is beleaguered on multiple sides, as indicated by the various techniques in this book, while the other team remains relatively affliction-free, you can venture to predict the game between them with better confidence.

The Three Levels of Karma

Fixed: Like your height or your gender, this is pretty unchangeable stuff—it would take a lot of effort to break through fixed karma. This is what we want to see in a game chart, since it makes prediction easier.

Mixed: Like your nationality or eyesight, this still takes some effort to change, but it is doable.

Nonfixed: Like what you wear, you can change clothes and give yourself a whole new look relatively easily. In nonfixed karma, any effort you make yields a commensurate result, such that you are starting with a clean slate. This is the type of karma we avoid in game charts because it indicates plenty of free will on the part of the players.

The games on page 24 also illustrate a question Krishnamurti asked about the charts of twins (though in his case, not the Minnesota Twins). Dissatisfied with standard astrological protocol, he wanted to know why certain siblings born just minutes apart (with therefore similar charts) sometimes led similar lives, while others led radically different existences. The meager degree differences in their charts was key to the system he developed, Krishnamurti Paddhati, which we will explore later.

In fact, in this book you will find many charts that look eerily similar. In some of these the underdog might prevail, in others the favorite. I will show you how to spot the combinations accounting for the subtle differences between them, as well as how to transfer that knowledge to other areas of Jyotisha, such as natal or electional astrology. This may be a departure from the type of astrology you are used to, but that's not such a bad thing. In fact, let's take a look at some of the things that make this book different from any other Jyotisha volume you may encounter.

Free Will and Grace in Toronto

In the fifth and deciding baseball game of the 2015 American League divisional series, the Texas Rangers faced the favored Toronto Blue Jays in Toronto in front of a sold-out stadium of raucous fans, where the din of the crowd was a palpable wave that reverberated over the entire field. By all accounts, the underdog had the better chart. I said to myself, *The only way Toronto gets out of this is by some divine intervention . . . or the effect of the crowd.* Neither was seeable in the chart. A cynic, I didn't think it would happen.

It happened.

Texas led until the seventh inning, when, in the most bizarre series of events that even the game commentators had ever witnessed, including three Texas errors and a noisy, belligerent crowd, Toronto piled up four runs to go ahead. They won that game, even though they shouldn't have. By sheer force of will they refused to lie down, even though the karma of the chart weighed against them. Sisyphus had made it up the hill and spiked the stone on top to boot.

By deciding they *would not lose,* Toronto's players wrote their own destiny. But such moments are rare, which is what makes them momentous. If it happened every day, astrology wouldn't work, and we'd be out of a job. But astrology does work, which means that in the majority of charts we should be able to judge an outcome and get it right.

Invisible Touch:
The Unseen Planets

Some of the techniques in this book make use of the unseen planets that are not part of traditional Jyotisha, including Uranus, Neptune, Pluto, and Ceres, along with the centaur* Chiron. I also use the *upagrahas* Upaketu and Gulika, which are shadow planets that are actually mathematical constructs. I call these dwarf planets, centaurs, and upagrahas *invisible planets* because they are, well, invisible to the naked eye. The reason to use them is simple: they work. Beyond that, the reasons may have more to do with consensus reality and the evolution of human society.

As soon as planets, or grahas, enter the collective consciousness, they awaken archetypal patterns within us, driving us to express their energies. For example, the discovery of Uranus in 1781 coincided with a century of revolutions, both on the battlefield as well as in the fields of science and industry, which Uranus rules.[†] Neptune's unveiling in 1846 coincided with the advent of ether (chloroform) as an anesthetic.[‡] That same year also witnessed the beginning of the modern history of petroleum (Neptune) with the refinement of paraffin from crude oil, not to mention the emergence of cults, government ideologies, and spiritual movements, all Neptune's domain.[§] Pluto's discovery in 1930 was

---

*Dwarf planets are bodies too small to carve out an orbit of their own, yet round enough due to their gravity to behave like planets. According to Wikipedia, Chiron is "the first-identified member of a new class of objects now known as centaurs—bodies orbiting between the asteroid belt and the Kuiper belt." All of these are grahas. It doesn't matter whether that sky influencer is a star, a moon, a planet, a comet, or a mathematical point; in astrology we are more concerned with its specific effect on human life. Therefore, for the purposes of this book, a graha may be any celestial object, even a mathematical construct like Rahu/Ketu and the upagrahas.

[†]"The discovery of Uranus has often been connected with both the American and French revolutions, but there was an important distinction between them. The Americans, acting before the discovery, created a new state based on existing principles; the French, in the full spirit of Uranus, attempted to create an entirely new society, with new laws, weights and measures, calendar, and religion" (David McCann, "The Birth of the Outer Planets," www.skyscript.co.uk/uranus.html).

[‡]Dreams, sleep, and altered states of consciousness are the realms of Neptune.

[§]Two years later, in 1848, Karl Marx published *The Communist Manifesto*.

followed two years later by the splitting of the atom and an acceleration to harness nuclear energy, the subtle but awesome power of nature. Just before that, in 1928, Alexander Fleming discovered penicillin, heralding the era of using nature to fight nature (literally, *anti-biotic*) in the biological realm. Pluto, one of the smallest grahas, can be the most transformational: it rules mass upheaval and the subtle power of the unseen. But discovery also works in the other direction. The recent demotion of Pluto to dwarf planet status could mean that his influence on charts and society in general is waning, just as the influence of other grahas like Ceres is rising.*

In astrology and mythology, Ceres, the whole of which fits nicely within the borders of Texas, is associated with agriculture, fertility, and nurturing. She is the embodiment of Mother Nature, and like her she can be convulsive in times of change. Discovered in 1801, then later demoted to an asteroid, Ceres's recent exploration and reclassification could mark a newfound respect for the feminine principle and a concurrent uptick in promoting women's rights and power. Increasingly there seems to be an acknowledgment on the part of society of the ills we have done to our planet, including the poisoning of Earth's waters, the mining of her minerals, the dumping of nuclear waste, overpopulation, and so much more. With the demotion of Pluto (along with its nuclear and patriarchal themes) to equal status with Ceres (Mother Nature), we may witness a necessary rebalancing between anima and animus, the masculine and the feminine, in the collective unconscious.

> **Ceres's recent exploration and reclassification could mark a newfound respect for the feminine principle.**

Chiron's discovery in 1977 came at a time when alternative forms of healing, including yoga, traditional Chinese medicine, and ayurveda, first took root in the West. With the end of the U. S. war in Vietnam, Chiron became the embodiment of the Wounded Warrior archetype and began to play a significant role

---

*At least in sports charts I find Pluto's effects to be less than one would expect, given its significations. More research is needed.

in modern chart interpretation, including natal astrology, astro locality,* and sports charts, in which Chiron can augur injuries and loss for a team when retrograde, or strength and victory when in direct motion.

If my using these outer planets seems like a marriage between Vedic and Western astrology, then you're in for a treat when in chapter 4 I introduce house cusps, the honeymoon fruit of that happy union. But ultimately this is a book on Jyotisha, and cutting-edge Jyotisha techniques like navamsha degrees and sublords, covered respectively in chapters 5 and 6, play a major role in predicting victory, as do the standard methods taught by the sage Parashara. Let's begin by looking at these methods, to see how they lured me into the unlikely journey of which this book is both a diary and a dissertation.

Summary

There are several important factors to keep in mind before engaging in speculation:

- Know your dharma type, as well as your life cycles as indicated by dasha and bhukti.
- Understand the major sandhis and avoid making predictions during those times.
- Correct predictions are easier when fixed karma plays into a chart—this book will help you find it.
- In addition to the standard grahas, unseen planets can also affect game outcomes.

---

*An astro locality map superimposes your birth chart on a map of the world, showing where on the planet each of your natal planets crosses the horizon, the meridian, and the paths of your other natal planets. For example, I have found that living on or near a Chiron line can evoke health issues and healing crises. How well one integrates these, like everything else in Jyotisha, depends on the rest of the chart.

3

Victory Houses

Basic Techniques for Predicting Outcomes

*As the night without a light, as the sky without the sun, so is a king
without an astrologer; like a blind man he stumbles on the road.*

VARAHAMIHIRA

It was an incredible game. Holland came from behind to rout a favored Spanish team 5 to 1 in the opening round of the World Cup. As I basked in the afterglow, a thought sparked: *You should pull the chart.*

Casting a horoscope is done in humans the moment a baby draws its first breath; for sporting events it is based on the exact time a match begins—tipoff, kickoff, or the first pitch. In this case, the chart would give me insight into why this game played out so dramatically, with the underdog routing the favored world champions—a mighty blowout indeed! But how would I read it?

Nah, too much work . . .

But the thought grew more insistent: *Pull the chart!*

C'mon, I just enjoyed the game, why spoil it by racking my brain with astrological analyses?

You should pull the chart!

Okay, okay . . .

I trust that inner voice, particularly when it's so insistent, since it usually knows something I don't. In this case, it knew that casting that horoscope would change my life forever.

So I did—easy enough, since I had just watched the game from beginning to end and knew exactly when it started and where it was played. There was one problem, however: no home team. Without a home team, how could I determine whether Holland or Spain should get the lagna? In Jyotisha, the lagna, or ascendant, is all important, since it's what ties down an event in space and time. So if I was born at 3 p.m. in Denver, Colorado, and you were born at the exact same moment in Delhi, India, we would have different lagnas and completely unique life experiences as a result.

Now, prevailing Jyotisha wisdom says that the home team should be represented by the ascendant, but what about when both teams are visitors, as is the case in tournaments like the World Cup where many nations play but only one country is host?

The same place from which the first thought sparked lit up again:

The favorite gets the lagna.

Well, okay, I could go along with that. After all, the favored team is the one most people think will triumph; it gets first billing and therefore the seat of honor. But how to find the favorite? A Google search and a few clicks later I arrived at that great modern hub of sports traffic, the online betting site. There I was smacked in the face by a barrage of decimal figures and terms like *moneyline, pick, over/under, spread*—a vernacular I hadn't heard since my last trip to Las Vegas (where I should have payed more attention). Undeterred from my mission to find the favorite team, I googled each of these terms and figured out that for the game I had watched, Holland was about a 4-to-1 underdog against the reigning world champions. In American odds it looked like this:

Spain −118   Holland +408

The minus in front of Spain's number indicates that they were the favorite, and that you had to wager $118 to win $100 on top of that, but a $100 wager on Holland would garner you $408 *in addition* to your initial $100 bet if they won. In other words, the favorite will have negative moneyline odds (less payoff for a safer bet), and the underdog will have positive moneyline odds (more payoff for a risky bet). In this case an underdog win looked like pretty good stuff.

In European odds lingo it looked like this:

Spain 1.85   Holland 5.08

This means that for every dollar you wagered on Spain you would get 85 cents back on top of your dollar should they win. For Holland, your dollar returned $4.08 in addition to your dollar wagered.*

Finally, in Indian odds, which are similar to the U.S. notation system save for the decimal point, the bet looked like this:

Spain −1.18   Holland 4.08

Here, the team with a minus (−1.18) is usually the favorite, and the team with nothing or a plus (4.08) is the underdog.

About half a dozen methods for representing odds are used in sports investing circles. Being a Yank, I have opted for the American method throughout this book.

Gambling Lingo

Moneyline shows you which team is the favorite and which is the underdog. The favorite will have the lower number, usually a negative digit. That means that if one team is +205 and the other is −180, the favorite is the second team. Sometimes both teams will be positive. In the case of, for example +205 and +180, the second team is still the favorite, since its number is lower than the first.

Over/under allows you to bet on whether the game will be over a particular score or under it. An over/under of 5.5 means that if the total team goals are 6 or higher, the *over* bet wins. If the total team goals are 5 or less, the *under* bet wins. Saturn tends to create *under,* or low-scoring games, while Uranus does the opposite.

So, why is this important, particularly if you're not interested in gambling? Because it illustrates that every day, for practically every professional sport, careful thinking goes into deciding who is going to win a particular game, and by how much. Around the world, experts vested in understanding the outcome of matches give their opinions, and out of that comes a consensus on who is the favored team. That consensus, I have found, is the most important factor in determining the lagna of a game chart. In Jyotisha this is tantamount to understanding *kala, desha,* and

---

*These are the actual odds for the game as reprented by www.oddsportal.com.

patra—the time and place of an event as well as the ability of the teams involved. This is discussed more in chapter 4.

Tie Me Down:
Fixing the Lagna

A horary chart, or *prashna,* is a chart for a question, specifically, for the moment the question is asked or the moment the astrologer sits down to analyze it. In horary charts for questions like "Will I find my ring?" the person asking (the querent) is usually represented by the lagna. The same is true for questions like "Will the Pittsburgh Steelers win the Super Bowl?" In this example, the Pittsburgh Steelers are assigned the ascendant and their chances of winning are evaluated in the resulting chart. That's because Pittsburgh is the subject of the question, and regardless of whether they're favored or not there is Shakti—primordial cosmic energy—and the desire to know, specifically referencing Pittsburgh and not any other team. This kind of energy and interest are vital for discovering outcomes, for the seed of the answer lies in the question *and how it was posed.* The querent could have worded it otherwise, but he didn't. Therefore, Pittsburgh gets the lagna, regardless of whether they're at home or away, the favorite or the underdog.

Now, if the question is "Who will win tonight's game between Pittsburgh and Cleveland?" you have two choices: (1) You can cast a prashna for the question itself; there, you can assign the ascendant to the first team mentioned (Pittsburgh) or use another method of allocating the lagna, such as finding the home team. Or (2) you can erect an event chart for the moment the match begins. The second is the technique we will use in this book. Like looking at the natal horoscope of a person based on his or her birth, this allows us to examine the chart for a particular game without the need for a horary chart. We can still supplement our analysis with prashna and read it separately from the game's birth chart to give us a clearer picture of the outcome, but it's not absolutely necessary.

The advantage of using an event chart is that games with no home team pose no problem astrologically. Also, doing horary charts requires a strong desire to know, either on the part of a team supporter (or a hater, for that matter—anywhere there's strong vested interest) or on your own part as an astrologer asking the question. But for the natal chart technique used in this book, no such energy is required, which means you don't need to hang around tailgates and parking lots anymore to find those rabid fans. The disadvantage is that you have to know who is favored in every match in order to assign the lagna. This may entail visiting sports information sites like www.sportsinsights.com or www.oddsportal.com. It also means you have to become familiar with basic gambling notation to understand who is the favorite in any given matchup, and by how much. Luckily, the box on page 32 will give you a heads-up to get you started.

To Pull or Not to Pull

"Man, this is so hard . . . I mean, finding start times, favorites, the time zone, latitude and longitude of the cities hosting the games . . . Wah! Why not just pull a prashna and be done with it?"

This is a good question, in a sniveling sort of way. Yes, sometimes it's hard to get the information you need to draw up a good event chart. Even if you find the right city, the stadium may be far enough from its center as to weigh on the placement of the house cusps (as is the case for the new home of the San Francisco 49ers). (Here's a tip: check Wikipedia for the exact longitude and latitude of the stadium, not the city.) In addition, some events, like the Super Bowl, are notorious for starting late, which can throw off the timing of your event chart. For these reasons you can simply ask, "Will this team win the Super Bowl?" and find your answer using standard prashna techniques. But the larger issue is this: do you do natal readings with only a prashna? Probably not. Prashna is typically a *supplement* to the natal chart for any given space-time event, and this is as true for games as it is for people. Also, when pulling charts for ten or twenty games on a given day it is difficult to do a prashna for each, as the horaries tend to be the same. Not practical.

Finally, and most importantly, prashnas are only effective when there is a *strong desire* to know. You may not have that desire for every chart you pull. As a result, having the natal game chart is vital.

> **When looking at a matchup between two opponents . . . , the favorite team is represented by the lagna, and their opponent by the 7th house.**

To summarize, when looking at a matchup between two opponents using the techniques in this book, the favorite team is represented by the lagna, and their opponent by the 7th house. If you are still in a quandary after analyzing the chart this way, for clarity you can pull a prashna as a second resort.

> **Everything that is born, lives, and dies is a space-time event.**
> **Sporting competitions are no exception.**

Like a human being, a game has a birth, a life span, and a termination, and the arc of its existence can be represented by the horoscope. Everything that is born, lives, and dies is a space-time event. Sporting competitions are no exception. The birth chart of an event gives us the summary of its existence; for our purposes, this means whether the favorite team (represented by the lagna) will triumph or be defeated by the underdog (represented by the 7th house), and what the manner of that victory or defeat may be.

Judging Physical Strength

Now, back to our World Cup game. Having assigned teams to the most important houses for outcome prediction (Spain, the favorite, got the lagna, and Holland, the underdog, fell in the the 7th house, or *kalatra bhava**), I looked at the chart using the one technique I understood: malefics in upachaya houses. Recall from the list of planets and their influences on page 6 that the malefic planets are Saturn, Mars, Rahu, Ketu, and the Sun, and that they do well in the upachaya houses. For this technique we do not use the outer, invisible grahas Uranus, Neptune, Pluto, Ceres, or Chiron or the upagrahas Upaketu and Gulika.† Don't worry, though, these Outsiders will all be invited to the party in the next chapter.

---

*The *kalatra bhava,* in Sanskrit, refers to the "house of the spouse." In both Western and Vedic traditions, the house of marriage and partnership is also the house of war, whereas the house of the paramour, the 5th, is also a house of fun and inspiration. Does this reflect a cynical mind-set about marriage on the part of our stargazing ancestors, or were they simply mirroring cosmic truths on the the photosensitive plate of the horoscope?

†Because Rahu and Ketu are always on opposite sides, their influences cancel each other out, though for the purposes of illustration I will continue using them in this book. In some rare cases, such as when one is exalted and the other debilitated, the exalted planet can take on a slightly greater influence.

- Upachaya houses from the ascendant (the favorite): 3, 6, 10, 11
- Upachaya houses from the 7th house (the underdog): 9, 12, 4, 5

This is the basis of what I refer to throughout this book as the *victory house technique*.

In addition to this, a Jyotishical precept says that a person with malefics in their lagna will generally be "harder" and more inclined to do battle than one without. In fact, a simple rule for judging the outcome of a match is this: *the team with the malefic in its lagna wins*. Yes, well, don't run to your bookie just yet. This rough-and-ready technique is great for a quick snapshot of a contender's strength, but it doesn't necessarily guarantee victory. Other factors, as we will learn in the coming chapters, also influence the outcome, which means that you'll have to read on to the end of this book before running off to Las Vegas.

I know—success ain't easy.

So, adding our *malefics in the 1st house* nugget, we get:

- Victory houses from the ascendant (i.e., the favorite) 1, 3, 6, 10, 11
- Victory houses from the 7th house (i.e., the underdog): 7, 9, 12, 4, 5

> **The favorite will be underlined throughout this book for extra clarity.**
> **The first team is always the visitor and the second the host,**
> **except where there is no home team.**

Now let's look at how this played out in our match (see chart on page 37). In addition to showing the American odds, the favorite will be underlined throughout this book for extra clarity. The first team is always the visitor and the second the host, except where there is no home team. (The reverse is how it's done in the UK and Europe.)

The Victory House Method in Brief

When malefics sit in victory houses (houses 1, 3, 6, 10, and 11 for the team considered the favorite, and houses 7, 9, 12, 4, and 5 for the underdog), they confer strength and fighting spirit.

Mo 07:13

SaR 23:44
Ra 02:57

Asc 11:42

Ma 18:36

Su 28:43

Ke 02:57
Ve 24:30

Ju 28:59
MeR 07:49

(North Indian chart houses numbered 1–12)

	Ke 02:57 Ve 24:30	Su 28:43	MeR 07:49 Ju 28:59
Mo 07:13	Asc 11:42	Ra 02:57 SaR 23:44	Ma 18:36

Spain (−118) vs. Holland (+408), 16:00 LT, June 13, 2014, Salvador, Brazil

Quickly, we see that the Sun, a malefic, occupied the 7th, the underdog's ascendant, while the favorite had no such luck. Good news for everyone dressed in orange, Holland's team color (even though they wore blue that day).

A look at the upachaya houses for each team shows that Holland had two malefics (Saturn and Rahu in the 12th, which is the 6th house from the 7th and therefore an upachaya for the underdog). Spain also had two (Mars and Ketu), but with the addition of the Sun, Holland won out with more malefics (three, against Spain's two) in victory houses.

But wait—they won 5 to 1, didn't they? How does this paltry margin of malefics explain such a stupendous win? There must be something more. I took out my metaphorical magnifying glass for a closer look . . .

Nothing. Then my little voice cleared its throat: *shubbha kartari yoga.*

Ah-ha! I noted the hemming-in of the 7th house by benefics. (Ketu, though a malefic, doesn't spoil this yoga, since he is a shadow planet and acting alone.) Termed *shubha kartari yoga*—the good scissors yoga—in Sanskrit, and abbreviated as SKY, this combination of natural benefics on either side of a house acts like a pair of guardian angels protecting the goal or basket of their team—a powerful force for good. The opposite of course happens when malefics hem in a team's house; in that case, they invite opponents to score and distract the owner of the house. Naughty angels!

> **Termed *shubha kartari yoga*... in Sanskrit, and abbreviated as SKY, this combination of natural benefics on either side of a house acts like a pair of guardian angels protecting the goal or basket of their team—a powerful force for good.**

For an example of SKY take a look at the chart on the top of page 39. Here the ascendant is Aries, but it could have been any sign. What's important is that it's hemmed in by the benefics Jupiter and Venus—and what benefics they are, both in their own signs, making them not only angels, but *dignified* ones—angels with attitude! We'll see this in action a little bit later. This doesn't have to be the case, though, as benefic grahas in ordinary status would work just fine.

When planets are debilitated,* on the other hand, as seen in the other example on page 39, there is less support. This is an instance where the angels on your shoulder have too much of their own problems—fighting off a bad cold or maybe even a hangover—to pay any serious attention to you.

> **Papa kartari yoga, or the "bad scissors combination," occurs when two or more malefics hem in a house by occupying the 12th *and* 2nd houses from it. In the context of game charts, this applies to the 1st and 7th houses, and includes the Sun as a malefic.**

And now an example of the opposite effect, *papa kartari yoga*. Abbreviated as PKY, the "bad scissors combination" occurs when two or more malefics hem in a house by occupying the 12th *and* 2nd houses from it (see page 40). In the context of game charts, this applies to the 1st and 7th houses, and includes the Sun as a malefic. Papa kartati yoga makes a person or a team vulnerable.

Note that for sports prediction, having only Rahu or Ketu on one side of a PKY is not enough to form the full negative yoga. The usual result is that a team plays well for half the game and poorly the other half, often allowing opponents to catch up and beat them.† One of the names of Rahu is ardhakaya, meaning

---

*For a list of planetary exaltation, debilitation, and dig bala, please refer to table 3.1 on page 46.
†Such was the case in the 2017 Super Bowl, where underdogs Atlanta were burdened by a PKY formed by Saturn and Ketu: they played extraordinarily well for one half until their PKY kicked in, allowing New England to come back and beat them. This happened for at least half a dozen games over the time that I observed this combination.

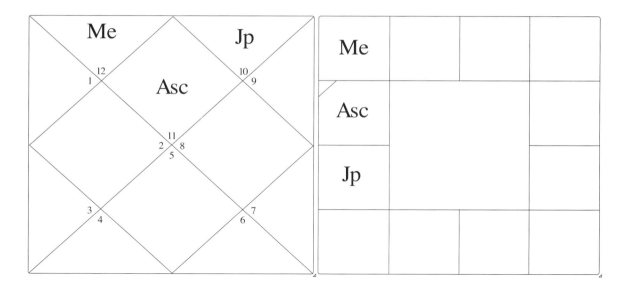

SKY (shubbha kartari yoga) for the ascendant

SKY with debilitated grahas—angels with a hangover

"half-bodied." This has a literal component when it comes to sports prediction. Likewise, when Rahu or Ketu mar a nice SKY, they only do so for half a game. Our Holland and Costa Rica matches bear this out, with the non-SKY team leading the first half, and their Ketu-marred SKY opponents coming back to beat them handily in the second. Finally, if Rahu or Ketu sit on top of an already formed PKY (by any among Saturn, Sun, or Mars), the addition of Rahu or Ketu adds to their negative effect and often seals the deal for that team.

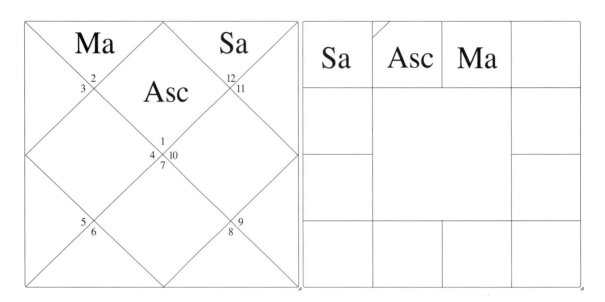

PKY (papa kartari yoga) of the ascendant formed by Saturn and Mars

---

H. R. Sheshadri Iyer

Okay, so I've mentioned him a few times already. What's all the fuss about this guy? Googling him, you'd find precious little about the personal life of this brilliant mathematician-turned-astrologer. A Wikipedia search turns up the eponymous Diwan of Mysore, who lived from 1845 to 1901. Close, but no cigar. Our Mr. Iyer was born in the twentieth century and, a researcher at heart, was not averse to testing his astrology in the office *and* on the racetrack. Like K. S. Krishnamurti, who refined his sublords and ruling planets theories playing cards, Iyer was no stranger to specula- tion because of the instant feedback and opportunities for fine-tuning techniques it provided. His two-volume book *New Techniques of Prediction*, first published in 1962, introduced the world to a host of old and new Vedic astrology techniques, including the *yogi, avayogi,* and *dagdha rashis,* as well as Iyer's unique system of D-chart inter- pretation. His third book, *Race Astrology,* details his work in horse racing.

Lucy in the SKY with Diamonds

Teams with SKY protecting their lagna do better than expected. That doesn't mean they always win, though. Take a look at the chart for the Brazil-Mexico matchup.

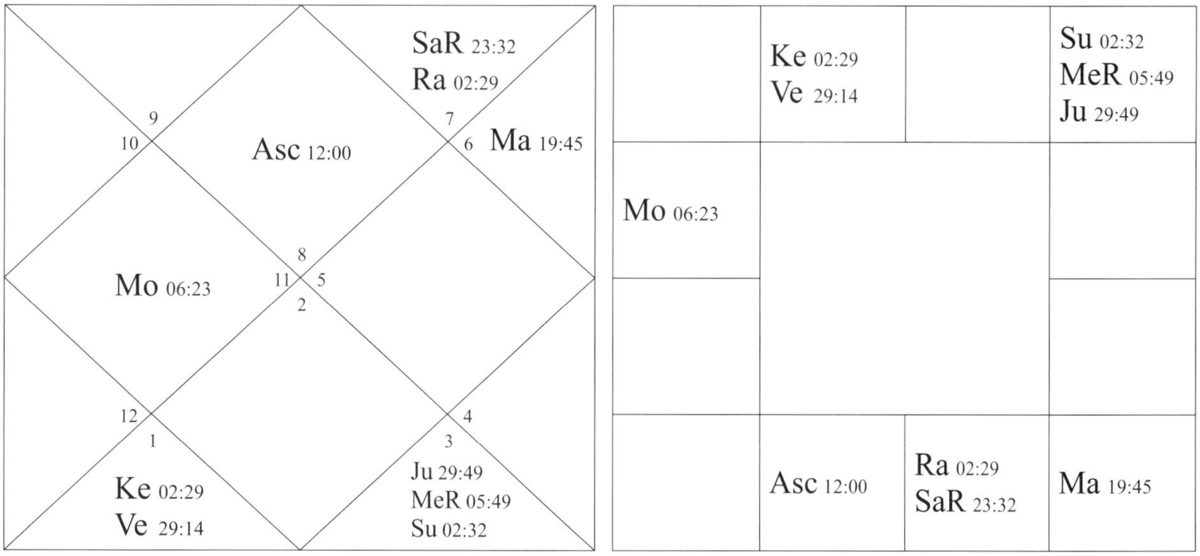

Left chart (North Indian style):

SaR 23:32
Ra 02:29

9
10 Asc 12:00

7
6 Ma 19:45

8
11 5
2

Mo 06:23

12
1

4
3
Ju 29:49
MeR 05:49
Su 02:32

Ke 02:29
Ve 29:14

Right chart (South Indian style):

Ke 02:29 Ve 29:14		Su 02:32 MeR 05:49 Ju 29:49
Mo 06:23		
Asc 12:00	Ra 02:29 SaR 23:32	Ma 19:45

Brazil (−278) vs. Mexico (+810), 16:01 LT, June 17, 2014, Fortaleza, Brazil

Here, the favored Brazilians had two malefics in upachaya houses, Ketu and Mars, against Mexico's Saturn and Rahu—an even matchup. However, an even matchup of upachaya planets suggests that both teams will play with an equal amount of physical force and toughness, which means the favored team is still likely to win since it is generally considered the better squad. For Mexico's victory, we would like to see a clear dominance of malefics in victory houses. To borrow a phrase from boxing, "To be the champ, you gotta *beat* the champ"—to triumph against a better opponent, you have to play above your game. Astrologically speaking, this means that you need convincing evidence for an underdog victory, and the bigger the dog, the more evidence required.

However, the trick card up Mexico's sleeve is the beautiful SKY formed by Jupiter, Mercury, and Venus. "Wait," you say, "what about the Sun and Ketu? Don't they do anything to mar this combination?" Good eye! Yes, the presence of the Sun and even Ketu in the SKY-forming houses diminishes this yoga but does not cancel it. If it were Saturn and Mars, the marring would have turned to scarring, making the SKY even less effective. But the Sun is only a mild malefic, and Ketu, as I mentioned above, is a shadow graha with less influence.

However, everything in astrology is cumulative. Having both millionaire and pauper combinations doesn't mean your finances will average out; more likely you'll experience very high highs along with very low lows in the same lifetime.

Astrology, and the karma it indicates, is cumulative, which means you have to add up all the techniques in this book to determine an outcome.

Astrology, and the karma it indicates, is cumulative, which means you have to add up all the techniques in this book to determine an outcome.

For this yoga, the Sun and Ketu made the job Mexico's angels had to do much harder, with miraculous saves by Mexico's goalkeeper, Guillermo Ochoa. It is also why the game ended in a 0-0 draw. Even so, one commentator suggested during the hard-fought match that "they're building statues to Ochoa in Mexico City." A more level-headed appraisal came after the game: "The Estadio Castelao crowd was treated to one of the most entertaining goalless draws in FIFA World Cup history as Mexican goalkeeper Memo Ochoa put in a performance for the ages."[*]

What made it even more lucky, countering the negative effects of the Sun and Ketu, was the presence of Mercury with the SKY, giving the angels some relief and ensuring that no goals came through. Lesson? Your angels may not be enough to win, but they will almost always ensure a lucky or better-than-expected performance. By the same token, the little devils in a PKY ensure that your team will endure more tough breaks and hardships than expected, though papa kartari yogas tend to not be as bad as shubbha kartari yogas are good—i.e., a team with a PKY can still win, though they will have to fight harder than if they did not possess the PKY in the first place. Don't ask me why PKY is less potent than SKY in sports; perhaps it has something to do with players getting a second wind after being beaten up, giving them fight and gusto to win.[†]

Papa kartari yogas tend to not be as bad as shubbha kartari yogas are good.

---

[*]"Ochoa Excels as Mexico Holds Brazil," www.fifa.com/worldcup/matches/round=255931 /match=300186509/match-report.html.

[†]For example, Arnold Schwarzennegger has a PKY around his lagna, and he has certainly benefited from his fighting spirit, though his lagna is also exceedingly strong.

What Happened Next

Again at the suggestion of my little voice, I studied the schedule for the following day's games. Here's what popped up:

Mo 22:06	SaR 23:41 Ra 02:49	
	Asc 09:10	Ma 18:53
Su 29:40		
Ke 02:49 Ve 25:41	Ju 29:11 MeR 07:22	

Ke 02:49 Ve 25:41	Su 29:40	MeR 07:22 Ju 29:11	
Mo 22:06	Asc 09:10	Ra 02:49 SaR 23:41	Ma 18:53

Costa Rica (+850) vs. <u>Uruguay (−210)</u>, 16:01 LT,
June 14, 2014, Fortaleza, Brazil

If you said it looks a lot like the Holland chart, you'd be right. Granted, the Moon has moved about 15 degrees, but the rest of the planets are right where we left them, more or less. *This is amazing,* I thought. *It's the same chart, therefore the same result should be expected.* With my full faith as a neophyte still not disabused by negative experience, I ventured out on a major limb to bet on this game to see if I was right. I wagered $75 on Costa Rica—$50 of my own money and a $25 bonus from the bookmaker.* I swore I'd give away part or all of the winnings and didn't tell a soul. The result? Uruguay scored first on a penalty, just like in the Holland-Spain game, where the champions opened with a penalty of their own. And just like in that game, the even bigger dog, Costa Rica (+850),

---

*Online bookmakers often give first-deposit incentives to attract bettors.

came back to win in a "miraculous" second half that witnessed three unanswered goals from their side. With fingernails chewed to the bone, I emerged with an unambiguous conclusion: Jyotisha works.

So why did this underdog win, but the same situation resulted in only a draw for Mexico in the matchup with Brazil, which happened a few days later? Take a look at the Sun. In the Holland and Costa Rica charts, the Sun, a malefic, sits on the underdog's lagna, a victory house, boosting their strength and competitiveness. In Mexico's chart, the Sun has moved to the 8th house, where it not only loses its victory house position but mars the otherwise brilliant SKY. Thus, instead of shocking the hometown favorite Brazilians with a brilliant victory, the Mexican squad shocked Brazil with a brilliant tie. Make sense?

That week followed with more games proving this rule, and the upachaya technique that shows that teams with malefics in the 1st, 3rd, 6th, 10th, and 11th houses from their lagna are physically strong and aggressive, while teams without these lack vigor.

Physical strength isn't the only determinant for victory, but it's a good start. Witness what happened the following day:

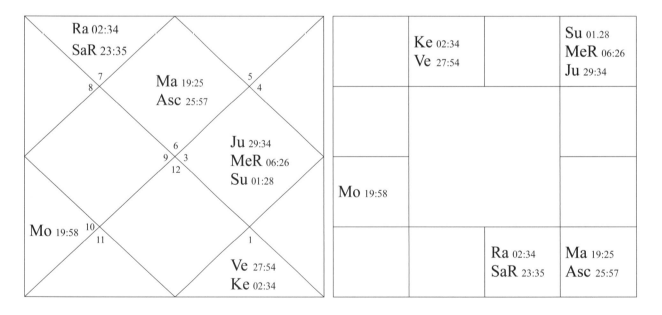

Germany (−110) vs. Portugal (+260), 13:01 LT,
June 16, 2014, Salvador, Brazil

Here, the favored Germans show a strong advantage—two malefics to none. "What about those nice benefics in the 10th house?" you ask. I asked that too, knocking on the door where my little voice lives. Out it came, none too pleased to see me: *Count benefics if they're strong and leave me alone now, will ya?* Fair enough. If we add two strong benefics—Mercury is retrograde and in its own sign, and Jupiter is in its own star, Punarvasu (we'll learn more about the stars, a more advanced technique, in chapter 8)—we get a total of four planets in victory houses to Portugal's zero. The final score was 4 to 0. You can also count the Moon, which is just past full and in its own star, as a strong benefic.

So, what makes benefics strong? Consider planets in their own sign and nakshatra strong, as well as exalted and retrograde planets (see table 3.1 on page 46). I have found that to really count as victory house grahas, benefics should ideally have an exaggerated condition. It takes exaggerated strength like exaltation, retrogression, or a full(ish) Moon to turn mild-mannered benefics into hard-core victory grahas. In sports, where nuance is not a necessity, we appreciate exaggerated planets.

Exalted, Debilitated, and Dig Bala

When planets occupy signs they own, they are considered strong; when they occupy signs that especially bring out their talents, they are said to be exalted. Think of it like this: If Bill Gates is at home, he feels comfortable and at ease—just like planets in their own signs. But when Bill Gates leaves home to go to Microsoft, he steps into his element, becoming a powerful computer mogul and boss. That's exaltation. If he were instead to step onto a deserted island, with no technology or connection to the world, he might feel helpless and unsupported. That's debilitation. Every planet has a sign it owns (except Rahu and Ketu), a sign where it is exalted, and a sign where it is debilitated.

Dig bala is another form of strength, but instead of placement in a sign, it depends on a planet's placement in a house. For example, Mars and Sun have dig bala in the 10th house of power and dominion. The 10th house represents high noon, when the Sun is in his full radiance. Jupiter and Mercury have dig bala in the 1st house, since the 1st is the house of the sunrise, and study is best done early in the morning. Jupiter and Mercury are both planets of study, knowledge, and education. Burning the midnight oil might be useful for passing a test the next day, but for long-term retention, study during the early morning hours just before and after sunrise is considered optimal according to Vedic astrology.

Moon and Venus have dig bala in the 4th house, since that represents deepest night, when the second and third brightest objects in the sky can really shine. Finally, Saturn has dig bala in the 7th, since that represents the sunset, or the death of the Sun. Saturn and Sun are mortal enemies, and Saturn feels empowered when his enemy is on his way down. Another way to look at it: if Saturn is the butler and Sun is the king, when the king goes to sleep, the butler finally has free reign over the castle. Either way, Saturn in the 7th house has strength.

TABLE 3.1. PLANETARY STRENGTH AND WEAKNESS

PLANET	OWN SIGNS	EXALTED	DEBILITATED	DIG BALA
Sun	5-Leo	1-Aries	7-Libra	10th house
Moon	4-Cancer	2 Taurus	8-Scorpio	4th house
Mercury	3-Gemini, 6-Virgo	6-Virgo	12-Pisces	1st house
Venus	2-Taurus, 7-Libra	12-Pisces	6-Virgo	4th house
Mars	1-Aries, 8-Scorpio	10-Capricorn	4-Cancer	10th house
Jupiter	9-Sagittarius, 12-Pisces	4-Cancer	10-Capricorn	1st house
Saturn	10-Capricorn, 11-Aquarius	7-Libra	1-Aries	7th house
Rahu/Ketu*	None	8-Scorpio	2-Taurus	None

*Different opinions exist for the exaltation/debilitation signs of Rahu and Ketu; use what works for you.

Table 3.2 is a breakdown of what makes planets stable and what makes them unstable and exaggerated.

TABLE 3.2. WHAT MAKES A PLANET STABLE, UNSTABLE, OR EXAGGERATED?

CONFERS STABILITY AND COMFORT	CONFERS INSTABILITY AND EXAGGERATED CONDITION
Planet in own sign, own nakshatra, or dig bala or unafflicted by malefics	Planet in exaltation, debilitation, retrogression, planetary war, combustion, full moon, new moon, or eclipse

What about Mercury's combustion in this chart?

Combustion occurs when a planet is too close to the Sun, especially less than 6 degrees. It's a primary source of weakness and instability, but in the case of Germany vs. Portugal it was not enough to diminish Mercury's effects. In this game, Thomas Muller, a wiry, Mercurial fellow, scored a hat trick for the German side—three goals in one game—which is just the sort of exaggerated outcome you'd expect from a planet that is *both* retrograde *and* combust. That is not to say that combustion helped the German cause, but that the strength of their chart was undiminished by it—in fact, Muller benefited from the heat and frustration of his opponents, one of whom was red-carded for head-butting him.

Retrograde—Good or Bad?

Like your uncle with the sideburns and bell-bottom jeans, retrograde planets are a little funky and, well, retro—going against the grain of their normal apparent motion. They are also quite bright in the sky, being closest to Earth when retrograde. They stand out (like your uncle) in a crowd. So how do we judge? Consider these points:

> Retrograde planets are unstable in that their movement is counter to regular motion. The houses they influence reflect where this instability plays out. This is not always a bad thing.

Retrograde planets are strong because they shine brightest in the sky during this period. When participating in yogas, for example, they can empower them, adding oomph to an otherwise ordinary combination.

For reading health in a horoscope, retrograde planets are rarely good; they usually indicate metabolic and cellular processes not working according to design, such as in the case of cancer.

In horary charts, especially those for health, retrograde planets also produce untoward results. In health prashnas they indicate relapse or having to repeat therapies. In other queries they show delay in achieving the desired object.

And the verdict?

Overall, retrograde planets are generally strong in natal charts and generally a nuisance in horary charts. For our purposes, retrograde benefics are empowered to become victory house planets and can be counted alongside malefics in terms of their effect, though perhaps not quite as strongly.

Using These Techniques Outside of Sports

All of the techniques in this book can be applied to other areas of interest, not just sports prediction. Sport is a laboratory, a testing facility in which we can quickly make sense of what works and what doesn't. The next step is to take these results from the lab into the "real world" with our daily use of *prashna* (horary), *muhurta* (electional), and *jataka* (natal) astrology.

> **All of the techniques in this book can be applied to other areas of interest, not just sports prediction. Sport is a laboratory, a testing facility in which we can quickly make sense of what works and what doesn't.**

For example, *protect the lagna* is a prime directive for a muhurta chart.

Whether you are planning an important event or you are a team playing in the World Cup, having SKY around the 1st house ensures that good angels are with you. If it is good enough for an entire nation and its soccer hopes, it's good enough for choosing when to take your poodle, Peaches, to the hairdresser. Or, for example, in a marriage chart, protecting the 7th house is vital. Instead of SKY around it, imagine a marriage muhurta with PKY on the 7th. With malefics all around, external factors will weigh heavily on such a marriage, regardless of how much two people love each other or how good that muhurta is otherwise.

In a natal chart, SKY for the lagna ensures that you have nine lives, are well liked, and are generally favored by the gods. SKY in the 7th house amounts to having *adhi yoga*, a special combination of benefics across houses 6, 7, and 8 that ensures status and command over others, such as in military or management careers. It is also a first-class wealth combo, conferring comfort and prosperity.

Finally, in a prashna chart, SKY or PKY around any house or planet gives us information about the comfort or discomfort of that house or planet—whether it is blessed and protected or in danger, surrounded by bad people. If the question is "Will Mom get home safely from her Eat, Pray, Love tour around the world?" and one or more among the Moon, 4th house, or 4th lord—all representing "mom"—is surrounded by benefics, then you can rest assured she's living it up and in good company. As to whether she will ever return home, that's another story.

Other Yogas

Parivartana yoga (PY), also called *mutual reception,* occurs when two planets occupy each other's signs, strengthening both planets in turn. If one of these is a benefic, it becomes eligible as a victory house planet, since strong benefics work like malefics in contest prediction. So, add PY to the list of ways benefics become eligible for the victory house technique. Frankly, most of the time I don't pay that much attention to this, though you may want to consider this as a subject for further research.

Of greater interest is when two planets fall within 1 degree celestial longitude of each other, a situation known as *planetary war,* or in Sanskrit *graha yuddha.* The victor on such occasions is the brighter planet—astronomically, the planet with lesser magnitude; failing to know this, look for the planet with the greater declination—that is, the one that is higher in the sky than its opponent.* Failing to know that, Vedic astrologers take the planet with the lesser longitude, but I do not recommend this technique. As a shortcut, consider that Venus is usually the third-brightest object in the sky, behind the Sun and the Moon, and therefore the easy winner in planetary wars involving it. Beyond that, planets are brighter when retrograde than when direct, since they are closer to Earth.

Only consider the lords of houses 1 and 10 for the favorite, and of houses 7 and 4 for the underdog, for this purpose; planetary wars between planets not ruling these houses do not concern us. Generally speaking, when one of these rulers is in a planetary war, it becomes destabilized, regardless of whether it proves the victor. This is true in natal charts as well, where a planetary war indicates instability in the area of life represented by those planets, as well as the planets' natural significations, such as relationships for Venus, or education and children for Jupiter.

When a planetary war is between the rulers of the 1st or 10th house on one side and the 7th or 4th house on the other, knowing the victor becomes more important, since it tells us which side gets the edge. Consider the side with the loser in a planetary war tarnished but not necessarily beaten. Remember, in Jyotisha as in life everything must play out—and we've still got more techniques to consider.

---

*Planetary brightness can be difficult to find, which is why other ways of determining victory in a planetary war were devised, the foremost being which planet owns the "higher ground" or greater declination. Of course, for game charts you can simply step outside and observe the conjunction yourself on the evening before the match. For charts of people, barring a time machine, it is likely you'll need good Vedic astrology software to determine planetary brightness on any given day in history. In general, planets are brighter when retrograde than when they are in their normal motion because they are closer to Earth. A planet moving relatively slower than its normal motion will also be brighter than usual, though not as bright as when it is retrograde. Declination is easier to find, and most good Vedic astrology programs show this.

These last two yogas, the parivartana and graha yuddha, are supplemental considerations to the victory house and SKY techniques described in this chapter and should not be used exclusively. Because parivartana yogas, especially those between the slow-moving outer planets, can last for weeks at a time, it is important to combine these with more time-sensitive methods like the navamsha and sublord techniques described later in this book for accurate prediction.

Finally, a technique involving the Moon says that when the Moon is strong, favorites tend to win. When the Moon is weak, underdogs do. I haven't seen much success with this on its own, but it is a common practice in India that you can test alongside those in this book.

Prashna

"The wallet is at your wife's house!" the chart announced, in no uncertain terms. The day before I had misplaced my money and credit card holder, and after searching everywhere, I finally decided to pull a prashna—a horary chart—asking the question, "Where is my wallet?" As valuables like money and jewelry are ruled by the 2nd house, I looked at the ruler of the 2nd, noting it was in the 7th house, conjunct exalted Jupiter. I could have drawn several other conclusions based on this and other planetary positions, but the chart grabbed me by the collar insistently, and so I made my way to my "wife's house" (I was house-sitting at the time, and therefore this showed up as two residences). "Well, I don't see your wallet anywhere. Are you sure it said *here*?" my wife asked, after looking in all the usual places.

"Yes," I replied, using my best imitation Hindi accent. "The chart said it's definitely at your wife's house!" I even added my Indian head lilt to show I was definitely, 100 percent sure it was there . . . guaranteed.

"Well, I don't know what to tell you, because I've looked everywhere. Are you sure the Jyotish is right, and it's not at *your* house somewhere?" she asked nonplussed, unconvinced of my Jyotish game, despite the many times we had done this to locate *her* lost keys, *her* earrings, *her* phone, and the like.

"Nope, definitely not there," I said resignedly, and I sat on the couch to watch TV, awaiting further inspiration.

In the movie *Men in Black III* (a remarkably philosophical and Jyotish-appropriate movie that explores alternate timelines and event possibilities) there is a great line that goes something like this: "When in doubt, have pie." It means that when you don't see a solution despite your best efforts, do something pleasurable to take your mind off the problem. Then as if on cue, a thought hit me: *Look between the cushions!* And voilà! There was my slim credit card case, safely snuggled between the cushions of my overstuffed and indecently comfortable couch. *Hmmm*, I thought. I hadn't considered Jupiter's effect—that the wallet would be near something big, heavy, nourishing, and brown (Jupiter rules the colors yellow and brown).

The techniques described in this chapter worked well enough in the World Cup. However, I also ran across games where SKY and victory house were not enough to explain some match outcomes. I turned to my inner voice again, but he was more reluctant this time, perhaps wanting me to work for the information. He left me one clue, however, muttering, *The victory house technique could be more refined.* I took this as a starting point, bid him farewell, and began to think about what this could possibly mean . . .

Summary

In summary, for this chapter, memorize the following:

- **Technique 1:** Malefics in victory houses (1, 3, 6, 10, and 11 for the favorite and 7, 9, 12, 4, and 5 for the underdog) indicate physical strength and toughness for their teams. All other factors being equal (there's more to this book, in case you haven't noticed), this indicates victory.
- **Technique 2:** SKY and PKY indicate luck or divine intervention, a powerful source of strength or debility for the team indicated, though PKY is not as bad as SKY is good.

- **Spot Plays:** (1) Mutual reception, or parivartana yoga (PY), especially between victory houses, gives some extra strength to the team indicated. (2) Planetary war, or graha yuddha, generally weakens planets and the houses they own but can give the winner of the planetary war a boost over the loser. For game charts consider only the lords of houses 1 and 10 for the favorite and 7 and 4 for the underdog.

4

On the Cusp of Greatness

Special Degrees of Victory

We write, we think, when writing please us
In truth, 'tis when the grahas seize us
May those Caesars in the sky
Be kind to us, before we die!

FROM THE AUTHOR'S UNPUBLISHED
POEM "BHAV' BALLADS"

As I pondered my inner voice's suggestion on how to make the victory house technique better, I turned my attention to the Women's World Cup, which witnessed the following matchup: Germany (−10,000) vs. Thailand (+ 4107).

Yes, you read it right—Germany was favored by −10,000 to win against Thailand. That means you had to bet $10,000 to win $100 on a German victory. On the other hand, if you wagered $100 on Thailand, you'd go home with $4207 if they won. Recall that the favorite will always have negative moneyline odds (less payoff for a safer bet) and the underdog will always have positive moneyline odds (more payoff for a risky bet).

This is about as astronomical as things get in soccer (okay, football for the rest of you). It's like Michael Jordan, in his prime, playing basketball with a member of the Thai women's soccer team. The Germans were bigger, stronger, and more skilled. Yet they still didn't cover the spread. What's a spread, and why wasn't it covered? I'm glad you asked.

We've learned how to read the *moneyline*—that's the (−10,000) and (+4107) notation next to a team indicating how likely they are to win. The *point spread*, on the other hand, is what experts think the likely difference in the score will be. For example, in this game the spread was six and a half goals, usually written like this:

$$-6\tfrac{1}{2} \text{ Germany} \qquad +6\tfrac{1}{2} \text{ Thailand}$$

This means that the Germans had to win by seven goals—i.e., more than 6½—for you to win this bet, and Thailand could lose by up to six goals and still win the wager, or "cover the spread" in betting lingo.

Huh? Why would you take a risk like that instead of just betting on Germany to win outright? Because of the payout. The full line looked something like this:

Team	Spread	Moneyline
Germany	−6½ (−175)	−10,000
Thailand	+6½ (+140)	+4107

If you bet on Germany to win by more than six goals, you would only have to wager $175 to win $100 (in addition to your bet). That's a lot better than wagering $10,000, though still not great. Part of that was due to Germany's having trounced Ivory Coast 10 to 0 a few days earlier; everyone expected a similar rout. On the other hand, betting on Thailand not to lose by more than six goals would win you $140 for every $100 you wagered (in addition to your bet)—not the killing you'd make by betting on them to win outright, but still a 140 percent return on your investment. Not bad for a couple of hours' work (and not something you typically get in the stock market). And that's exactly what happened. To see why, we need to consider the role that cuspal strength plays in a chart, and in doing so we'll dive into what is for most traditional Jyotishis some unfamiliar territory: the outer, invisible planets.

What Exactly Is a Cusp?

As I sat rubbing a sore shoulder, thinking *What could make the victory house technique more specific, more powerful?* I hit on a nerve. In ayurveda there are special points on the human body called *marmani* (literally, "killer points") that represent junctures where *prana,* or life force, is tied up with nerve plexi, blood vessels, or other vulnerable tissues. Ayurveda uses these points to access the body-mind matrix for healing; martial artists use them to incapacitate an opponent. *What if astrology had such points?*

I reasoned. In fact astrology does—they're called house cusps, and they represent the exact degree where a specific house ends and another begins. For example, the 5th house cusp is the beginning of the 5th house and the end of the 4th, at least in the house system we will employ. Think of cusps like invisible property lines in space. (They may not seem like much, but try throwing a party in your neighbor's yard and see what happens!)

Think of cusps like invisible property lines in space.

Even if you've never worked with them, you still know at least one important cusp: the ascendant. The lagna degree represents the cusp of the 1st house, and exactly 180 degrees opposite lies the 7th house cusp. Similarly, every house has a cusp that can be calculated in a number of ways. In fact, there are many house systems with different techniques of allocation, some of them with funny names like Porphyry, Regiomantus, Shripati, and others. For our purposes, we will use the Placidus system, a staple of Western astrologers, which has had a renaissance in Jyotisha thanks to K. S. Krishnamurti, who used it with great success, as did mathematician, astronomer, geographer, and astrologer Ptolemy. If it's good enough for them, it's good enough for us.

Cusps represent the concentrated essence of a house, or bhava: the place where that bhava's meanings manifest most strongly. For example, if the 6th house represents strife, and the planet Venus rules relationships, then Venus placed in the 6th could indicate general relationship problems. Now put that Venus within a degree or two of the 6th *cusp,* and you have a recipe for knock-down, drag-out disputes.

In addition to holding concentrated energy, cusps are *sandhis,* transitions from one state to another, junctures between two realities. For example, the lagna represents the rising point of any planet or constellation over the eastern horizon (hence the appellation *rising sign*). This is a transition from dark to light, from below-the-horizon invisible to above-the-horizon visible—a major sandhi.

**Cusps are *sandhis,* transitions from one state to another,
junctures between two realities.**

In addition to the lagna, there is another prime cusp, called the MC, or *medium coeli,* literally the "middle of the sky." The MC represents the culmination point of any planet, meaning that to the observer at any given locality that planet has reached its highest possible point in the sky. The MC is the epitome of the 10th house, which stands for glory and victory. After planets attain the MC, they appear to fall away, down toward the western horizon, or 7th house cusp—another major sandhi and an important point for considering the outcome of events, since it also represents the lagna degree of the underdog.

The *imum coeli,* literally "bottom of the sky," abbreviated as IC, represents the nadir, or 4th cusp. The IC is the point opposite the MC and represents midnight, another important transition, as it is the 10th cusp for the underdog team.

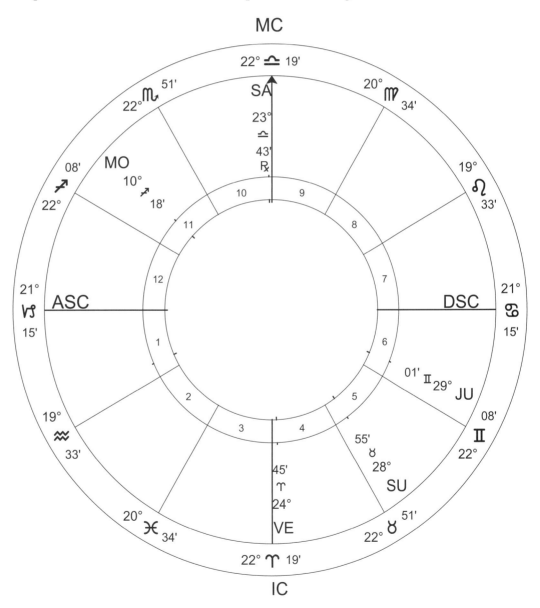

A Western chart showing the four major cusps: the ascendant (ASC) on the left; the medium coeli (MC) on top; the descendant (DSC) to the right; and imum coeli (IC) on the bottom. In this chart, Saturn is on the MC while Venus hugs the IC, each within 2°30' of orb.

Because Vedic astrology's square charts do not lend themselves to displaying the cusps as well as the pie-shaped charts of Western astrology, we use a table like the one below. The first column shows the house (bhava) number. The second shows the cuspal degree and sign. For this chart, the 4th cusp is 21°36' Sagittarius, and the 10th is its opposite, 21°36' Gemini (remember that the charts show this in degrees:minutes or degrees:minutes:seconds). Notice that these degrees are the same; thus, when the lagna cusp is a certain degree, the 7th will be the same degree in the opposite sign. This applies to every pair of opposing cusps: 1st and 7th, 2nd and 8th, 3rd and 9th, 4th and 10th, 5th and 11th, and 6th and 12th. Planets located on either side of the cusps have a powerful effect on the team they represent.

Bhava	Cusp
1st h.	18:10:48 Vir
2nd h.	13:44:23 Lib
3rd h.	15:09:56 Sco
4th h.	21:36:12 Sag
5th h.	26:33:08 Cap
6th h.	25:24:19 Aqu
7th h.	18:10:48 Pis
8th h.	13:44:23 Ari
9th h.	15:09:56 Tau
10th h.	21:36:12 Gem
11th h.	26:33:08 Can
12th h.	25:24:19 Leo

So, the crucial question is: which cusps go with which team? To get the answer, recall the victory houses:

- Houses 1, 3, 6, 10, and 11 for the favorite
- Houses 7, 9, 12, 4, and 5 for the underdog

Because cusps are microcosms of the houses they represent, the cusps of houses 1, 3, 6, 10, and 11 affect the favorite. Likewise, those of houses 7, 9, 12, 4, and 5 affect the underdog. For outcome prediction we throw out the 3/9 and 5/11 cusps, since their effects are negligible. This leaves us with:

- 1st, 6th, and 10th cusps for the favorite
- 7th, 12th, and 4th cusps for the underdog

> **Because cusps are microcosms of the houses they represent, the cusps of houses 1, 3, 6, 10, and 11 affect the favorite. Likewise, those of houses 7, 9, 12, 4, and 5 affect the underdog.**

Some astrologers sneer at the 6/12 axis, utilizing only the core 1, 10, 7, and 4 cusps for prediction. I have included the 6/12 axis here because it works. Try it and decide for yourself.

Cusps in a Nutshell

The 1st and 7th cusps represent a team itself; the 1st is the favorite, the 7th their opponent.

The 10th and 4th cusps represent their respective team's glory and victory.

The 6th and 12th cusps represent their respective team's fighting spirit.

Page 60 shows the chart and table together. This is for the Germany-Thailand game mentioned earlier. Looking from one to the other, can you spot any planets within 2°30' on either side of the 1/7, 6/12, or 4/10 cusps?

If you said Pluto, you'd be correct. In this chart, Pluto falls in the underdog's 10th house, boosting their chances. They may not win, but they'll try damn hard. By only looking at the victory houses, we see that the favorite has a distinct advantage: all malefic grahas in upachaya houses with the addition of exalted Jupiter. And certainly Germany won the game. But seeing Pluto on the 4th cusp gave me a feeling in the pit of my stomach, a certainty that the underdog would outperform, and the favorite wouldn't play up to their expected level. As it was, Thailand held the Germans 1 to 0 at the half and lost the game 4 to 0—two goals below the expected total, and good enough to win our over/under bet.

To find out the effects of the different planets when they fall on a cusp, let's now take a look at . . .

The Actors

The Usual Suspects

Sun acts as a negative force, burning up the cusps it touches much as it burns up planets that come too close, a phenomenon called *combustion,* which translates into loss for the indicated team.

		Uk 00:25 Me 11:09 Mo 20:58	Ma 00:06 Su 00:25
Ur 25:52 Ke 12:49			
NeR 15:50			Ve 15:27 Ju 24:55
PlR 20:47	SaR 05:58		Ra 12:49 Asc 18:10

North Indian chart: SaR 05:58 (8/7); Ra 12:49, Asc 18:10 (5/4); Ju 24:55, Ve 15:27; PlR 20:47 (6/9/3/12); Su 00:25, Ma 00:06; Ke 12:49, Ur 25:52 (10/11, 2/1); Mo 20:58, Me 11:09, Uk 00:25; NeR 15:50

Bhava	Cusp
1st h.	18:10:48 Vir
2nd h.	13:44:23 Lib
3rd h.	15:09:56 Sco
4th h.	21:36:12 Sag
5th h.	26:33:08 Cap
6th h.	25:24:19 Aqu
7th h.	18:10:48 Pis
8th h.	13:44:23 Ari
9th h.	15:09:56 Tau
10th h.	21:36:12 Gem
11th h.	26:33:08 Can
12th h.	25:24:19 Leo

Germany (−10,000) vs. Thailand (+4107), 15:00 LT,
June 16, 2015, Winnipeg, Canada

Moon, not as strong as the other planets, lends a lazy influence on all the cusps, leading to lackluster performance.

Mars on the cusps acts the way you'd think, as a galvanizing force impelling a team to victory. It does this for the 6/12 and 1/7 cusps, but like the Sun's effect it is not as generous on the 4/10 cusps. This was a big surprise for me, as I expected Mars to perform well here; instead, he appears to give loss, though more research is needed.

Rahu on the cusps gives force and ambition. But because it is a shadow graha it does not impel with the same force as the visible planets do. I use a 2-degree orb for it as well as for all the other invisible grahas. This includes the outer planets Uranus and Neptune, as well as the dwarf planets Pluto and Ceres, the centaur Chiron, and the upagraha Upaketu. And since Rahu and Ketu are always 180 degrees apart, whenever we speak of Rahu as positive on a cusp, we could also say that it is Ketu acting negatively on the opposite cusp, though in practice these are taken as one.

Jupiter, as you may have guessed, is an equal opportunity benefic, granting favor and victory to every cusp it touches.

Saturn on the 6/12 and 4/10 cusps brings victory. On the 1st and 7th he does the opposite, slowing and handicapping the indicated team.

Mercury's position requires more research. On the 6/12 axis he may be a positive influence for his team, but on the 4/10 and 1/7 he is, well, mercurial, which is why I don't use him much. If you decide to employ Mercury, consider the houses he rules. When he rules victory houses for a team, he may act positively for that team. When the opposite is the case, he may become a negative influence.

Ketu, Rahu's opposite, is unilaterally negative on a cusp.

Venus exerts a positive if mild influence on all cusps he touches—the opposite of what the Moon does.*

Upaketu and Gulika, the invisible lurkers, make their way onto our list as representatives of their oft-overlooked ilk, the upagrahas, who, like the invisible outer planets and Rahu/Ketu, all take a tight orb of 2 degrees. They exert a lesser effect on game outcomes than the visible planets do. Like Ketu, Upaketu ("little Ketu") is negative all around, while Gulika is a special case. Negative on the 1st and 7th houses, Gulika behaves like his daddy, Saturn, on the 4th and 10th houses, helping teams earn victory. I have also observed that when the lord of the 1st or 7th house is tightly conjunct Gulika (within a 1-degree orb), the team represented by that planet is highly detrimented. Nonetheless, I do not use Gulika much and have left him out of most of the chart illustrations in this book, except where he has a direct influence on an outcome.

While Upaketu and Gulika seem to have some effect on game charts, the remaining upagrahas (along with the asteroids Pallas, Vesta, and Juno, as well as outer-system objects like Sedna and Makemake) are candidates for further graha research, especially in Jyotisha, where to my knowledge no one has used them so far.

---

*Note that all planets are male in Vedic astrology; all nakshatras are female.

The Outsiders

In considering the outer, invisible planets that have not been a part of traditional Jyotisha, always remember that they only use a 2-degree maximum orb (unlike the visible grahas, to whom I allot a wider berth of 2°30'). But first, a word about the retrograde effects of the outer planets when they fall on a cusp.

As a rule, all the outer planets (Uranus, Neptune, and the neoplanets Chiron and Ceres) except for Pluto, when retrograde, tend to give the opposite effect of their normal influence. So, for example, retrograde Neptune can actually empower a team with inspiration that leads to victory, while Uranus, normally a positive force, turns psycho against a cusp when retrograde. Chiron, the Wounded Warrior, expresses his noble nature when direct, but his self-pitying, vindictive side emerges when he turns backward. And Ceres, a nurturer, abandons her nurturing qualities for a more vampirish demeanor, draining cusps of energy when retrograde. The exception to this rule is Pluto; being lord of the underworld, he seems to work the same whether retrograde or direct.

> **All the outer planets (Uranus, Neptune, and the neoplanets Chiron and Ceres) except for Pluto, when retrograde, tend to give the opposite effect of their normal influence.**

Uranus rules electricity and unconventional energy. It is refreshing and eccentric, a galvanizing force for everything it touches, therefore asserting a positive effect on the house cusps it connects with, provided it is in direct motion. When retrograde, that electricity goes haywire, and instead of being a galvanizing force it can short-circuit a team's chances.

Neptune is the ruler of the oceans and life's deepest mysteries. He is associated with dreams, sleep, and the subconscious mind, including altered states of consciousness and meditation. He is the antithesis of the primal physical energy necessary for competition and is therefore a downer when it comes to winning in sports. Neptune conjunct any cusp counts against the team that cusp represents, unless he is retrograde, in which case he does the opposite. Pay special attention to when these planets are stationary (*kutila* in Sanskrit), as the effect of their stations can last for a week or more and make their effects less certain.

Pluto, a dwarf planet, is shrouded in mystery and intrigue. As the traditional ruler of the underworld, Pluto doesn't like authority and may have a grudge against favorites—he spoils their chances when conjunct the 1st house. He does this for the 7th as well, though perhaps with less vehemence. However, like Saturn, Pluto on the 4/10 cusps can exert a positive influence. Discovered late in Western astronomy, Pluto was recently downgraded as a "sub" or dwarf planet, which could subdue his effects on human psychology and performance. Nonetheless, it is still worth noting his position, even as we acknowledge his fellow dwarf planet, Ceres.

Ceres, the largest object in the asteroid belt, was recently upgraded to dwarf planet. Scientists believe that Ceres, despite being about the size of Texas, contains more fresh water than Earth does. Its influence, like all planets not visible to the naked eye, is less than that of a true planet but is nonetheless very real with respect to determining event outcomes. Ceres is beneficial on cusps when direct, and detrimental when retrograde.

Chiron behaves like Ceres, helping grant victory. But when retrograde on a cusp, Chiron, the archetypal Wounded Warrior, indicates that injuries and poor play are likely for the team indicated.

TABLE 4.1. PLANETARY AND CUSPAL RELATIONSHIPS

PLANET	CUSPS 1/7	CUSPS 4/10	CUSPS 6/12	GENERAL EFFECTS
Sun	–	–	–	Burns up the cusps it touches
Moon	–	–	–	Generally lazy and inauspicious, though not as strong as the Sun or Saturn
Mars	+	–	+	Gives fight and will to win, but also anger and frustration on the 4/10 axis
Rahu	+	+	+	Gives ambition, but is not as strong as visible grahas
Jupiter	+	+	+	A powerful benefic force on all cusps
Saturn	–	+	+	Gives discipline on the 4/10 and 6/12 axis, but slows teams down when on the 1/7
Mercury	+/–	+/–	+	Mercury's position is precarious and requires more research—I do not use it; on the 6/12 axis he seems to be favorable, but overall his influence may vary depending on the houses he rules; when ruling victory-house houses for a team, he may act more positively, but otherwise the influence is negative
Ketu	–	–	–	Gives confusion and loss on all cusps; not as strong as visible grahas

PLANET	CUSPS 1/7	CUSPS 4/10	CUSPS 6/12	GENERAL EFFECTS
Venus	+	+	+	A benefic influence, though not as strong as Jupiter; gives grace, talent, and victory
Uranus	+/−	+/−	+/−	Gives electricity, wakefulness, and inspiration when direct; gives eccentricity and blunders when retrograde
Neptune	−/+	−/+	−/+	Negative when direct, inspirational when retrograde
Pluto	−	+	−	A mildly negative influence on 1/7 and 6/12, but can give victory on the 4/10 axis
Upaketu	−	−	−	Behaves like a mild malefic on all cusps
Gulika	−	+	+/−	Gulika's effects are hard to discern, though I have seen it behave like Saturn—negatively on the 1/7 axis, but positively on the 4/10. The 6/12 needs more research. Special use: when conjunct within a 1-degree orb of the lord of the 1st or 7th house he spoils that team's chances.

2015: Year of the Dwarf Planet

Asteroids and dwarf planets are some of the most exciting players in the area of event prediction, and a tagline in a number of astronomy magazines singles out the year 2015 as "the year of the dwarf planet."* The growing number of space bodies that we are aware of in our solar system, and the almost countless such objects beyond our solar system, means that more than ever there are new grahas in the game to account for. Knowing how they affect us can help us build and refine new techniques of prediction. The dawn of discovery that has witnessed space probes (named *Dawn* and *New Horizons,* incidentally) reach Ceres and the protoplanet Vesta, as well as the far reaches of Pluto, means that we are living in an age that could very well redefine what planets are.

---

*"2015 Will Be the Year of the Dwarf Planet, and You Need to Tell People About It!" by Emily Lakdawalla, www.planetary.org/blogs/emily-lakdawalla/2014

The Vulcan Death Grip

We already know that planets anywhere in the victory houses can empower their respective teams. But if these planets happen to sit within 2°30′ on either side of the cusps of houses 1/7, 4/10, or 6/12 (2 degrees for invisible grahas), they become doubly powerful to affect the nature of the game. Imagine it like a Vulcan death grip, a point that exerts an exceptional effect on the nervous system. Achilles is a famous example of a warrior who was undefeatable, save for the sensitive point on his eponymous heel. In the same way, favored teams can be defeated if they have unfavorable planets on their cusps.

> **Planets anywhere in the victory houses can empower their respective teams. But if these planets happen to sit within 2.5 degrees on either side of the cusps of houses 1/7, 4/10, or 6/12 (2 degrees for invisible grahas), they become doubly powerful to affect the nature of the game.**

Moreover, the closer the bond within this tight orb, the more powerful that particular planet's effect on the cusp. Three degrees or more distance from the cusp simply amounts to a planet occupying a house, not conjoining a cusp. (The exception may be a strong Jupiter, which seems to exert its influence up to 3 degrees from a house cusp on either side. Other exalted planets may also have their orb extended, so use your discretion.) But less than 3 degrees incrementally makes the planet's effect stronger. Less than 1 degree from a cusp is very strong indeed, and within 30 minutes is a case of extra-special effect, one that can color the entire chart.

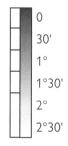

A planet's ability to affect a cusp is directly related to its distance from it; the closer the planet, the more "heat" it can apply, and therefore the more powerful its effect.

Let's take a look at an example of how this works in the chart on page 66.

Pittsburgh was favored in this match, but they were cut down 7 to 4 by the struggling Milwaukee Brewers. Why? If you said Sun in the 7th house, making the underdog stronger, you'd be wrong. In fact, using the victory house technique in this case we find no clear winner, since the favorite gets two malefics and the underdog one. Even if you factor the afflicted SKY for the 7th house, formed by Venus and Mercury, you'd still be hard-pressed, since that yoga is marred to some extent by Mars and Rahu.

Ke 07:07
UrR 25:58

CeR 1:36

Mo 00:38

Asc 10:28
NeR 14:24
ChR 25:42

PlR 19:07

Sa 05:03

Ju 10:41
Su 15:15

Uk 15:15
VeR 20:47
Ma 21:26

Me 12:11
Ra 07:07

UrR 25:58 Ke 07:07	Mo 00:38		
ChR 25:42 NeR 14:24 Asc 10:28			Uk 15:15 VeR 20:47 Ma 21:26
CeR 1:36			Ju 10:41 Su 15:15
PlR 19:07	Sa 05:03		Ra 07:07 Me 12:11

Bhava	Cusp
1st h.	10:28:50 Aqu
2nd h.	29:04:11 Pis
3rd h.	00:15:40 Tau
4th h.	22:50:29 Tau
5th h.	13:11:06 Gem
6th h.	06:11:01 Can
7th h.	10:28:50 Leo
8th h.	29:04:11 Vir
9th h.	00:15:40 Sco
10th h.	22:50:29 Sco
11th h.	13:11:06 Sag
12th h.	06:11:01 Cap

<u>Pittsburgh Pirates (−167)</u> vs. Milwaukee Brewers (+141), 19:11 LT,
Sept. 1, 2015, Milwaukee, Wisconsin

The real dealmaker in this chart is Jupiter. Take a closer look at the 7th cusp (called the *descendant*) in the table below the chart. In fact, you don't even need the table—just look at the ascendant degree: the 7th cusp is the same degree in the opposite sign. Notice how closely Jupiter hugs the descendant. This serves as a powerful nerve pinch that energizes the underdog. Jupiter's effect superceded everything else in the chart to bring the dogs victory. Irrespective of which houses Jupiter rules, its placement on a cusp shows success for the indicated team. This, coupled with the planetary war between Venus and Mars, ensured victory for underdog Milwaukee.*

*Venus, being the brightest object in the night sky after the Moon, wins this and most planetary wars; being retrograde, it was even brighter than usual, ensuring the underdog's 10th house got all the glory. An imperfect SKY is also present for the 7th house. Note how the multiple factors indicating victory for the underdog denote fixed karma, a case where no matter how hard the other team tries, victory is just not in the stars for them.

Now here's a game with Jupiter just outside a 2°30' orb:

North Indian chart (left):

- House 12 / 1 area: Ke 07:10, UrR 25:53
- Top center (11): Asc 08:32, NeR 14:19, Ch 25:30
- House 10 / 9: CeR 1:24, PlR 19:05
- House 2 / 8 / 5 center: Mo 12:28 (left), Sa 05:12 (right)
- House 3 / 4 bottom left: Uk 18:07, VeR 20:27, Ma 23:19
- House 6 / 7 bottom: Ju 11:20, Su 18:07, Me 15:08, Ra 07:10

South Indian chart (right):

UrR 25:53 Ke 07:10		Mo 12:28	
Ch 25:30 NeR 14:19 Asc 08:32			Uk 18:07 VeR 20:27 Ma 23:19
CeR 1:24			Ju 11:20 Su 18:07
PlR 19:05	Sa 05:12		Ra 07:10 Me 15:08

Bhava	Cusp
1st h.	08:45:52 Aqu
2nd h.	24:44:23 Pis
3rd h.	26:48:09 Ari
4th h.	20:37:43 Tau
5th h.	12:00:26 Gem
6th h.	05:37:18 Can
7th h.	08:45:52 Leo
8th h.	24:44:23 Vir
9th h.	26:48:09 Lib
10th h.	20:37:43 Sco
11th h.	12:00:26 Sag
12th h.	05:37:18 Cap

Atlanta Braves (+141) vs. Washington Nationals (−169), 19:06 LT,
Sept. 4, 2015, Washington, D.C.

Here, the saintly benefactor Jupiter is in the 7th house, slightly out of orb of the 7th cusp to really pinch a nerve. Remember, when exalted, Jupiter's influence can extend beyond the 2°30' orb, but here he is in ordinary condition and just a little too far removed to exert his magnanimous influence. Atlanta, having lost 15 to 1 the night before, made a game of it against the favored Nationals, pushing into extra innings. But finally they gave out and lost 5 to 2, as Washington, ever stylish and dramatic, hit a three-run homer to end the game. If only Jupiter had been closer . . .

Well, above is a case from the same day where Jupiter *was* closer.

Left chart:
- Ke 07:10, UrR 25:53 (house 12/1)
- CeR 1:24 (house 10)
- Asc 09:21, NeR 14:19, Ch 25:30 (house 9/11)
- PlR 19:05 (house 9)
- Mo 14:10 (house 2/5)
- Sa 05:13 (house 8)
- Ju 11:22, Su 18:14 (house 7)
- Uk 18:14, VeR 20:26, Ma 23:24 (house 3/4)
- Me 15:15, Ra 07:10 (house 6)

Right chart:
- UrR 25:53, Ke 07:10
- Mo 14:10
- Ch 25:30, NeR 14:19, Asc 09:21
- Uk 18:14, VeR 20:26, Ma 23:24
- CeR 1:24
- Ju 11:22, Su 18:14
- PlR 19:05 | Sa 05:13
- Ra 07:10, Me 15:15

Bhava	Cusp
1st h.	09:21:28 Aqu
2nd h.	24:36:32 Pis
3rd h.	26:39:07 Ari
4th h.	20:40:55 Tau
5th h.	12:18:47 Gem
6th h.	06:11:02 Can
7th h.	09:21:28 Leo
8th h.	24:36:32 Vir
9th h.	26:39:07 Lib
10th h.	20:40:55 Sco
11th h.	12:18:47 Sag
12th h.	06:11:02 Cap

Seattle Mariners (+124) vs. Oakland Athletics (−127), 19:07 LT,
Sept. 4, 2015, Oakland, California

Here, Jupiter falls within orb, about 2 degrees from the 7th cusp, giving the underdog a much better chance. That, along with their so-so SKY, meant victory. Though down early, Seattle rallied and never looked back, winning 11 to 8.

Okay, had enough of Jupiter? The point in showing these very similar charts is that though they all possess the same SKY and victory house configurations, they produced different outcomes. The reason? The presence of a planet on a sensitive cusp—in this case Jupiter. If you're especially clever, you'll notice that the proximity of Jupiter to the 7th cusp is directly proportional to its influence on the game: very close ensured victory; loosely on the cusp but within range (as in the Seattle game above), and the underdog had to fight to come back from behind; and out of range? Well, you guessed it, tough luck for the underdog.

Other Planets in Action

Astronomers call Chiron a centaur because he is half asteroid, half comet. Riding between Uranus and Saturn, he also exemplifies the qualities of the mythological centaur Chiron, who was Achilles's half-human, half-horse teacher. When in direct motion on a cusp, he displays his warrior abilities to promise strength and fighting spirit to its team. When retrograde or stationary, however, watch out! Injuries, penalties, and loss entail as the *wounded* nature of this warrior gets literal, hampering the cusp he happens to straddle.

Let's take a closer look at the two sides of this mythic monster:

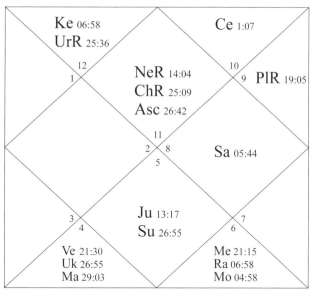

Bhava	Cusp
1st h.	26:42:40 Aqu
2nd h.	07:09:30 Ari
3rd h.	06:34:43 Tau
4th h.	00:21:01 Gem
5th h.	23:17:37 Gem
6th h.	19:59:46 Can
7th h.	26:42:40 Leo
8th h.	07:09:30 Lib
9th h.	06:34:43 Sco
10th h.	00:21:01 Sag
11th h.	23:17:37 Sag
12th h.	19:59:46 Cap

New York Giants (+245) vs. <u>Dallas Cowboys (−312)</u>, 19:33 LT, Sept. 13, 2015, Arlington, Texas

In this game, Dallas barely squeezed out a last-second win, despite being heavily favored. Note retrograde Chiron lurking near the lagna, which augured injuries to Dallas's key players as well as turnovers and sloppy play for much of the game. So why did the Cowboys win at all? Chiron's conjunction is not very tight, whereas the defending team had the Sun almost *exactly* on its cusp, the 7th house. This is a major problem. Couple that with Venus on the 6th cusp for the favorite and you get enough firepower to overcome Chiron's retrograde influence. Nonetheless, everything indicated in Jyotisha must play out, and it did. The Cowboys looked lost until the final seconds of the game.

On the flip side is an instance of Chiron helping his team to victory in the chart below. What's the difference between this chart and the previous one? Here, Chiron is direct in motion atop the MC, or 10th house cusp. While this

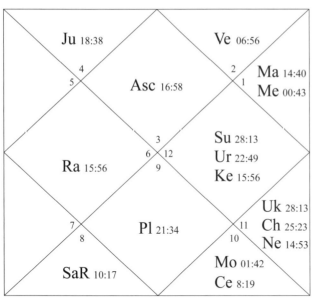

Bhava   Cusp
1st h.   16:58:40 Gem
2nd h.   06:36:53 Can
3rd h.   28:30:31 Can
4th h.   25:57:26 Leo
5th h.   01:27:45 Lib
6th h.   11:33:07 Sco
7th h.   16:58:40 Sag
8th h.   06:36:53 Cap
9th h.   28:30:31 Cap
10th h.   25:57:26 Aqu
11th h.   01:27:45 Ari
12th h.   11:33:07 Tau

Barcelona (+220) vs. Atletico Madrid (−286), 12:16:30 LT,
April 12, 2015, Madrid, Spain

placement didn't help much because Chiron is in a stolen cusp—we'll learn about stolen cusps a bit later—the favorites also have Saturn on the 6th cusp as well as a *perfect* SKY, driving them to an easy win in their Spanish League basketball game, 91 to 78.

Note that sometimes when it rains it pours, and this game presents a plethora of factors to consider. Beginning with the victory house technique, we see overwhelming support for the favorite. Coupled with the absolutely stunning SKY, which features an exalted Jupiter and Venus in its own house, this should be more than enough to signal fixed karma and a blowout win for them. However, there is a fly in the ointment in the form of the Sun atop the 10th cusp. This is a big minus for the favorite team, though not enough to offset the help from the aforementioned Saturn on their 6th cusp and Chiron on the 10th. It wasn't a blowout, but it was an easy win nonetheless.

In the chart on page 72 the Sun is also on the MC, burning up the 10th cusp, but here he has help. Do you see Saturn exactly on top of the ascendant, also depressing the favorite? This is gold for predicting, since it aligns two strong indicators to point to the same conclusion: that the favorite must lose. And they did, 7 to 5.*

"But wait!" you say. "Don't both Saturn and the Sun count *for* the favorite in the victory house technique? Isn't a malefic on the ascendant good?" The answer is yes—and had these two baddies not been within orb of their respective cusps, they would have helped their team. However, cuspal strength outweighs victory house strength, just like the Vulcan death grip overcomes mere mortal fisticuffs.

> **Cuspal strength outweighs victory house strength, just like the Vulcan death grip overcomes mere mortal fisticuffs.**

Why do I emphasize underdog victories? Simple—fewer people give them a chance, which makes their accomplishments extra-special. Favorites only need

---

*"Why so close, though?" I like the way you think. Hold on, I'll be addressing that very question when we look at the influence of sublords in chapter 6. If you haven't tired of me saying it yet, you will: everything in Jyotisha is cumulative, and we will learn how to weigh multiple factors in the chapters to come.

PlR 19:04

CeR 1:18 10 9

Asc 05:07
Sa 05:18
                    7   Me 16:44
                    6   Ra 07:09

NeR 14:16
ChR 25:29
           8
        11   5   Su 19:51
        2   Ju 11:43

Ke 07:09
UrR 25:50   12
           1   4   Ma 24:28
                    3   Ve 20:24
                        Uk 19:51

            Mo 06:19

UrR 25:50 Ke 07:09			Mo 06:19
NeR 14:16 ChR 25:29			Uk 19:51 Ve 20:24 Ma 24:28
CeR 1:18			Ju 11:43 Su 19:51
PlR 19:04	Asc 05:07 Sa 05:18		Ra 07:09 Me 16:44

Bhava	Cusp
1st h.	05:07:22 Sco
2nd h.	06:17:30 Sag
3rd h.	12:22:03 Cap
4th h.	18:42:56 Aqu
5th h.	19:41:29 Pis
6th h.	14:27:51 Ari
7th h.	05:07:22 Tau
8th h.	06:17:30 Gem
9th h.	12:22:03 Can
10th h.	18:42:56 Leo
11th h.	19:41:29 Vir
12th h.	14:27:51 Lib

Chicago White Sox (+179) vs. <u>Kansas City Royals (−217)</u>, 13:12:25 LT,
Sept. 6, 2015, Kansas City, Missouri

a decent chart to get by; underdogs, especially heavy underdogs, need an exceptional one to see them through.

So let's continue with another example of two planets working together to ensure victory for the underdog in the chart on page 73.

The Cubs came in heavily favored at more than 2-to-1 odds, which is about as biased as it gets in baseball, unlike other sports where the odds can soar dramatically higher (e.g., Germany vs. Thailand at the beginning of this chapter).

The victory house technique shows both teams with two malefics (Saturn/Ketu for the favorite and Mars/Rahu for the underdog) in victory houses, with the underdog also sporting Mercury, a benefic that is eligible to be a victory house graha because he is exalted. You can also add in Venus, as it is retrograde, thus giving the underdog a decent edge using this technique. I say decent because benefic planets, no matter how tough they become by being exalted or retrograde, are still not as gritty as the malefic grahas. In essence, they get invited to the fight club by

UrR 26:00 Mo 15:07 Ke 07:06			
NeR 14:26 ChR 25:45			Uk 14:14 Ma 20:47 VeR 20:59
CeR 1:41 Asc 21:47			Ju 10:28 Su 14:14
PlR 19:08	Sa 05:00		Ra 07:06 Me 11:04

Bhava	Cusp
1st h.	21:47:20 Cap
2nd h.	08:35:07 Pis
3rd h.	14:09:05 Ari
4th h.	09:49:38 Tau
5th h.	01:23:21 Gem
6th h.	23:22:52 Gem
7th h.	21:47:20 Can
8th h.	08:35:07 Vir
9th h.	14:09:05 Lib
10th h.	09:49:38 Sco
11th h.	01:23:21 Sag
12th h.	23:22:52 Sag

<u>Chicago Cubs (−220)</u> vs. Cincinnati Reds (+185), 19:07 LT, Aug. 31, 2015, Cincinnati, Ohio

being retrograde (or by knowing Brad Pitt), but they're never quite as rough-and-tumble as the bad guys.

Is this victory house advantage enough to beat a heavily favored opponent? Probably not, though it might keep them close. But Cincinnati had Mars *and* Venus within 2 degrees of their 7th house cusp, giving their opponent not only the finger but the Vulcan death grip with both hands. They blew them out, 13 to 6. Indeed, when two or more planets together indicate the same outcome, it is convincing evidence of fixed karma; no matter how hard the other team tries, victory is just not in the stars for them.

> **When two or more planets together indicate the same outcome, it is convincing evidence of fixed karma; no matter how hard the other team tries, victory is just not in the stars for them.**

Cuspal strength does not require other techniques for it to work. Cincinnati could have been down zero planets to three in the victory house department and still won this game—that's the power of the cusps, which goes deeper than physical strength all the way to the level of skill and inspiration, or in Eastern terminology, prana, chi, or ki.

A Lesson from Yoga

Yoga philosophy considers multiple "bodies" or layers of influence, called *kosha*s in Sanskrit. The most basic kosha is the food body, relating to brute physical strength, the flesh and muscles that propel us across the field to score a goal. A more subtle layer is the breath or prana body, which rules the electricity and coordination in our nervous systems that control the physical body. The victory house technique represents physical strength while the cuspal strength and SKY/PKY techniques both stand for the higher-tier influence of the prana body.

TABLE 4.2. RELATIONSHIPS BETWEEN THE KOSHAS AND VEDIC ASTROLOGY TECHNIQUES

KOSHA	TECHNIQUE	TIER
Anna, the food body	Victory house	1
Prana, the breath body	Cuspal strength, SKY/PKY	2

Think of David and Goliath, the story of an inspired combatant taking on and defeating a larger, stronger opponent because of his focus, skill, and determination, all qualities of the prana body. Jyotisha accounts for these differences, and when judging a horoscope we can see which yogic body is activated and the extent of its influence. The example on page 75 will show us how it's done.

In this chart the favorite, Pittsburgh, has no useful planets in upachaya houses, while the underdog has three (counting an exalted and retrograde Jupiter). This is a clear case of physical strength on the dog side. Nevertheless, the favorite won 5 to 1. Look carefully at the 7th cusp and you'll see why: it is within orb of the Sun *and* Neptune, two grahas that are detrimental when placed on the 1st or 7th cusps. Despite the dog's greater physical presence (dominance of upachaya houses, or the food body), prana and skill proved more important in this hockey matchup.

North Indian Chart

```
         Ra 16:30              JuR 21:34
              6            4
                   Asc 11:51  3
    Sa 10:38      5
              8   2
              11
  Pl 20:52      Su 10:02      1  Mo 05:14
  Ce 23:26   9    Ne 13:10     12
           10    Ch 22:28        Ur 20:11
    Uk 10:02                      Ke 16:30
    Me 13:21                      Ve 08:38
                                  Ma 08:18
```

South Indian Chart

Ur 20:11 Ke 16:30 Ve 08:38 Ma 08:18	Mo 05:14		
Ch 22:28 Ne 13:10 Su 10:02			JuR 21:34
Me 13:21 Uk 10:02			Asc 11:51
Ce 23:26 Pl 20:52	Sa 10:38		Ra 16:30

Bhava   Cusp
1st h.   11:51:52 Leo
2nd h.   05:37:35 Vir
3rd h.   04:25:58 Lib
4th h.   07:40:41 Sco
5th h.   12:11:41 Sag
6th h.   14:02:33 Cap
7th h.   11:51:52 Aqu
8th h.   05:37:35 Pis
9th h.   04:25:58 Ari
10th h.   07:40:41 Tau
11th h.   12:11:41 Gem
12th h.   14:02:33 Can

**Florida Panthers (+301) vs. <u>Pittsburgh Penguins (−137)</u>, 18:08 LT,
Feb. 22, 2015, Pittsburgh, Pennsylvania**

While Florida played harder, with double shots on goal for most of the game, they just could not score, while Pittsburgh made the most of fewer opportunities. The announcer even noted that the Panthers had arrived at 5 a.m. that morning and were playing on very little sleep. Neptune, which rules sleep and dreams, played the foil here, as did the Sun, who rose too early for them, burning up their chances altogether.

> **When a SKY is marred by two or more malefics,
> it is basically rendered useless.**

Note that the SKY around the 7th house didn't help the underdog either, because it was influenced by multiple malefics. We've seen this in previous charts as well; when a SKY is marred by two or more malefics, it is basically rendered useless. Guardian angels, it appears, are fragile creatures.

Finally, you may have spotted a planetary war between the 10th lord and the 4th lord, which the 10th lord won (Venus is brighter), again favoring Pittsburgh. All in all, the Florida Panthers should have slept in that day.

Rah Rah Rashi

Though the victory house technique is trumped by cuspal strength, it can mean the difference when there is no cuspal strength present or when there is a tie, or an even amount of cuspal influence on both sides, as in the chart below.

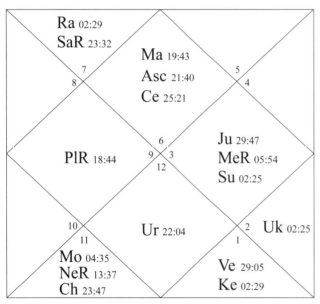

Bhava	Cusp
1st h.	21:40:21 Vir
2nd h.	24:59:49 Lib
3rd h.	22:17:13 Sco
4th h.	17:14:30 Sag
5th h.	13:31:39 Cap
6th h.	14:34:28 Aqu
7th h.	21:40:21 Pis
8th h.	24:59:49 Ari
9th h.	22:17:13 Tau
10th h.	17:14:30 Gem
11th h.	13:31:39 Can
12th h.	14:34:28 Leo

Belgium (−286) vs. Algeria (+885), 13:00 LT, June 17, 2014,
Belo Horizonte, Brazil

In this World Cup game, the heavily favored Belgians faced an Algerian team with outer-planet trump cards—namely, Uranus on their 1st cusp and Pluto on their 10th. When direct, Uranus gives a huge boost, often in unusual ways. In addition, the favorite was belabored, at least initially, by having Neptune on their 6th cusp, making them appear uninspired and lazy. Remember, the 6th cusp represents your work ethic, and the planet of sleep and dreams occupying that space does not bode well for sports competition, at least when he is in direct motion. But when retrograde, as he was here, Neptune often turns around, giving the opposite effect.

As the match unfolded, underdog Algeria was awarded an early penalty, giving them the lead at halftime. But the favorite also showed strength, with Mars on their 1st cusp. In addition, Neptune's retrogression meant that while at first he may have appeared lackadaisical and sleepy, he was likely to reverse this during the game. This is exactly what happened, as Belgium got a late burst of inspiration to win it. However, Mars and Neptune may not have been enough to earn this late win if it weren't for the dominant victory house effect, which shows Belgium with *four* victory house planets and Algeria zero. Here I am counting the benefic Mercury because he is exalted and retrograde, and Jupiter because he occupies Punarvasu, his own nakshatra (we'll learn more about them in chapter 8), something you can opt not to do if you choose. In either case, even with three victory planets in addition to Mars and retrograde Neptune, Belgium tied in the seventieth minute of the game and squeaked out a win with an eightieth-minute goal.

Let's look at another example of multiple planets contributing to an outcome on page 78.

The slight underdogs Zawisza (remember, even when there are two plus signs, the team with the lower number is the favorite) have three planets on their sensitive cusps: Saturn on their 10th, Jupiter on their 6th, and Neptune on their 1st house cusps. Note that Neptune has an orb of 2 degrees, which is about the limit for invisible planets. Saturn, on the other hand, is exactly conjunct their 10th cusp. Despite Neptune's unfavorable effect as a result of being in direct motion in this chart, this situation gives a preponderance of positive cuspal evidence for the underdog. This, coupled with their victory house superiority, ensured a favorable result: Zawisza won 4 to 1. Perhaps the one goal against them could be attributed to Neptune's placement on their 1st house cusp.

North Indian chart planets:
Ra 15:57 (6/7), Asc 16:40, Ju 18:38 (4/3), SaR 10:16 (8/2/5/11), Ve 07:06, Pl 21:34 (9/10), Ne 14:53, Ch 25:23, Uk 28:21 (12/1), Ma 14:46, Me 01:00, Mo 03:35, Ce 08:21, Su 28:21, Ur 22:49, Ke 15:57

South Indian chart:

Su 28:21 Ur 22:49 Ke 15:57	Me 01:00 Ma 14:46	Ve 07:06	
Uk 28:21 Ch 25:23 Ne 14:53			Ju 18:38
Ce 08:21 Mo 03:35			Asc 16:40
Pl 21:34	SaR 10:16		Ra 15:57

Bhava	Cusp
1st h.	16:40:53 Leo
2nd h.	08:05:07 Vir
3rd h.	05:48:33 Lib
4th h.	10:33:53 Sco
5th h.	18:10:07 Sag
6th h.	20:35:50 Cap
7th h.	16:40:53 Aqu
8th h.	08:05:07 Pis
9th h.	05:48:33 Ari
10th h.	10:33:53 Tau
11th h.	18:10:07 Gem
12th h.	20:35:50 Can

Zawisza (+181) vs. Belchatow (+160), 15:31 LT, April 12, 2015,
Belchatow, Poland

In the chart on page 79, Jupiter loosely joins the 10th cusp while Uranus has a vise grip on the 6th—note the tight orb. These are both signs of victory for the favorite. Why do I mention Jupiter, even though he is barely within the 2°30' orb? My gut tells me to, that's why. And also because it's polite to give exalted planets a wider berth, as I noted earlier—like their retrograde cousins, they'll respect you more when you do.* In this matchup, the favored White Sox, won 5 to 1.

---

*My experience shows that when planets are retrograde, even outer invisible planets, you can push their orb of influence a bit, in the order of 15 to 30 minutes of arc. Retrograde planets are brighter in the sky and have a bigger aura. Use your own good sense.

North Indian chart (diamond):

- SaR 04:40 (8)
- Ra 10:19 (6)
- PlR 20:09 (9)
- Asc 17:44
- Ve 03:35 (5)
- CeR 10:59 (10)
- (7)
- Ju 29:39 (4)
- (1)
- NeR 15:37 (11)
- ChR 27:26 (12)
- Su 25:14, Ma 17:34, Me 11:42 (3)
- (2)
- Ke 10:19, Ur 26:26
- Uk 25:14, Mo 03:40

South Indian chart (square):

Ur 26:26 / Ke 10:19	Mo 03:40 / Uk 25:14	Me 11:42 / Ma 17:34 / Su 25:14	
ChR 27:26 / NeR 15:37			Ju 29:39
CeR 10:59			Ve 03:35
PlR 20:09	SaR 04:40	Asc 17:44	Ra 10:19

Bhava	Cusp
1st h.	17:44:40 Lib
2nd h.	16:55:06 Sco
3rd h.	20:58:05 Sag
4th h.	27:09:17 Cap
5th h.	29:46:13 Aqu
6th h.	26:18:58 Pis
7th h.	17:44:40 Ari
8th h.	16:55:06 Tau
9th h.	20:58:05 Gem
10th h.	27:09:17 Can
11th h.	29:46:13 Leo
12th h.	26:18:58 Vir

<u>Chicago White Sox (−120)</u> vs. Chicago Cubs (−102), 15:07 LT,
July 11, 2015, Chicago, Illinois

Stolen Cusps

All cusps used in this book are based on the Placidus house system. As their calculation is based on the length of the day—and this changes when days are very long or very short, such as in midsummer or midwinter—a cusp may be said to be "stolen" when it occupies a different house in the whole-sign charts used in standard Vedic astrology. This means, for example, that the 10th house cusp (the MC) could actually fall in the 9th, 10th, or 11th houses of the rashi chart based on the length of day/time of year.

There are three types of stolen cusps: power-to-neutral, neutral-to-power, and power-to-power. The example on page 80 shows a power-to-neutral stolen cusp, meaning that a power cusp (1/7, 6/12, or 4/10) has shifted to one of the neutral houses (3/9, 5/11). A power-to-neutral stolen cusp reduces the effect of any planets conjoined with that cusp. In this example, the 10th house cusp

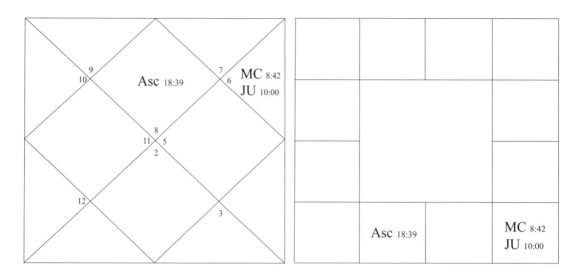

Bhava   Cusp
1st h.   18:39:34 Sco
2nd h.   22:49:45 Sag
3rd h.   02:24:41 Aqu
4th h.   08:42:28 Pis
5th h.   07:03:42 Ari
6th h.   29:19:59 Ari
7th h.   18:39:34 Tau
8th h.   22:49:45 Gem
9th h.   02:24:41 Leo
10th h.   08:42:28 Vir
11th h.   07:03:42 Lib
12th h.   29:19:59 Lib

Power-to-neutral stolen cusp

actually falls in the 11th sign from the ascendant. Any planet conjoined with a stolen cusp like this may lose power. Even though the favorite has Jupiter within orb of this 10th house cusp, because its placement falls in the 11th house of the whole-sign chart it will lose some of its effectiveness, making the favored team less impressive than if it had Jupiter on the 10th cusp in the tenth sign. Likewise, if it had Ketu or the Sun on this cusp, both of which are negative influences, this negative influence too would be significantly reduced.

> **A power-to-neutral stolen cusp reduces the effect of any planets conjoined with that cusp.**

In the top chart on page 81 we have the neutral 11th cusp shifted to the 12th house. This is an example of a neutral-to-power stolen cusp. If there is a planet within orb of this cusp, it will exert an effect for the indicated team.

In the neutral-to-power example on the bottom of page 81, Saturn is less than

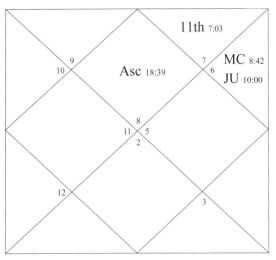

Bhava   Cusp
1st h.   18:39:34 Sco
2nd h.   22:49:45 Sag
3rd h.   02:24:41 Aqu
4th h.   08:42:28 Pis
5th h.   07:03:42 Ari
6th h.   29:19:59 Ari
7th h.   18:39:34 Tau
8th h.   22:49:45 Gem
9th h.   02:24:41 Leo
10th h.   08:42:28 Vir
11th h.   07:03:42 Lib
12th h.   29:19:59 Lib

Neutral-to-power stolen cusp

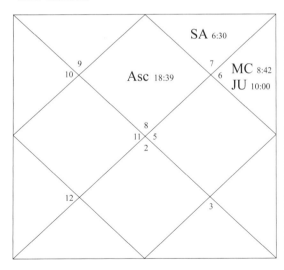

Bhava   Cusp
1st h.   18:39:34 Sco
2nd h.   22:49:45 Sag
3rd h.   02:24:41 Aqu
4th h.   08:42:28 Pis
5th h.   07:03:42 Ari
6th h.   29:19:59 Ari
7th h.   18:39:34 Tau
8th h.   22:49:45 Gem
9th h.   02:24:41 Leo
10th h.   08:42:28 Vir
11th h.   07:03:42 Lib
12th h.   29:19:59 Lib

Neutral-to-power stolen cusp

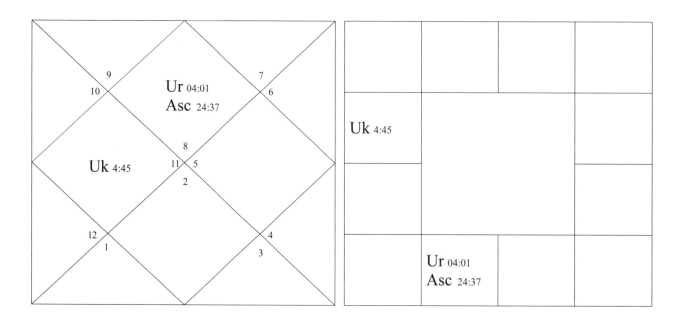

Bhava / Cusp table:

Bhava	Cusp
1st h.	24:37:13 Sco
2nd h.	28:02:37 Sag
3rd h.	05:16:38 Aqu
4th h.	10:25:09 Pis
5th h.	09:24:41 Ari
6th h.	03:12:18 Tau
7th h.	24:37:13 Tau
8th h.	28:02:37 Gem
9th h.	05:16:38 Leo
10th h.	10:25:09 Vir
11th h.	09:24:41 Lib
12th h.	03:12:18 Sco

Power-to-power stolen cusp

a degree away from the 11th cusp, which normally doesn't mean much save that now that cusp is in the 12th house of the whole-sign chart, making it eligible to affect the outcome of a match. In this example, Saturn would empower the underdog as if he actually sat on their 6th house cusp (remember, Saturn on the 4/10 or 6/12 axis helps his teams win; on the 1/7 he is not so kind).

Similarly, if Neptune occupied Saturn's position in this example, the underdog would be detrimented, since Neptune in direct motion dulls a team's fighting spirit.

We normally ignore the cusps of the 3rd, 5th, 9th, and 11th houses because these have negligible strength to affect game outcomes. However, when they happen to occupy houses other than 3, 5, 9, or 11 in the rashi chart, they become neutral-to-power stolen cusps.

The final example is that of a power-to-power stolen cusp (above).

Power-to-power stolen cusps can only happen between the 6th and 7th houses and their opposite, the 12th and 1st houses. For example, a planet on the 6th cusp can move into the 7th house of the whole-sign chart, thereby affecting the underdog (represented by the 7th house cusp) instead of the favorite (represented by the 6th house cusp). In our example, Uranus has moved from helping the underdog in the 12th house to helping the favorite in the 1st. Also note here the neutral-to-power cusp move of Upaketu from the harmless 3rd house into the 4th, which spells double doom for the underdog, as Upaketu now hovers over its 10th house. With the addition of Uranus in the favorite's ascendant, stolen cusps have robbed victory from the underdog and handed it to the favorite, a type of astrological reverse Robin Hood story.

Let's now look at these in a real chart (see below).

In this chart, Saturn on the 12th cusp is shifted to the lagna of the whole-sign chart due to a power-to-power stolen cusp scenario. Whether on the 12th or the 1st, Saturn helped the underdog. Can you see why? Either way, the heavily favorite

Bhava   Cusp
1st h.   24:37:13 Sco
2nd h.   28:02:37 Sag
3rd h.   05:16:38 Aqu
4th h.   10:25:09 Pis
5th h.   09:24:41 Ari
6th h.   03:12:18 Tau
7th h.   24:37:13 Tau
8th h.   28:02:37 Gem
9th h.   05:16:38 Leo
10th h.   10:25:09 Vir
11th h.   09:24:41 Lib
12th h.   03:12:18 Sco

<u>Washington Nationals (−200)</u> vs. Atlanta Braves (+168), 19:11 LT, July 2, 2015, Atlanta, Georgia

Nationals lost this game 2 to 1. Not helping them either is the power-to-neutral stolen cusp that shifted their Rahu on the 10th house (a helpful influence) into the 11th house of their whole-sign chart, basically neutralizing his positive effect. Saturn on the stolen 1st house cusp also worked to keep the game a low-scoring affair.

Burning Down the House

Down twelve points at the half, the New Orleans Pelicans surged to upset the favorite Golden State Warriors 103 to 100. Note the multiple influences on the cusps in this chart on page 85, most of them in favor of the underdog Pelicans.

This chart is an extreme example of cusps bombarded by planets. You will rarely see such busy configurations, though when you do you need to weigh the influences. First, find the closest conjunction; that is likely the dominant player. Second, count how many influences favor each side and weigh them against one another. This is where judgment becomes subjective. Here are the planets, their placement in the chart, and which team they favor:

Uranus, 7th cusp: underdog
Sun, 7th cusp: favorite
Mercury, 7th cusp: N/A (we are not using Mercury to judge except on the 6/12 houses)
Chiron, 6th cusp: favorite
Upaketu, 6th cusp: underdog
Pluto, 4th cusp: underdog

Uranus sits almost exactly on the 7th cusp; the closeness of this aspect dominates everything around it, energizing the underdog for a favorable outcome. The Sun on the 7th cusp is bad for the underdog Pelicans and perhaps explains why New Orleans was down early; however, Pluto on the 4th cusp, a loose conjunction, may have slightly boosted their chances. Upaketu on the 6th cusp was bad for the favorite (we're building a case against them and it's starting to look solid), but the favorite was also helped by Chiron's placement there. Overall, however, the underdog had one more cuspal planet in its

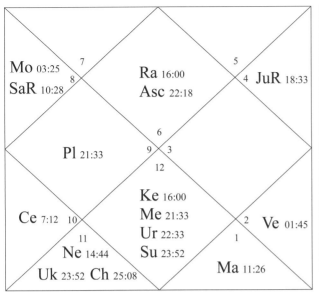

Su 23:52 Ur 22:33 Me 21:33 Ke 16:00	Ma 11:26	Ve 01:45	
Ch 25:08 Uk 23:52 Ne 14:44			JuR 18:37
Ce 7:12			
Pl 21:33	Mo 03:25 SaR 10:28		Ra 16:00 Asc 22:18

Bhava   Cusp
1st h.   22:18:49 Vir
2nd h.   20:45:21 Lib
3rd h.   21:21:45 Sco
4th h.   23:17:36 Sag
5th h.   25:17:27 Cap
6th h.   25:29:42 Aqu
7th h.   22:18:49 Pis
8th h.   20:45:21 Ari
9th h.   21:21:45 Tau
10th h.   23:17:36 Gem
11th h.   25:17:27 Can
12th h.   25:29:42 Leo

<u>Golden State Warriors (−192)</u> vs. New Orleans Pelicans (+162), 19:11:22 LT,
April 7, 2015, New Orleans, Louisiana

favor than the favorite did, helping to offset the slight victory house advantage Golden State possessed, and leading the Pelicans to a narrow margin of victory.

It's worthwhile to note that on the same day this configuration led to victories for underdog teams across multiple sports, including baseball, soccer, and basketball. That's because many events begin at the same time across the world and therefore often share the same chart.

> **Many events begin at the same time across the world and therefore often share the same chart.**

The Ones That Got Away

There will always be charts that confound us, in which our techniques just don't work. I have run across many such examples and sometimes come out with new methods or corollaries as a result. But at other times there is simply no explanation. This is when we must surrender to the cosmos, acknowledging the 70/30 doctrine, in which astrologers were cursed to be correct only 70 percent of the time at best.

A long time ago astrologers became so enamored of their ability to predict that they declared themselves omniscient, pushing out the role of the gods and the divine. They even wrote horoscopes for clients yet to be born (which are now accessible through a specific branch of astrology called Nadi-Jyotisha). But such knowledge comes at a price—just like the wiseacres in your family, karma always comes a-calling to put them in their place. These celestial know-it-alls were cursed, and every astrologer today bears the burden of their conceit.

I too have been a victim of self-deception and conceit, breaking my own rules and betting on days I knew were bad for me because I was overly confident in an outcome. And this didn't turn out well for me. Predicting and, worse yet, betting on games when you shouldn't puts you on track to enter alternate timelines where bad things happen to good Jyotishis.

As well, sometimes who the favorite is changes between the time the odds are first posted and the actual start of a game. This can happen when two teams are pretty equal, or when there is a last-minute change in one team's roster, as when a superstar player is taken out of a game. This frustrating reality of sports betting can be catastrophic for sports predictors like us, for whom the favorite/underdog distinction is crucial. During my time wagering, this alone cost me thousands of dollars.

In one basketball example, the early favorite, Detroit, was supposed to easily beat the Philadelphia 76ers, who had the Sun conjunct their 7th cusp. Instead, Philadelphia won by 11. The moneyline changed to make them the favored team just minutes after I had bet on Detroit. Moneyline changes and other unpredictable events are the reason Jyotishis must remain humble and connected to a higher source of wisdom. In my case, losses came when I didn't listen to my inner voice and played only on intellect, relying on the strength of technique to win while ignoring grace. These are lessons I encourage you to avoid.

Honor the Bookie:
Kala, Desha, and Patra

In the Germany-Thailand matchup at the beginning of this chapter, Thailand had little to no chance of winning, even had they had a stronger chart—victory house and SKY all in their favor. The physical laws of the universe would have had to significantly bend to allow them a victory. We know this because of the number assigned Germany, −10,000, which represents the pledge bookies make, staking their reputations and significant sums of money on the veracity of an outcome.

Skilled bookmakers, like Jyotishis, earn their living judging the likelihood of potential outcomes. The better the bookmaker, the closer their prediction is to actual events. This means knowing which teams are going to win, and by how much—even things like which player went out on the town the night before if it affects his or her game. With this kind of confidence in Germany, a major rift in time and space would have had to intercede for a Thailand win. This is why knowing the *kala* (time), *desha* (setting), and *patra* ("vessel," i.e. the individual) is vital to good Jyotisha, which means the *setting in time and space* and the *capacity of the person or team.*

Let's say a ninety-year-old man walks into your house asking if he can become a ballerina. You pull the chart for the question, and it's a strong yes. All the techniques indicate a positive answer. Does that mean you break out a toast and predict the Bolshoi for him? Considering kala, desha, and patra—i.e., the reality of the client's age, sex, background, and physical condition—you may venture the following: "It appears that if this is your strong desire, in your next lifetime you will definitely have the opportunity to be a ballerina. And if you do not believe in reincarnation, it may be that you pass down the gene, and one of your descendants becomes a ballerina in her own right. Either way, your desire will be fulfilled, just not in the current kala, desha, and patra." In sports investment, this reality is represented by the moneyline odds, and secondarily by the spread. I have included them in this book for just this reason; ignore them at your peril.

> **Every day, for practically every professional sport, careful thinking goes into deciding who is going to win a particular game, and by how much.**

Summary

While physical strength can be judged using the victory house technique, skill, coordination, and willpower are better assessed by considering the house cusps, which are like celestial trigger points that enliven the effects of any planets close enough to them. This cuspal effect is stronger than mere physical strength. Here is some homework to help you put them to use:

- Memorize first the visible planets and their effects on the cusps. Then slowly work on the outer, invisible grahas. What's Saturn's effect on the 10th house? How about on the 1st?
- Memorize the orbs—2°30' for visible planets and 2 degrees for invisible ones. Remember, the closer a planet is to its cusp, the more powerful its effect. Keep in mind the exceptions for exalted or retrograde planets (which get a little extra orb).
- Stolen cusps with key planets on them are fairly rare but should also be memorized. Learn the difference between power-to-neutral and neutral-to-power.

This has been the most difficult chapter to write. The sheer volume of possible outcomes related to planets on the cusps means that I could easily spend additional years (and gray hairs) researching the topic. Instead, I have decided to publish what results I have in order to begin a discussion and hopefully encourage other Jyotishis to join me in this research.

For whatever errors exist here, I apologize in advance. Nonetheless, I hope this chapter may initiate you into the power of house cusps for sports prediction and more—indeed, to make sense of practically any chart, from when to get married to the best time to divorce (though if you use them correctly for the first purpose, you won't need them for the second).

5

The Power of Nine

Using the Navamsha for Precise Prediction

*Jnāninām api cetānsi / devī bhagavatī hi sā / Bālād ākrishya
    mohāya / mahāmāyā prayacchati
(The Divine Mother wrenches even the minds of the wise into
    delusion.)*

From the Devi Mahatmyam

Mr. Spock left Vulcan too soon, else he would have discovered a technique twice as powerful as his Vulcan death grip. Of course, had he stayed we never would have heard of it because his planet was destroyed. I guess the point is moot. But the navamsha technique is not, for it can affect event outcomes more powerfully than any other technique in this book. Whereas the victory houses show physical power, and cuspal strength the force of prana, or chi, the navamsha seems to reveal mental and emotional fortitude. Physical strength is subordinate to pranic force, and pranic force ultimately is directed by and subordinate to mental attitude, which is why this technique, which I have not found described anywhere else, yields such strong results.

TABLE 5.1. RELATIONSHIPS BETWEEN THE KOSHAS AND VEDIC ASTROLOGY TECHNIQUES

KOSHA	TECHNIQUE	TIER
Anna, the food body	Victory house	1
Prana, the breath body	Cuspal strength, SKY/PKY	2
Manas, the mental/emotional body	Navamsha cuspal strength	3

Navamsha means "nine portions." It is derived from the division of each of the twelve signs of the zodiac into nine segments. The navamsha is just one of many subcharts used in Vedic astrology—sort of like children of the main, or rashi, charts we've been looking at up to this point. Each of these subcharts is dedicated to a specific theme or themes. For example, the D7, or "seventh division," pertains mainly to children, while the D24 pertains to education. Outside of it being useful in contest prediction, the navamsha, or D9, is mainly used to analyze relationships. Note that as a kind of shorthand, we use the letter D (for division) plus a number (from 1 to 150) to indicate which divisional subchart we are referencing. D9 is shorthand for the ninth division; it is easily the most important of all the subcharts, which is why it is often shown side by side along the D1, which refers to the rashi, or main horoscope.

> D9 is shorthand for the ninth division; it is easily the most important of all the subcharts, which is why it is often shown side by side along the D1, which refers to the rashi, or main horoscope.

The number 9 is sacred among many ancient traditions and represents completion or fulfillment. In essence, the navamsha is the fulfillment potential of the rashi chart, meaning that what your main chart promises as a potential is often actualized or denied in the navamsha. That is why in this chapter we will look at both charts, in order to compare. Sometimes a beautiful tree (D1/rashi) produces only sour fruit (D9/navamsha), and sometimes the sweetest-tasting fruits (or results) ripen from the gnarliest of trees. In contest prediction we use the navamsha to confirm or deny the results we might expect based on the main rashi chart, sometimes turning predictions 180 degrees on their heads.

> In contest prediction we use the navamsha to confirm or deny the results we might expect based on the main rashi chart, sometimes turning predictions 180 degrees on their heads.

Calculating the Navamsha

Now let's take a look at how the navamsha is calculated. Since there are twelve signs with nine navamshas each, we have a total of 108 navamshas in the zodiac, each 3°20' wide. Table 5.2 on page 92 indicates how these divisions are apportioned. Briefly, in Fire signs the first navamsha is always Aries, in Earth signs it is always Capricorn, in Air signs it is always Libra, and in Water signs it is always Cancer.

How the Navamsha Technique Works

Now let's take a look at how the navamsha technique works. First, we need to assign degrees to the planets and ascendant in the navamsha. Normally we do not use degrees in the D9 when using it for purposes other than contest prediction, but for this technique we do. It is not too hard to calculate, and it's even easier if you have your computer do it for you. To do it yourself, read on. Otherwise it takes a split second with Jyotisha software.

The rule: if a planet sits within 2°30' on either side of the navamsha lagna degree for the favorite, or the navamsha 7th house (descendant) degree for the underdog, it is a powerful indicator of success or failure, depending on the planet involved.

How to Calculate the D9 Lagna Degree

To find the degree of the navamsha lagna, you can simply turn this feature on in your Jyotisha program.

If you don't have Jyotisha software, all it takes is a little math. Here's how to do it:

- Each navamsha is 3°20'. Convert these 3 degrees to minutes. Each degree has 60 minutes, so 3 degrees are 180 minutes. Add the 20 minutes remaining and you get a total of 200 minutes of arc for each navamsha.
- Next, find exactly how far the D1 lagna has progressed in its navamsha. Let's say your main chart ascendant is at 12°20' Capricorn. Looking at the table 5.2, you can see that this falls in the fourth navamsha of Aries. Since the span of this navamsha is from 10° to 13°23', we can see that the ascendant has traveled 2 degrees and 20 minutes.
- Converting this span to minutes, we get 140 (2°20' = 60 x 2 + 20).
- Divide 140 by the constant 6.67 (remember this number!). We derive this constant by subtracting the total possible minutes in one navamsha (200) by the total number of degrees (30). Dividing by 6.67 converts your minutes into navamsha degrees. This gives you your D9 lagna degree. For this example it is 21 degrees.

TABLE 5.2. THE NINE NAVAMSHAS FOR THE TWELVE SIGNS WITH THEIR DEGREE POSITIONS

SIGN	1ST NAVAMSHA	2ND NAVAMSHA	3RD NAVAMSHA	4TH NAVAMSHA	5TH NAVAMSHA	6TH NAVAMSHA	7TH NAVAMSHA	8TH NAVAMSHA	9TH NAVAMSHA
Aries	Ari 0°–3°20'	Tau 3°20'–6°40'	Gem 6°40'–10°	Can 10°–13°20'	Leo 13°20'–16°40'	Vir 16°40'–20°	Lib 20°–23°20'	Sco 23°20'–26°40'	Sag 26°40'–30°
Taurus	Cap 0°–3°20'	Aqu 3°20'–6°40'	Pis 6°40'–10°	Ari 10°–13°20'	Tau 13°20'–16°40'	Gem 16°40'–20°	Can 20°–23°20'	Leo 23°20'–26°40'	Vir 26°40'–30°
Gemini	Lib 0°–3°20'	Sco 3°20'–6°40'	Sag 6°40'–10°	Cap 10°–13°20'	Aqu 13°20'–16°40'	Pis 16°40'–20°	Ari 20°–23°20'	Tau 23°20'–26°40'	Gem 26°40'–30°
Cancer	Can 0°–3°20'	Leo 3°20'–6°40'	Vir 6°40'–10°	Lib 10°–13°20'	Sco 13°20'–16°40'	Sag 16°40'–20°	Cap 20°–23°20'	Aqu 23°20'–26°40'	Pis 26°40'–30°
Leo	Ari 0°–3°20'	Tau 3°20'–6°40'	Gem 6°40'–10°	Can 10°–13°20'	Leo 13°20'–16°40'	Vir 16°40'–20°	Lib 20°–23°20'	Sco 23°20'–26°40'	Sag 26°40'–30°
Virgo	Cap 0°–3°20'	Aqu 3°20'–6°40'	Pis 6°40'–10°	Ari 10°–13°20'	Tau 13°20'–16°40'	Gem 16°40'–20°	Can 20°–23°20'	Leo 23°20'–26°40'	Vir 26°40'–30°
Libra	Lib 0°–3°20'	Sco 3°20'–6°40'	Sag 6°40'–10°	Cap 10°–13°20'	Aqu 13°20'–16°40'	Pis 16°40'–20°	Ari 20°–23°20'	Tau 23°20'–26°40'	Gem 26°40'–30°
Scorpio	Can 0°–3°20'	Leo 3°20'–6°40'	Vir 6°40'–10°	Lib 10°–13°20'	Sco 13°20'–16°40'	Sag 16°40'–20°	Cap 20°–23°20'	Aqu 23°20'–26°40'	Pis 26°40'–30°
Sagittarius	Ari 0°–3°20'	Tau 3°20'–6°40'	Gem 6°40'–10°	Can 10°–13°20'	Leo 13°20'–16°40'	Vir 16°40'–20°	Lib 20°–23°20'	Sco 23°20'–26°40'	Sag 26°40'–30°
Capricorn	Cap 0°–3°20'	Aqu 3°20'–6°40'	Pis 6°40'–10°	Ari 10°–13°20'	Tau 13°20'–16°40'	Gem 16°40'–20°	Can 20°–23°20'	Leo 23°20'–26°40'	Vir 26°40'–30°
Aquarius	Lib 0°–3°20'	Sco 3°20'–6°40'	Sag 6°40'–10°	Cap 10°–13°20'	Aqu 13°20'–16°40'	Pis 16°40'–20°	Ari 20°–23°20'	Tau 23°20'–26°40'	Gem 26°40'–30°
Pisces	Can 0°–3°20'	Leo 3°20'–6°40'	Vir 6°40'–10°	Lib 10°–13°20'	Sco 13°20'–16°40'	Sag 16°40'–20°	Cap 20°–23°20'	Aqu 23°20'–26°40'	Pis 26°40'–30°

That was pretty easy, right? Now the hard part: you have to do this for every planet in order to see if any of them fall within 2°30' of this D9 ascendant degree, or its opposite in the 7th house. For example, let's pretend your Saturn falls at 23 degrees Gemini. Consulting table 5.2, you'll see that it falls in the seventh navamsha (again, Aries). Within this Aries division it has spanned 3 degrees, or 180 minutes. Dividing 180 by 6.67, we get 27 degrees. Conclusion? This is too far from the D9 lagna of 21 degrees to have the powerful effect we're looking for.

Let's look at another example. This time consider Mercury at 22°30' Leo. Looking at table 5.2, we find that this falls in the Libra navamsha and is therefore a candidate for our consideration since the Libra holds the 7th house cusp of the D9. Mercury at 22°30' has traveled 2°30' in its division. Converting this to minutes, we get 150 (2 × 60 + 30 = 150). Dividing 150 by 6.67, we get 22°24'—close enough to the 7th cusp to make a difference. Underdog wins. Hooray!

How the Planets Influence the Navamsha

Here's how the planets fare in the navamsha chart:

Sun conjunct the 1/7 cusps "burns up" the team indicated, making them less likely to score. This is nothing but the combustion of cusps that we saw in chapter 4 carried over to the navamsha. While not the strongest indicator for loss (Mars is worse), it is definitely not a positive influence.

Mars conjunct the D9 ascendant spells doom for the favorite team, while on this degree in the 7th house Mars delivers the same fate to the underdog. Unlike his role in the rashi chart, where he is beneficial on the 1/7 axis, Mars in the D9 is an equal-opportunity terrorizer. Don't ask me why this is so, it just is. This indicator alone earned countless accurate predictions in game charts.

Ketu on the D9 1/7 axis does pretty much what you'd expect—confuses and scares the party it represents. Not good. Opposite Ketu lurks Rahu, who is rabid about success, though he does not achieve it as often as he'd like, or as often as real planets conjoining a cusp. Such is the fate of these shadow planets.

Moon in the D9, like his position in the D1, seems to engender laziness and instability. I say "seems to" because more research is needed on this position, and because Moon is the most unstable graha.

Jupiter on the D9 1st or 7th cusps gives grace, luck, and a well-rested, strong, and optimistic attitude—he's a big plus.

Venus on the 1st or 7th cusp of the D9 indicates laziness, complacency, and/or inattention. The team or person expects to win and acts like a prima donna, and unlike its placement in the rashi chart, Venus here encourages losses, though not as strongly as Mars or Saturn.

Mercury on the navamsha lagna or 7th cusp gives speed, cleverness, and a youthful enthusiasm to its teams—another strong indicator for victory.

Saturn on the navamsha lagna or 7th cusp, much like Mars, harms a team's chances by depressing and uninspiring them. Like your grandfather, he is also slow, old, and conservative. Sitting on a cusp, he is a good indicator for loss and low-scoring games.

Uranus is a strange bird. As mentioned previously, when direct in the rashi chart he galvanizes teams with an electric energy, an out-of-this-world excitement that can result in blowouts and flashy victories. When retrograde or stationary, however, he does the opposite. He behaves the same in the D9. Like AC and DC currents, he switches roles, making Jyotishis' heads spin. Outer planets, because they move slowly, can spend a lot of time being retrograde and stationary. In fact, this is one of the reasons why it took so long to discover Uranus. Well before William Herschel pointed his telescope at it in 1781, the astronomer P. Le Monier "observed Uranus eight times in four weeks but failed to realise it was a planet because it was in its station."* Unlike faster-moving planets, Uranus was sitting still like just another star in the pinhole majesty of the sky.

Neptune, like Uranus, is slow and seems to switch roles, which makes predicting with these outer planets in the navamsha a hassle. Normally negative, he can turn positive while retrograde, just as in the rashi.

Pluto, on the other hand, seems to behave like the grouchy ruler of the underworld that he is, whether retrograde or direct. He tends to give intensity and misfortune in the D9, though more research is needed here.

Upaketu does in the navamsha chart what he does in the rashi: he acts like Ketu—a negative influence.

---

*David McCann, "The Birth of the Outer Planets," www.skyscript.co.uk/uranus.html.

Gulika can be used with success in the navamsha to indicate defeat when it conjoins the 1st or 7th cusps. We haven't looked at Gulika much yet, but you can also use it in the main rashi chart with similar indications, except for in the 10th house, where, like his daddy, Saturn, he favors victory.

Since subcharts are mathematical abstracts of the main chart, planetary positions in these divisional charts bear no relationship to astronomical reality, which is why Rahu and Ketu can occupy the same house, and the Sun and Mercury can be opposite each other, something that can't happen in this solar system.

You can also extrapolate a 10th and 4th house cusp using the same degree of the navamsha lagna. For example, if the D9 lagna was 8°30' Pisces, then the 4th cusp would be 8°30' Gemini and the 10th cusp 8°30' Sagittarius. I do not use the 10th and 4th cusps of the navamsha in this book, as this requires further investigation and is not as solid as the 1st and 7th cusps for indicating victory or defeat. I'm bringing it up for you, dear reader, to take into consideration if you wish to follow up with your own research. Until then, do not even think about using the 3/9, 5/11, or even 6/12 cusps or houses in the navamsha, though they are used in the rashi chart. The only cusps we use in the D9 are the 1st and 7th, and, maybe, possibly, secondarily, the 10th and 4th. Period.

> **The only cusps we use in the D9 are the 1st and 7th, and, maybe, possibly, secondarily, the 10th and 4th.**

Table 5.3 below presents a list of the planets and how they affect the D9 cusps. I've starred those planets whose effects in the navamsha are the opposite of what they are in the rashi.

TABLE 5.3. EFFECTS OF THE PLANETS IN THE NAVAMSHA

PLANET	EFFECT ON 1/7	REASON
Moon	Negative	A lazy influence, but can also sometimes inspire its teams (more research needed)
Mars★	Negative	Gives frustration, anger, and self-undoing
Rahu	Positive	Gives ambition to win
Jupiter	Positive	Gives luck and a well-rested, positive attitude

PLANET	EFFECT ON 1/7	REASON
Saturn	Negative	Restricts; team feels old, tired, weak
Mercury★	Positive	Gives skill and speed
Ketu	Negative	Gives confusion, unusual circumstances leading to defeat
Venus★	Negative	Gives laziness and a laissez-faire attitude; not as negative as other influences
Sun	Negative	Tends to give a cautious, conservative attitude, which often results in losses and low-scoring games; not as strong as other malefic influences
Uranus	Positive/Negative	Unpredictable: gives a positive boost when direct; when retrograde it can be quite negative
Neptune	Negative/Positive	Watch carefully: rules sleep, smoke, and confusion; therefore when direct it is a negative factor, and when retrograde it can give a sort of inspiration that pushes teams ahead
Pluto	Negative	Generally negative, conferring a heaviness to everything it touches
Ukaketu	Negative	Acts like Ketu to spoil a team's luck
Gulika	Negative	A negative influence on the 1st or 7th cusps

How to Use the Navamsha Technique

Find the navamsha lagna degree. The 7th house cusp in the navamsha will also be the same degree in the opposite sign. If there are planets within 2°30' of either cusp they will exert a strong influence on the respective team. For outer planets, use a 2-degree orb, just like in the main chart.

Take Me Out to the Ball Game

Let's now start plugging in the navamsha technique. We will be looking at the D1 alongside the D9 to add up the influences. Here's a match that took place even as I was writing this book (see charts on page 97). I turned this game on in the second inning and the favored Giants already led 2 to 0. Something told me to check the chart. I'm glad I listened.

RASHI

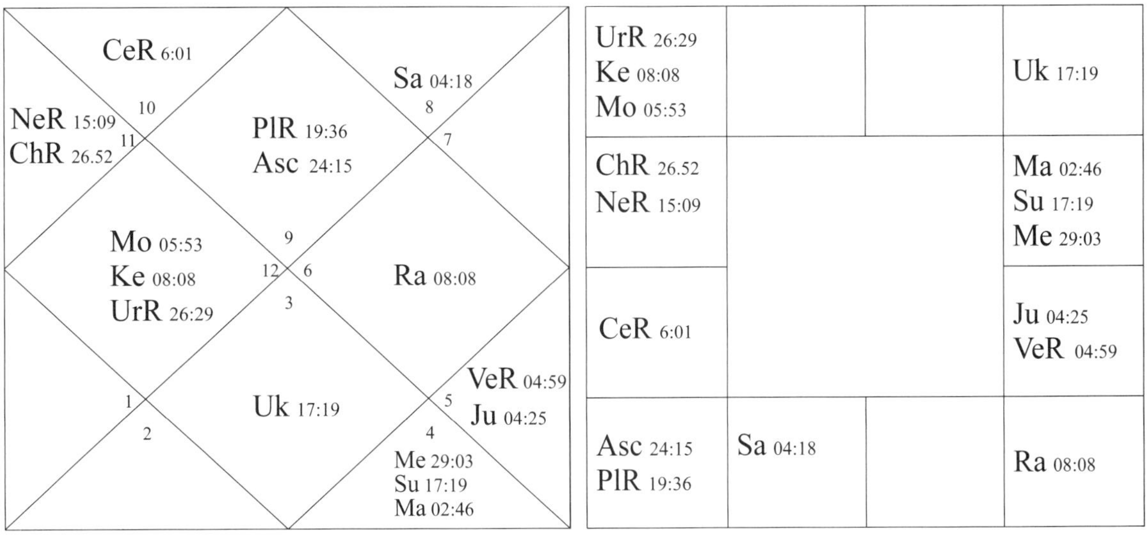
CeR 6:01
NeR 15:09
ChR 26.52
Sa 04:18
PlR 19:36
Asc 24:15
Mo 05:53
Ke 08:08
UrR 26:29
Ra 08:08
Uk 17:19
VeR 04:59
Ju 04:25
Me 29:03
Su 17:19
Ma 02:46
UrR 26:29
Ke 08:08
Mo 05:53
Uk 17:19
ChR 26.52
NeR 15:09
Ma 02:46
Su 17:19
Me 29:03
CeR 6:01
Ju 04:25
VeR 04:59
Asc 24:15
PlR 19:36
Sa 04:18
Ra 08:08

Bhava	Cusp
1st h.	24:15:38 Sag
2nd h.	03:52:14 Aqu
3rd h.	12:44:30 Pis
4th h.	13:57:43 Ari
5th h.	08:46:41 Tau
6th h.	00:53:13 Gem
7th h.	24:15:38 Gem
8th h.	03:52:14 Leo
9th h.	12:44:30 Vir
10th h.	13:57:43 Lib
11th h.	08:46:41 Sco
12th h.	00:53:13 Sag

NAVAMSHA

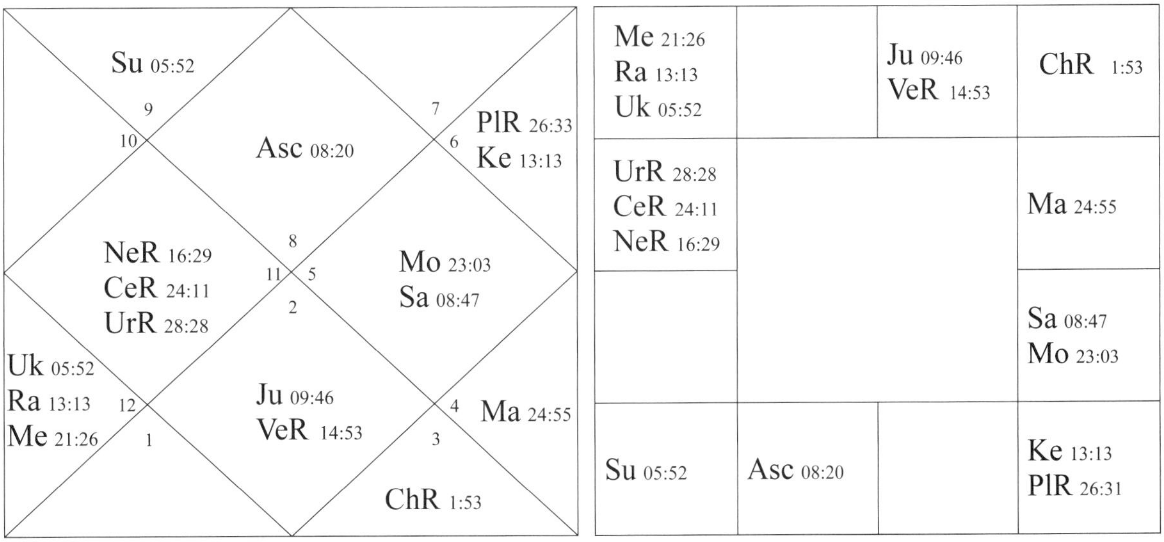
Su 05:52
Asc 08:20
PlR 26:33
Ke 13:13
NeR 16:29
CeR 24:11
UrR 28:28
Mo 23:03
Sa 08:47
Uk 05:52
Ra 13:13
Me 21:26
Ju 09:46
VeR 14:53
Ma 24:55
ChR 1:53
Me 21:26
Ra 13:13
Uk 05:52
Ju 09:46
VeR 14:53
ChR 1:53
UrR 28:28
CeR 24:11
NeR 16:29
Ma 24:55
Sa 08:47
Mo 23:03
Su 05:52
Asc 08:20
Ke 13:13
PlR 26:31

San Francisco Giants (−141) vs. Atlanta Braves (+120), 19:11 LT,
Aug. 3, 2015, Atlanta, Georgia

There in the D9 7th house sat Jupiter, close enough to the cusp to pique my interest. Surely Atlanta won't lose, I thought, and even if they do, it won't be by this margin. No, not happening... To document this sentiment I logged on to my favorite betting site and placed a live wager for $10 once, and once more for good measure: that Atlanta wouldn't lose by two runs. See the ticket below.

Aug 3, 2015 7:50 PM	#601197881 Placed by Web	Single #601197881 Baseball - Runline San Francisco Giants @ Atlanta Braves **Atlanta Braves 2.5 (+102)** Aug 3, 2015 7:10 PM Outcome: **Win** Date settled: Aug 3, 2015 11:04 PM	$10.00	$10.20
Aug 3, 2015 7:50 PM	#601200683 Placed by Web	Single #601200683 Baseball - Runline San Francisco Giants @ Atlanta Braves **Atlanta Braves 2.5 (EVEN)** Aug 3, 2015 7:10 PM Outcome: **Win** Date settled: Aug 3, 2015 11:04 PM	$10.00	$10.00

Live wager for San Francisco Giants vs. Atlanta Braves

To my chagrin, in the next inning the score climbed to 4 to 0 in favor of the Giants. In the one after that, San Francisco turned it into a 6 to 0 lead. By the end of the fourth inning, my team losing 6 to 0 and my Jyotisha skills in question, I did what any self-respecting astrologer does: I shut off the TV and ate cookies. It wasn't about the twenty bucks; when I make bad predictions, it's an awful feeling, and I like to put my head in the sand, which for me means sitting on the couch gratifying some sugar craving. But an hour later, out of curiosity, I checked the score just to make sure. It was the ninth inning, and Atlanta had come back in the bottom of the ninth to tie it, 7 to 7. Two innings later, they won it all, 9 to 8. A miracle! And even though for my bet I didn't need the victory, this shows the power of the navamsha cusps.

Why was it so bad early on? Sans navamsha, it's an unexceptional chart, and in such cases the favorite usually triumphs. Remember, underdogs need to play better than usual to have a chance at beating favorites. Atlanta wasn't a dog by much, but without Jupiter protecting its D9 in the 7th house, they would have been toast. And perhaps more relevantly, Jupiter likely wasn't exactly conjunct that 7th cusp (I didn't catch the first pitch so we'll never know), which means he had to telephone in his assistance long distance, and with delay. During the wait, San Francisco scored six runs.

To illustrate how important orbs of influence are, take a look at the example on page 100, which is a precise chart.

This chart appears loaded against the favorite. A close inspection shows the factors weighing against them that indicate an underdog victory: Sun on the rashi 10th cusp and Jupiter on the navamsha 7th cusp, both slightly out of orb. Though Ketu sits on the 6th rashi cusp, halting the favorite's momentum, the Sun and Jupiter are unable to give the underdog the push they need to win. Thanks to Ketu, they kept it close but couldn't scratch off a victory as the Giants prevailed 2 to 1. Had the game started moments later, with Jupiter closer to the navamsha 7th cusp, a victory for Oakland was assured. If only they had spent more time lacing up their shoes . . .

Let's take a look at another example on page 101.

Here we have a case of conflicting testimonies in the main rashi chart: two bad placements for the favorite (Sun on the 10th and Ketu on the 6th) and one bad placement for the underdog (Ceres retrograde on the 4th—their 10th—cusp). While this looks good for the underdog, as Seattle has fewer damaging planets in the rashi, we get a more complete picture of the game by looking at the D9. Do you see Mercury conjunct the 1st house cusp? That's the game. Done! Though favored Toronto was down 6 to 3 in the middle innings, they came back to win it 8 to 6.

> **The navamsha chart shows the fruit of
> the main chart and is the most powerful influencer on
> games we have studied so far.**

The navamsha chart shows the fruit of the main chart and is the most powerful influencer on games we have studied so far. Yes, the favored Blue Jays have problems, but with Mercury in the D9 lagna and Ceres retrograde in the rashi, it was enough to get them by.

RASHI

Ur 26:31 Ke 09:01			Uk 08:35 Ma 26:48
NeR 15:22 ChR 27:08			Su 08:35 Me 10:55
CeR 7:59			Ju 02:30 VeR 06:47
PlR 19:49	SaR 04:21	Asc 02:09 Mo 27:26	Ra 09:01

Bhava	Cusp
1st h.	02:09:56 Lib
2nd h.	00:20:09 Sco
3rd h.	02:01:44 Sag
4th h.	06:00:52 Cap
5th h.	08:58:44 Aqu
6th h.	07:57:25 Pis
7th h.	02:09:56 Ari
8th h.	00:20:09 Tau
9th h.	02:01:44 Gem
10th h.	06:00:52 Can
11th h.	08:58:44 Leo
12th h.	07:57:25 Vir

NAVAMSHA

CeR 11:57 Ra 21:14	Ju 22:30		VeR 01:08 Ma 01:17 ChR 4:20 Mo 06:57
Ur 28:44 NeR 18:18			
			SaR 09:09
Uk 17:21		Me 08:21 Asc 19:29	Su 17:21 Ke 21:14 PlR 28:21

Oakland Athletics (+168) vs. San Francisco Giants (−200), 13:05:30 LT,
July 25, 2015, San Francisco, California

RASHI

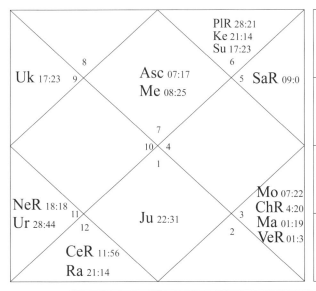

Ur 26:31 Ke 09:01			Uk 08:35 Ma 26:48
NeR 15:22 ChR 27:08			Su 08:35 Me 10:56
CeR 7:58			Ju 02:30 VeR 06:47
PlR 19:49	SaR 04:21	Asc 00:48 Mo 27:29	Ra 09:01

Bhava   Cusp
1st h.   00:48:39 Lib
2nd h.   27:57:44 Lib
3rd h.   00:44:08 Sag
4th h.   07:25:32 Cap
5th h.   11:22:57 Aqu
6th h.   09:02:06 Pis
7th h.   00:48:39 Ari
8th h.   27:57:44 Ari
9th h.   00:44:08 Gem
10th h.   07:25:32 Can
11th h.   11:22:57 Leo
12th h.   09:02:06 Vir

NAVAMSHA

CeR 11:56 Ra 21:14	Ju 22:31		VeR 01:08 Ma 01:19 ChR 4:20 Mo 07:22
Ur 28:44 NeR 18:18			
			SaR 09:09
Uk 17:23		Asc 07:17 Me 08:25	Su 17:23 Ke 21:14 PlR 28:21

Toronto Blue Jays (−133) vs. Seattle Mariners (+112), 13:11 LT, July 25, 2015,
Seattle, Washington

Does Mercury always win when it joins a D9 cusp? No. In fact, no technique is perfect. I've seen games go down quite the opposite of how they were supposed to on paper, which, instead of discouraging us, should inspire us to do more research in this area. The fact is that these techniques work—most of the time, and certainly more than not using them. Remember that before making any bold claims. This is why Jyotisha is a tough profession. Study any field for twelve years—medicine, law, crocodile hunting—and likely you'll become a pretty good doctor, lawyer, or croc wrestler; you may even get your own reality TV show. But study Jyotisha for twelve years and you'll still have days when you look at a chart, draw a blank, and wonder whether you shouldn't move to the jungle and talk to animals. Or maybe it's just me.

Now let's take a look at the chart on page 103 in which two planets make the difference in the navamsha.

As you can see, Milwaukee wasn't a strong favorite, as the difference between the two teams was minimal, at least in the eyes of the bookies (never forget kala, desha, and patra—time, place, and circumstance). Nonetheless, the favored Brewers racked up a worthy blowout against their star-struck and star-crossed opponents. Why? Consider Saturn and Mars, both major oppressors in the D9, conjunct the D9 7th house. This, together with the lazy Moon on the rashi 7th cusp, meant one thing: the dogs should have stayed home.

Happy Together:
Navamsha Combos

There's another, simpler way to look at the D9 to give a snapshot of a game without considering degree position. This is a level of strength similar to the victory house technique; it doesn't supercede D9 cuspal strength but can supplement it when present. See table 5.4 on page 104 for some examples of D9 combos that work.

When these combinations occur in either the 1st or the 7th house of the navamsha, they give the indicated result for that team. They don't have to be within orb of the cusps of those houses either. Aside from these, planetary combos with the Sun generally tend to lose; this includes the Sun and Saturn and the Sun and Jupiter. On the other hand, combos with the Moon generally tend to win. Other surprising combos, like Venus and Ketu (winner) and Venus and Rahu

Sa 04:19

Ra 08:10

Ju 05:00
Me 04:09
VeR 03:48

8

PlR 19:33   9

Asc 14:23

5

7

CeR 5:26

10   4

Su 19:59
Ma 04:34

1

NeR 15:05
ChR 26:46   11

Mo 15:46

3   Uk 19:59

12

2

Ke 08:10
UrR 26:28

UrR 26:28 Ke 08:10	Mo 15:46		Uk 19:59
ChR 26:46 NeR 15:05			Ma 04:34 Su 19:59
CeR 5:26			VeR 03:48 Me 04:09 Ju 05:00
PlR 19:33	Sa 04:19	Asc 14:23	Ra 08:10

Bhava   Cusp
1st h.   14:23:07 Lib
2nd h.   13:11:48 Sco
3rd h.   17:01:50 Sag
4th h.   23:19:07 Cap
5th h.   26:11:01 Aqu
6th h.   22:55:49 Pis
7th h.   14:23:07 Ari
8th h.   13:11:48 Tau
9th h.   17:01:50 Gem
10th h.   23:19:07 Can
11th h.   26:11:01 Leo
12th h.   22:55:49 Vir

NAVAMSHA

Ra 13:32
Uk 29:56

Asc 09:28
NeR 15:53
CeR 19:02
UrR 28:16

10

12

9

1

Su 29:56

VeR 04:16
Me 07:28
Ju 15:07

11

2   8

5

ChR 1:03   3

Sa 08:54
Ma 11:14
Mo 21:54

7

4

6

PlR 26:00
Ke 13:32

Uk 29:56 Ra 13:32		VeR 04:16 Me 07:28 Ju 15:07	ChR 1:03
UrR 28:16 CeR 19:02 NeR 15:53 Asc 09:28			
			Sa 08:54 Ma 11:14 Mo 21:54
Su 29:56			Ke 13:32 PlR 26:00

**San Diego Padres (+104) vs. Milwaukee Brewers (−122), 13:11 LT, Aug. 6, 2015,
Milwaukee, Wisconsin**

(loser), have no rhyme or reason that I can discern. Finally, Mars combos such as Mars and Saturn and Mars and Jupiter also favor victory, but more study is needed to develop consistency. For this technique, we do not consider the invisible grahas except for Rahu and Ketu.

TABLE 5.4. D9 COMBINATIONS AND THEIR EFFECTS

PLANET COMBOS	EFFECT
Sun + Ketu	Loss
Venus + Ketu	Win
Sun + Jupiter	Loss
Moon + Rahu	Win
Moon + Saturn	Loss
Venus + Rahu	Loss

Let's take a look at the example on page 105.

Minnesota, though having positive odds (+124), is still the favorite because their number is lower than their opponent's. This happens in cases where a draw in regular time is also a likely outcome, or where oddsmakers want to encourage betting.

In the rashi chart, Upaketu exactly on the 6th house cusp is the strongest cuspal activation; it shows the favorite's desire to fight is diminished. Alone, it is good for the underdog but does not necessarily confer victory. Looking at the D9 chart, however, we find Venus and Ketu in the 7th house, a nice combo that supports the underdog's chances. They won 3 to 2. Similar rashi charts without this kind of D9 combination resulted in victories for the favorite, underscoring the need to consult the D9 before making final predictions.

Up, Uranus

In the chart on page 106, underdog Tampa Bay won 8 to 5 because of Uranus on the navamsha 7th cusp. That Uranian current that normally galvanizes cusps with energy also tends to run the score up, especially when Uranus alone is involved—good for players who like to place over bets in the over/under.

RASHI

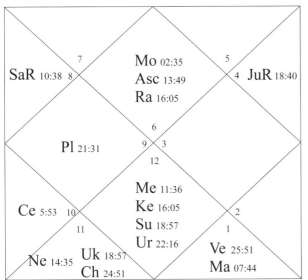

Ur 22:16 Su 18:57 Ke 16:05 Me 11:36	Ma 07:44 Ve 25:51		
Ch 24:51 Uk 18:57 Ne 14:35			JuR 18:40
Ce 5:53			
Pl 21:31	SaR 10:38		Mo 02:35 Asc 13:49 Ra 16:05

Bhava   Cusp
1st h.   13:49:26 Vir
2nd h.   09:47:40 Lib
3rd h.   10:41:40 Sco
4th h.   15:27:08 Sag
5th h.   19:38:43 Cap
6th h.   19:22:00 Aqu
7th h.   13:49:26 Pis
8th h.   09:47:40 Ari
9th h.   10:41:40 Tau
10th h.   15:27:08 Gem
11th h.   19:38:43 Can
12th h.   19:22:00 Leo

NAVAMSHA

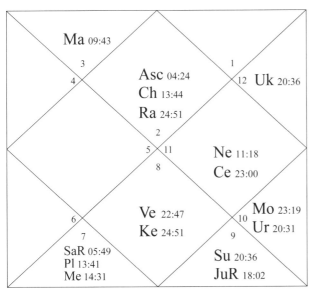

Uk 20:36		Asc 04:24 Ch 13:44 Ra 24:51	Ma 09:43
Ne 11:18 Ce 23:00			
Mo 23:19 Ur 20:31			
Su 20:36 JuR 18:02	Ve 22:47 Ke 24:51	SaR 05:49 Pl 13:41 Me 14:31	

New York Rangers (+184) vs. <u>Minnesota Wild (+124)</u>, 19:10 LT, April 2, 2015,
Minneapolis, Minnesota

RASHI

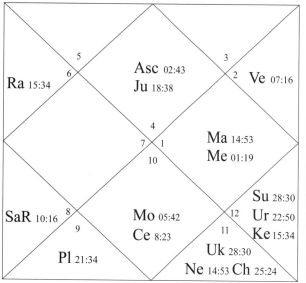

Su 28:30 Ur 22:50 Ke 15:34	Me 01:19 Ma 14:53	Ve 07:16	
Uk 28:30 Ch 25:24 Ne 14:53			Asc 02:43 Ju 18:38
Ce 8:23 Mo 05:42			
Pl 21:34	SaR 10:16		Ra 15:34

Bhava   Cusp
1st h.   02:43:10 Can
2nd h.   26:36:07 Can
3rd h.   23:58:17 Leo
4th h.   25:40:57 Vir
5th h.   29:41:14 Lib
6th h.   02:31:22 Sag
7th h.   02:43:10 Cap
8th h.   26:36:07 Cap
9th h.   23:58:17 Aqu
10th h.   25:40:57 Pis
11th h.   29:41:14 Ari
12th h.   02:31:22 Gem

NAVAMSHA

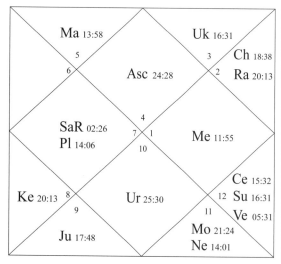

Su 16:31 Ce 15:32 Ve 05:31	Me 11:55	Ch 18:38 Ra 20:13	Uk 16:31
Mo 21:24 Ne 14:01			Asc 24:28
Ur 25:30			Ma 13:58
Ju 17:48	Ke 20:13	SaR 02:26 Pl 14:06	

Tampa Bay Rays (+106) vs. <u>Miami Marlins (−128)</u>, 13:11 LT, April 12, 2015,
Miami, Florida

The Over/Under

Sometimes you don't have to bet on a team to win. Knowing whether the final score will be a high or low number relative to the over/under figure set by odds-makers is enough. The over/under is what analysts believe the total score will be when you add up both sides' points. For example, in a soccer game the over/under may be 2.5 goals. That means that if you think the total number of goals scored by both teams will be three or higher, you make a wager on the "over." If instead you feel it will be a low-scoring game (under three goals), then you would bet the "under." In the game between Tampa Bay and Miami (page 106), the over/under was 7.5, which means that if you bet on the over, you would win with a combined score of eight or more runs. This game gave us thirteen, well over the expected. If you bet on the under, you were hoping that the combined score would be seven runs or less. With Uranus on a cusp, unless it's blocked by other factors, it's likely that wouldn't be the case. Opposite Uranus are Saturn and the Sun, which tend to give lower-scoring games.

The World I Know

Applying the D9 to Other Areas of Life

So, is this information only good for contest charts? Goodness no! You can use it in jataka, prashna, or muhurta—three of the six limbs of Jyotisha corresponding to natal, horary, or electional astrology. Would you want to set the grand opening of your flower shop based on a time and date that has Pluto on the D9 lagna? Not unless you cater to the Mafia (as Pluto rules the underworld), which, on second thought, may be a new and possibly lucrative business model. However, if you want to be embraced by the public, why not have the Moon or Jupiter conjunct the D9 lagna instead?

Once, a friend was leaving for a seven-hour road trip, and I pulled the chart to analyze how it would progress. To my dismay I found Saturn and Ketu both lurking near the D9 lagna. I asked her to delay her trip, but she was pressed. I exhorted her to at least wait until Saturn and Ketu were both out of orb of the navamsha ascendant degree (more than 2°30'). She did, hanging on a few minutes to depart, taking Saturn and Ketu out of orb but still in the D9 lagna. A few hours later she was caught in a terrible rainstorm that reduced visibility to a few meters (Ketu rules smoke and obfuscation). Then she hit a rock on the road (Saturn). Pulling over, she found that the rock had fortunately disintegrated and the car was alright. Nonetheless, it was a scare for both of us. Had she left when Saturn or Ketu were within orb of the D9 lagna, the circumstances may not have been so forgiving.

Poor Billy Crystal . . .

Tsk, tsk. How did the Yankees get themselves into this mess of the chart on page 109?

The New York Yankees have a lot of famous fans who were badly let down as the Houston Astros shut their team out 3 to 0 in this wildcard playoff game. If the Yanks had known Jyotisha, perhaps they could have picked a better game to prolong instead of ending their baseball season. The culprit? Consider the PKY on the 7th house to begin with. The coup de grace, however, is the Sun's D9 position on the 7th cusp, which burns up the underdog and ensures a low-scoring, dull affair.*

Double Whammy

A double whammy is when two bad things happen at the same time, or when a single planet delivers a double dose of trouble by hugging a rashi cusp so tightly that its effect transfers to the D9. Consider the chart on page 110, which we saw in chapter 4.

In the previous chapter we noted that the underdog Milwaukee Brewers have Jupiter exactly on the 7th cusp, their lagna. What we didn't know is that this bear hug of a cuspal influence puts Jupiter within orb (2°30') of the navamsha 7th cusp as well, ensuring that the underdog is utterly protected by this powerful graha. Pay attention to very close conjunctions to the 1/7 cusps in the rashi chart, as they may also affect the navamsha. See another example on page 111, from the Wounded Warrior, Chiron.

This is a beast of a chart for the underdog, who dominates in every category, including victory house and SKY. The knockout blow comes from retrograde

---

*The cherry on top is the nakshatra marker star Altair (main star of Shravana nakshatra), which exactly joins the 10th cusp. Though we haven't covered the nakshatras and their marker stars yet, in chapter 8 we will see how this star's symbolism directly reflected on the final score.

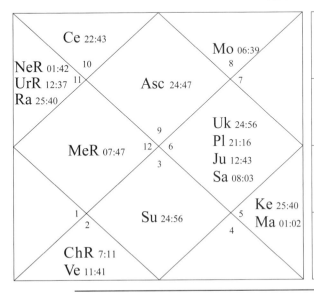

UrR 24:44 Ke 06:11	Asc 29:25		
NeR 13:31 ChR 24:07			Mo 14:04
Ce 2:31			Ve 04:37 Ma 13:26 Ju 18:04 Uk 19:26
Pl 19:01	Sa 07:33		Ra 06:11 MeR 07:31 Su 19:26

Bhava   Cusp
1st h.   29:25:13 Ari
2nd h.   25:23:17 Tau
3rd h.   16:22:29 Gem
4th h.   07:50:30 Can
5th h.   04:23:27 Leo
6th h.   11:55:49 Vir
7th h.   29:25:13 Lib
8th h.   25:23:17 Sco
9th h.   16:22:29 Sag
10th h.   07:50:30 Cap
11th h.   04:23:27 Aqu
12th h.   11:55:49 Pis

NAVAMSHA

MeR 07:47		ChR 7:11 Ve 11:41	Su 24:56
Ra 25:40 UrR 12:37 NeR 01:42			
Ce 22:43			Ma 01:02 Ke 25:40
Asc 24:47	Mo 06:39		Sa 08:03 Ju 12:43 Pl 21:16 Uk 24:56

<u>**Houston Astros (−114)**</u> **vs. New York Yankees (+110), 20:10:25 LT, Oct. 6, 2015,**
Bronx, New York

RASHI

Bhava	Cusp
1st h.	10:28:50 Aqu
2nd h.	29:04:11 Pis
3rd h.	00:15:40 Tau
4th h.	22:50:29 Tau
5th h.	13:11:06 Gem
6th h.	06:11:01 Can
7th h.	10:28:50 Leo
8th h.	29:04:11 Vir
9th h.	00:15:40 Sco
10th h.	22:50:29 Sco
11th h.	13:11:06 Sag
12th h.	06:11:01 Cap

NAVAMSHA

Pittsburgh Pirates (−167) vs. Milwaukee Brewers (+141), 19:11 LT, Sept. 1, 2015,
Milwaukee, Wisconsin

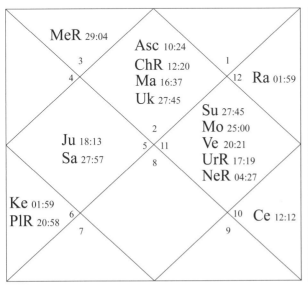

North Indian chart (left):

- House 12: Ke 06:53, UrR 25:15
- House 10/9: Ce 1:21, Mo 06:06, PlR 18:59
- Center-left: NeR 13:49, Asc 24:29, ChR 24:42
- House 8/5: Sa 06:26
- House 3/4: Ma 05:10, Uk 06:25, Ju 15:21
- Ve 25:35
- House 6/7: MeR 19:53, Ra 06:53, Su 06:25

South Indian chart (right):

UrR 25:15, Ke 06:53			
ChR 24:42, Asc 24:29, NeR 13:49			Ve 25:35
Mo 06:06, Ce 1:21			Ma 05:10, Uk 06:25, Ju 15:21
PlR 18:59	Sa 06:26		Su 06:25, Ra 06:53, MeR 19:53

Bhava	Cusp
1st h.	24:29:24 Aqu
2nd h.	09:42:30 Ari
3rd h.	08:18:31 Tau
4th h.	00:06:02 Gem
5th h.	20:53:52 Gem
6th h.	15:50:26 Can
7th h.	24:29:24 Leo
8th h.	09:42:30 Lib
9th h.	08:18:31 Sco
10th h.	00:06:02 Sag
11th h.	20:53:52 Sag
12th h.	15:50:26 Cap

NAVAMSHA

North Indian chart (left):

- MeR 29:04
- Asc 10:24, ChR 12:20, Ma 16:37, Uk 27:45
- Ra 01:59
- Su 27:45, Mo 25:00, Ve 20:21, UrR 17:19, NeR 04:27
- Ju 18:13, Sa 27:57
- Ke 01:59, PlR 20:58
- Ce 12:12

South Indian chart (right):

Ra 01:59		Asc 10:24, ChR 12:20, Ma 16:37, Uk 27:45	MeR 29:04
Su 27:45, Mo 25:00, Ve 20:21, UrR 17:19, NeR 04:27			
Ce 12:12			Ju 18:13, Sa 27:57
			Ke 01:59, PlR 20:58

Celta Vigo (+550) vs. Barcelona (−200), 20:00 LT, Sept. 23, 2015, Vigo, Spain

Chiron, who has the main chart ascendant in such a headlock that it transfers into the D9—an example of hitting someone so hard that his ancestors feel it. The underdog stunned perennial favorite Barcelona, 4 to 1. (Remember that outside grahas, when retrograde, tend to give opposite results.)

The Tracks of My Tiers

Smokey Robinson probably wasn't thinking about Vedic astrology when he recorded his Motown classic, but then again maybe he was. Whatever the case, we can save ourselves a lot of suffering by organizing the principles we've learned thus far into tiers, according to their ability to influence an outcome. We saw this earlier; let's now take another look. Tier three represents the strongest advantage, tier one the weakest. We'll be assessing techniques according to strength like this throughout this book, adding more as we go along. See table 5.5 for what we have so far.

TABLE 5.5. THREE TIERS OF STRENGTH

TIER	TECHNIQUE	STRENGTH
Tier 3	Navamsha cuspal strength	Super strong; indicates victory by itself
Tier 2	SKY/PKY, cuspal strength	Strong; indicates victory unless tier 3 techniques oppose it
Tier 1	Victory houses, navamsha combos	Weak; indicates victory unless tier 2 or 3 techniques oppose it

Note that third-tier techniques are powerful but don't come around often. Your bread and butter will likely be second- and first-tier techniques, because you can use them in practically every chart. Memorize table 5.5; knowing the tiers will help you break ties when some techniques point in one direction and others in a different direction. For example, all factors being equal, a strong navamsha will almost always trump a strong rashi, as we have seen in the preceding examples. Just as the mind moves the body, so the D9 (navamsha) controls the D1 (rashi).

> **Just as the mind moves the body, so the D9 (navamsha)
> controls the D1 (rashi).**

I will end this chapter with another reminder that these techniques are not limited to event charts or sports. Take this prashna I cast for the question "Will the Los Angeles Dodgers win the World Series?" Okay, it's still about sports, but the question could have been about anything requiring a yes or no answer.

Here I point your attention to the D9, which, in the chart on page 114, shows Jupiter glued to the 7th house, indicating, among other things, that the other, the opponent, would take the trophy, rather than the self, the lagna, or in this case, the Los Angeles Dodgers. Sorry, not this year.

"Jyotisha Works!"

. . . I exclaimed, raising my arms exultantly and turning to my wife, eyes peeled in quasidisbelief. I said it as much to her as to my inner, doubting self. In your face, doubting self!

We had just finished watching a soccer match in which our team came back from a 1 to 0 deficit to win 2 to 1 in the twilight minutes of the game—a nail-biting, stomach-churning affair that, ironically, didn't need to be had I possessed greater faith in my craft. But there is something nerve-wracking about watching a game, or a life, unfold, as the veil of maya confounds even the stoutest of intellects.

A sports match is a microcosm of a lifetime: a space-time event with a beginning, a life span, and an ending, that, like our own human lives, ebbs and flows with drama, giddy exultation, and abject desperation, and in such a compressed format that it makes the event even more poignant. Its triumphs soar on a dopamine high, and its lows feel like a vampire sucking your lifeblood until all that's left is abject torpor. But there can come a point during a game—or during a lifetime—in which you resign yourself: "Thy will, Lord, not mine, be done." This is surrender, and it's a good thing, a positive outcome of the spiritual practice that is being a sports fan. At other times, surrender gives way to a sense of knowing, a trust in your own inner self that says, "No! This will not stand! If Jyotisha works, this must be so!" That certainty born of experience (or innocence) is so

RASHI

Diamond chart (North Indian):

- Ma 17:36
- NeR 11:23, ChR 20:23 — 10, 11
- Mo 01:08, Asc 11:58, Pl 17:02 — 9
- Sa 26:31, Ce 25:13, Me 07:32 — 8, 7
- UrR 20:49, Ke 25:51 — 12, 6
- Ra 25:51, Su 13:37, Ve 07:14 — 3
- Uk 13:37 — 1, 2, 5, 4
- Ju 21:56

Square chart (South Indian):

Ke 25:51 UrR 20:49			
NeR 11:23 ChR 20:23			Ju 21:56
			Uk 13:37
Pl 17:02 Asc 11:58 Mo 01:08	Ma 17:36	Me 07:32 Ce 25:13 Sa 26:31	Ve 07:14 Su 13:37 Ra 25:51

Bhava	Cusp
1st h.	11:58:47 Sag
2nd h.	19:30:17 Cap
3rd h.	28:52:08 Aqu
4th h.	02:00:43 Ari
5th h.	28:03:58 Ari
6th h.	20:11:27 Tau
7th h.	11:58:47 Gem
8th h.	19:30:17 Can
9th h.	28:52:08 Leo
10th h.	02:00:43 Lib
11th h.	28:03:58 Lib
12th h.	20:11:27 Sco

NAVAMSHA

Diamond chart (North Indian):

- Uk 02:35, Ra 22:40 — 5
- Asc 17:49 — 3, 2
- Sa 28:47, Ce 17:00, Su 02:35
- Pl 03:24 — 6
- ChR 3:34, Mo 10:20 — 4, 7, 1, 10
- UrR 07:29, NeR 12:32, Ju 17:24 — 8, 9
- Ve 05:10 — 12, 11
- Me 07:50, Ma 08:26
- Ke 22:40

Square chart (South Indian):

Ve 05:10	ChR 3:34 Mo 10:20	Su 02:35 Ce 17:00 Sa 28:47	
Ke 22:40			Asc 17:49
Ju 17:24 NeR 12:32 UrR 07:29			Uk 02:35 Ra 22:40
Ma 08:26 Me 07:50			Pl 03:24

Will the Los Angeles Dodgers win the World Series? 14:05 LT, Sept. 30, 2014, Albuquerque, New Mexico

strong that it also engenders a serenity that in this case is born not of surrender, but of knowing.

And that's exactly what I said, watching sullenly as our team crept closer to being shut out, just a dozen minutes from the end.

"No, Jyotisha works! This can't be!" I said with the self-assurance only faith in a higher power—or madness— instills. Mind you, we couldn't tie; I had predicted a win, and a win it had to be. Just a few minutes later, we tied the game—a good start. And then, minutes after that, we got our win. Call it what you will, madness, faith, or knowing, on this day we prevailed.

Summary

- Navamsha cuspal strength: planets on the D9 1st or 7th cusps affect the teams they represent according to their nature with third-tier strength (the strongest possible influence). Use the same orbs as you did with the rashi cuspal strength technique (chapter 4): 2°30' for visible planets and 2° for invisible planets.
- Navamsha combinations: certain combinations of planets in the D9 lagna or 7th house have a first-tier effect.

6

A Quantum of Solace

Factoring in Sublords and Putting It All Together

The universe is like a safe to which there is a combination.
But the combination is locked up in the safe.
PETER DE VRIES

Discovered and popularized in the midtwentieth century by K. S. Krishnamurti, sublords offer precise predictions based on minute increments of time. The question of sublords arose out of Krishnamurti's frustration with whole-sign Vedic astrology's inability to explain the differences between identical twins. Though some people who are born as twins display relatively similar personalities, many do not, often leading dramatically different lives though their rashi charts are virtually identical. Krishnamurti reasoned that there must be some finer demarcation within each sign that accounts for such differences.

The Sublord Theory

There are currently twenty-seven nakshatras used in Vedic astrology (see table 6.1), reflecting the number of days in a sidereal month (modern value: 27.32 days) and the time it takes the moon to traverse each nakshatra (about 1 day). An older tradition of Jyotisha uses twenty-eight nakshatras—a subject we'll return to in chapter 8, where you will find a complete list of the twenty-eight nakshatras and their specific marker stars, or yogataras (also called taras).

One of the nine grahas is assigned to each of the nakshatras as a governing "lord," in the following sequence: Ketu, Venus, Sun, Moon, Mars, Rahu, Jupiter, Saturn, and Mercury. This cycle repeats itself three times to cover all twenty-seven nakshatras. The lord of each nakshatra determines the planetary period known as the *vimshottari dasha,* which is considered of major importance in forecasting the life path of the person in Hindu astrology.

TABLE 6.1. VEDIC NAKSHATRAS

NAKSHATRA	VIMSHOTTARI DASHA RULER
Ashvini	Ketu
Bharani	Venus
Krittika	Sun
Rohini	Moon
Mrigashira	Mars
Ardra	Rahu
Punarvasu	Jupiter
Pushya	Saturn
Ashlesha	Mercury
Magha	Ketu
Purva Phalguni	Venus
Uttara Phalguni	Sun
Hasta	Moon
Chitra	Mars
Svati	Rahu
Vishakha	Jupiter
Anuradha	Saturn
Jyeshtha	Mercury
Mula	Ketu

NAKSHATRA	VIMSHOTTARI DASHA RULER
Purva Ashadha	Venus
Uttara Ashadha	Sun
Dhanishta	Mars
Shravana	Moon
Shatabhisha	Rahu
Purva Bhadrapada	Jupiter
Uttara Bhadrapada	Saturn
Revati	Mercury

Since the dashas of planets are long, ranging from six to twenty years in length, they are further broken down into subperiods—called *bhuktis*—to help us give more precise predictions. Krishnamurti's genius was taking the dasha-bhukti division of *time* and turning it into a division of *space* by dividing nakshatras into nine parts, but instead of calling them *bhuktis* (which are divisions of time), he called them *sublords* (which are divisions of space). Thus, every nakshatra has a *lord* (for the whole nakshatra) and a *sublord* (for a subdivision of the nakshatra). Each sublord is proportional in length to its span in the vimshottari dasha scheme. Here are the dasha periods in their natural order, along with their span in years in the vimshottari dasha.

Ketu—7 years
Venus—20 years
Sun—6 years
Moon—10 years
Mars—7 years
Rahu—18 years
Jupiter—16 years
Saturn—19 years
Mercury—17 years

A full dasha cycle equals 120 years (*vimshottari* in Sanskrit), which perhaps also indicates the optimum human life span according to Jyotisha and ayurveda.

Of course, in contest prediction we do not use the dasha at all, since games have such a short life span.

Let's see how this nakshatra division works:

TABLE 6.2. PURVA PHALGUNI 13.20–26.40 LEO

NAKSHATRA LORD	SUBLORD	SPAN
Venus	Venus	(13°20'00"–15°33'20" Leo)
Venus	Sun	(15°33'20"–16°13'20" Leo)
Venus	Moon	(16°13'20"–17°20'00" Leo)
Venus	Mars	(17°20'00"–18°06'40" Leo)
Venus	Rahu	(18°06'40"–20°06'40" Leo)
Venus	Jupiter	(20°06'40"–21°53'20" Leo)
Venus	Saturn	(21°53'20"–24°00'00" Leo)
Venus	Mercury	(24°00'00"–25°53'20" Leo)
Venus	Ketu	(25°53'20"–26°40'00" Leo)

This example is for the Venus-ruled nakshatra Purva Phalguni, which spans from 13°20' to 26°40' in the sign Leo. Since this nakshatra is ruled by Venus, its first division is also ruled by Venus. Thus, if a graha or cusp were placed between 13°20' and 15°33'20" in Leo, Venus would be both its lord (nakshatra ruler) and its sublord, as that graha or cusp would lie within the Venus portion of the nakshatra. Let's say instead that your ascendant was 20 degrees Leo. Then its lord would still be Venus (because Venus rules the entire nakshatra), but its *sublord* becomes Rahu, conferring a different personality and life experience, even though your rashi chart—ascendant, Moon, and rising nakshatra—all remain the same.

And, since the vimshottari dasha is determined by the placement of the Moon, if in the example above your Moon fell between 13°20' and 15°33'20" Leo at birth, you would have been born in Venus dasha, Venus bhukti. If your Moon were at 20 degrees Leo, then you would have been born in Venus dasha, Rahu bhukti. Capisce?

Krishnamurti found great success with his sublord method, as it solved the dilemma of twin births whose exact timing, though even only minutes apart, was often enough to change the ascendant sublord of each person, thereby indicating different planetary influences and different life experiences.

> **Krishnamurti's genius was taking the dasha-bhukti division of *time* and turning it into a division of *space* by dividing nakshatras into nine parts, but instead of calling them *bhuktis* (which are divisions of time), he called them *sublords* (which are divisions of space).**

In appendix 1 you will find the full list of sublords for the entire zodiac. Don't worry if this table doesn't make sense now—all we need to do is to familiarize ourselves with the concept that the zodiac can be divided into lords (nakshatra rulers) and sublords (nakshatra division rulers), precisely the same way dashas and bhuktis are allotted. From there we can begin to apply the principles of sublords to contest prediction.

The Sublord Technique Explained

Every house cusp has a sublord based on where it falls in the horoscope. The first step of our technique is to find the sublord of the 1st and 7th house cusps. Take a look at the chart below. You are already familiar with the first two columns, bhava (house) and cusp; now we will learn to use the rest of the information it contains.

HOUSE SIGNIFICATORS

Bhava	Cusp	Lord/Sub/SS	D	C	B	A
1st h.	00:06:39 Sco	Ju/Mo/Me	Sa, Ke	Sa		Ma
2nd h.	00:36:16 Sag	Ke/Ke/Sa				Ju
3rd h.	05:50:48 Cap	Su/Me/Su			Sa, Ke	Sa
4th h.	12:02:58 Aqu	Ra/Sa/Ra	Ju	Ke	Sa, Ke	Sa
5th h.	13:37:44 Pis	Sa/Ra/Sa				Ju
6th h.	09:05:19 Ari	Ke/Ju/Ra				Ma
7th h.	00:06:39 Tau	Su/Ra/Me	Mo, Me	Mo	Su	Ve
8th h.	00:36:16 Gem	Ma/Me/Ve			Ma, Ve	Me
9th h.	05:50:48 Can	Sa/Me/Ve	Su	Ma, Ju, Ve	Mo, Me	Mo
10th h.	12:02:58 Leo	Ke/Me/Ve	Ra	Su, Ra	Ra	Su
11th h.	13:37:44 Vir	Mo/Ra/Mo	Ma, Ve	Me	Ma, Ve	Me
12th h.	09:05:19 Lib	Ra/Ju/Sa			Su	Ve

This chart is an example from a specific game. Depending on your software, you should have a similar printout for any chart that requires Krishnamurti analysis. (I use Parashara's Light software.) Note here that the 1st house cusp lies at 0°06' (0 degrees, 6 minutes) Scorpio. Shifting to the third column, titled Lord/Sub/SS, you will see Ju/Mo/Me. The first planet is the nakshatra lord, in this case Jupiter. The second planet is the sublord, Moon—this is the information we want—and the third column gives something we will not be using, the sub-sublord, a nicety that computer software makes available to us, but one too fine for our purposes. Ignore it. You can also verify this information using the table in appendix 1 (see page 193): for 0°06' Scorpio the sign ruler is Mars, the nakshatra ruler Jupiter, and the sublord Moon.*

Thus, the sublord of the 1st house is Moon and the sublord of the 7th house is Rahu.

Step two is determining which houses each sublord signifies. For this you will use the rest of the information in this box. Scan across from column D to column A for each house. If Moon or Rahu show up anywhere in these four columns, they become *a significator* for the indicated house. For example, scanning across the 1st house we see Saturn and Ketu under column D, Saturn again under column C, nothing under column B, and Mars under column A. Therefore only Saturn, Ketu, and Mars are significators of the 1st house. Looking across the 2nd house, we see nothing under columns D, C, and B, and only Jupiter under column A. Therefore only Jupiter is a significator for the 2nd house. Now do this for each of the remaining houses: scan across to find the significators for each house and familiarize yourself with this technique. Go ahead, I'll wait.

Did you see which houses are signified by the Moon and Rahu? If you got the 7th and 9th for the Moon and the 10th house for Rahu, pat yourself on the back and exhale. Alright, now let's go a little deeper.

Modern Jyotisha software is a great boon as it provides tables like this to make things easy. But it is useful to know how the tables are calculated and what exactly a significator is. In Krishnamurti Paddhati (Krishnamurti Method), planets become

---

*Recall that for this and all other calculations in this book, I use the Krishnamurti ayanamsha. You can experiment with other ayanamshas for other techniques, but when using sublords it is best to stick with Krishnamurti's version of the sidereal offset, which is just slightly different from Lahiri.

significators of houses in four major ways (note that the letters below match the columns on the chart on page 120):

A. By being the sign lord of the house cusp (owning the cusp). If, for example, the house cusp falls in Aries, then Mars owns the cusp because Mars rules Aries.

B. By tenanting the nakshatra of the owner of a house cusp. Since Mars owns the cusp in question, if a planet sits in any of Mars's nakshatras (Mrigashira, Chitra, or Dhanishta), it becomes a significator of that house. You don't have to have the nakshatras or their rulers memorized; table 6.1 (page 117) provides this information, but it would be a good idea to shoot for this kind of knowledge eventually if you want to deepen your overall knowledge of Jyotisha.

C. By residing in the house. This way uses Placidus houses, not signs. Thus, to occupy the 5th house in the chart on page 120, a planet would have to be between 13°38' Pisces and 9°05' Aries (notice that I round up the seconds). If it sits at 10 Pisces it is not considered as being in the 5th house, even though it tenants the fifth sign. If it sits at 8 Aries, it is still in the 5th house, even though it has moved to the sixth sign in the Parashari whole-sign house system. Placidus houses are a staple of Western astrology, and one Krishnamurti took to, since it works well for prediction.

D. By tenanting the nakshatra of the resident of a house (like B above). Since Saturn resides in the 1st house, we are looking for any planets that sit in the Saturn-ruled nakshatras (Pushya, Anuradha, or Uttara Bhadrapada).

Since we've already looked across and seen the significators for the 1st house, let's work out how we determined that. On page 123 you'll find the full horoscope. Let's start with the last column on the right (A), which shows Mars, who owns the sign on the 1st house cusp. This column will *always* have a significator since every cusp falls somewhere in the twelve signs of the zodiac.

Then, in the column next to it (B), we have the planets that occupy the owner's nakshatra; in this case we have nothing, since no planet occupies a nakshatra of Mars. Again, refer to the table in appendix 1 if you don't have the nakshatras and their rulers memorized.

In the next column to the left (C), we have the occupant of that house, Saturn,

RASHI

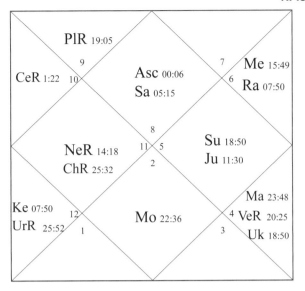

UrR 25:52 Ke 07:50		Mo 22:36	
NeR 14:18 ChR 25:32			Uk 18:50 VeR 20:25 Ma 23:48
CeR 1:22			Ju 11:30 Su 18:50
PlR 19:05	Asc 00:06 Sa 05:15		Ra 07:50 Me 15:49

Bhava	Cusp	Lord/Sub/SS	D	C	B	A
1st h.	00:06:39 Sco	Ju/Mo/Me	Sa, Ke	Sa		Ma
2nd h.	00:36:16 Sag	Ke/Me/Sa				Ju
3rd h.	05:50:48 Cap	Su/Me/Su			Sa, Ke	Sa
4th h.	12:02:58 Aqu	Ra/Sa/Ra	Ju	Ke	Sa, Ke	Sa
5th h.	13:37:44 Pis	Sa/Ra/Sa				Ju
6th h.	09:05:19 Ari	Ke/Ju/Ra				Ma
7th h.	00:06:39 Tau	Su/Ra/Me	Mo, Me	Mo	Su	Ve
8th h.	00:36:16 Gem	Ma/Me/Ve			Ma, Ve	Me
9th h.	05:50:48 Can	Sa/Me/Ve	Su	Ma, Ju, Ve	Mo, Me	Mo
10th h.	12:02:58 Leo	Ke/Me/Ve	Ra	Su, Ra	Ra	Su
11th h.	13:37:44 Vir	Mo/Ra/Mo	Ma, Ve	Me	Ma, Ve	Me
12th h.	09:05:19 Lib	Ra/Ju/Sa			Su	Ve

NAVAMSHA

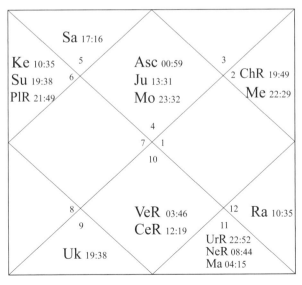

Ra 10:35		ChR 19:49 Me 22:29	
UrR 22:52 NeR 08:44 Ma 04:15			Asc 00:59 Ju 13:31 Mo 23:32
VeR 03:46 CeR 12:19			Sa 17:16
Uk 19:38			Ke 10:35 Su 19:38 PlR 21:49

Milwaukee Brewers (+116) vs. Cincinnati Reds (-133),
13:11:20 LT, Sept. 5, 2015, Cincinnati, Ohio

and finally, in the column next to this, the planets that tenant the nakshatras of that occupant, Ketu and again Saturn, since Saturn is in his own nakshatra. These are the four columns corresponding to the four major ways planets can signify a house.

You might want to draw this out for yourself and do it for all twelve houses, noting which planets signify each house based on the four criteria above. It takes a bit of doing to familiarize yourself, but once it clicks it will become second nature and will make you a better astrologer.

In the chart on page 123 you can see that the favorite has a victory house advantage as well as a massive cuspal strength ace card with Jupiter less than a degree from the MC, which should give them an easy victory. And that's how it appeared as the game started, with the favorite Cincinnati Reds racking up a 5 to 1 early lead.

In the navamsha, Venus is ever so slightly out of orb of the 7th cusp, which would have further helped the favorites, sealing the deal for an easy win. But with cuspal and victory house strength both on their side you wouldn't think they'd need any more help. As it turns out, the underdog Brewers came back to beat them 8 to 6.

Why? Was it the parivartana yoga between Moon and Venus? Is it Mars's debilitation? Did I miss the correct start time of the game?

These are questions I asked too, for many outcomes that didn't make sense . . . until I found sublords. You'd be hard pressed to predict a victory for the underdog using the techniques we've learned so far. That's why learning to quantify sublords and the other techniques of this book is essential.

Putting It All Together

Once you are familiar with using the house significators box, which is found in all the charts we'll be examining for the sublords technique, it's time to rate the strength of our significators. In my system I allot points to each column:

- Column A, which represents the lord of the sign holding a cusp, is the weakest influence, and planets in this one get one point.
- Column B, which shows planets occupying the nakshatra of the cusp ruler, is more important. Planets here get two points.
- The third column, C, is for planets tenanting a house, and they get three points.
- Finally, planets in the nakshatra of planets tenanting a house in column D are the strongest significators of that house. They get four points.

This point allotment system is something I use to rate influences in contest charts. To my knowledge, Krishnamurti did not use a point-allocation system, though he did weigh the significators in the way I've shown, with planets in column A being weakest and those in column D the strongest significators of a house.

> **For the sublord technique we exclusively consider the strength of the lagna sublord versus the 7th house sublord.**

For the sublord technique we exclusively consider the strength of the lagna sublord versus the 7th house sublord. To do this, we will add up the points for each house these represent. The points work like this:

- Houses 1, 3, 6, 10, and 11 get positive points. House 2 gets half positive points.
- Houses 4, 5, 7, 8, 9, and 12 get negative points.
- Houses 2 and 8 are subject to further research in game charts, as they are not part of the victory house technique and the active cusps we look at to influence a chart. Currently, I give the 8th house full negative points, and the 2nd house half positive points.

For our example we will calculate points for the Moon (1st house sublord) and Rahu (7th house sublord) to judge which planet (and team) has greater strength, and thus who is more likely to win the match. Remember, the ascendant and its sublord represent the favorite; the descendant and its sublord represent the underdog. Let's begin with the Moon. Working down from the 1st house, we see that the Moon first becomes a significator for the 7th house, with entries in both columns D and C. It gets −4 and −3 points for a total of −7. Moving further down we see that the Moon is also a significator of the 9th, another negative house. Adding columns A and B we get −1 + −2 = −3.

$$
\begin{array}{r}
\text{7th house} = -7 \\
\text{9th house} = -3 \\
\hline
\textbf{Total} = \ -10
\end{array}
$$

Now let's do the same thing for Rahu. Since Rahu signifies only the 10th house, we can add up his points thus: 4 + 3 + 2 (columns D, C, and B, respectively) = +9 points.

As a result, we have the Moon −10 vs. Rahu +9, which tells us that the sublord of the 1st house gets −10 points (not good) and the sublord of the 7th house gets +9. This is a major discrepancy, a difference of *nineteen points*, which means the underdog, represented by the sublord of the 7th cusp, is strongly favored to win. You will rarely find such dramatic differences, and when you do, they're a pretty good indication of fixed karma and victory for the team with the point advantage, *provided other influences in the chart do not indicate otherwise.* Remember my mantra: everything in Jyotisha is cumulative.

"But wait, how do you score rows in which only two columns are filled?"

Ah, yes, I asked myself that. For the sake of this example, let's say that Jupiter was the sublord of the 1st house, and Mars the 7th sublord. Starting from the top down, we see that Jupiter is the only significator for the 2nd house as the cuspal rashi lord. Normally this gets one point. However, when a house has only one significator, that significator gets a full four points, plus or minus depending on the house. Thus, Jupiter gets +4 points. However, the 2nd house is not a strong house for sports prediction, as noted above, so I only allot *half* the points to it. You can do what you like—allot full points, allot half points, or leave it completely out of your judgment. Try it out and let me know what works for you. The 8th house is less of a dilemma, and currently I'm inclined to give it full negative points.

> **When a house has only one significator,**
> **that significator gets a full four points.**

Here's how Jupiter's significations boil down:

> 2nd house: +2 (half given)
> 4th house: −4
> 5th house: −4 (as the only significator for the
>   5th, he gets a full −4 points)
> 9th house: −3
> ──────────
> **Total: Jupiter −9**

Now we can do the same for Mars. Before we do, take a look at the 8th house. Here there are only two columns of significators. When columns A and B contain the only significators, column A gets two points and column B four points.

TABLE 6.3. HOW POINTS ARE ALLOTED TO SIGNIFICATORS

COLUMN D	COLUMN C	COLUMN B	COLUMN A	
4	3	2	1	If 3 or 4 columns have planets
		4	2	If only columns A and B have planets
			4	If only column A has planets
	3		1	If 2 columns that are not only A and B have planets

Now let's calculate Mars's points:

1st house: +1
6th house: +4
8th house: −4
9th house: −3
11th house: +6

Total: +4

Thus we get Jupiter −9 vs. Mars +4, a thirteen-point difference that indicates victory for the underdog. When judging sublords, the total point difference between the 1st and 7th sublords is the key to interpretation. With a difference of three points or less, it is virtually a draw—very difficult to show an advantage one way or another. For example, sublord X +6 vs. sublord Y +8, a two-point difference, is not enough to warrant a conclusive judgment; it indicates a close match, and you should therefore look at other techniques for predicting the winner.

> **When judging sublords, the total point difference between the 1st and 7th sublords is the key to interpretation.**

Now let's return to the example on page 123. As noted on page 124, the favorite had significant victory house and cuspal strength placements over the underdog. However, the *nineteen-point* sublord advantage sported by the underdog was enough to overwhelm these, granting the Milwaukee Brewers an unlikely come-from-behind victory.

Whereas the victory house technique shows physical strength and cuspal strength shows prana and inspiration, I liken the sublords to spiritual force or luck. Large sublord differences, like in this example, give a clearer picture of which team has the stronger spiritual fortitude—or grace and luck—on their side. Consider this a second-tier technique, on par with main chart cuspal strength. With a big margin like this one, though, it was like having *two* planets directly on a cusp. We'll take a look at how exactly to quantify these points in a moment. First, look at table 6.4, which builds on earlier tables.

TABLE 6.4. RELATIONSHIPS BETWEEN THE KOSHAS AND VEDIC ASTROLOGY TECHNIQUES

KOSHA	TECHNIQUE	TIER
Anna, the food body	Victory house, navamsha combinations	1
Prana, the breath body	Cuspal strength, sublord strength, SKY/PKY	2
Manas, the emotional body	Navamsha cuspal strength	3
Vijnana, the spiritual body	Sublord strength	2

> **Whereas the victory house technique shows physical strength and cuspal strength shows prana and inspiration, I liken the sublords to spiritual force or luck.**

Every three points of difference can stand for one score in the final goal differential of a soccer match and most baseball games. For example, a four-point sublord difference could indicate a final score in which the victor triumphs by one goal or run. A six-point difference could indicate a two-goal differential.

"Wait—I thought you said three points was a draw? And what about a ten-point difference?"

I said three points was a close match. You have to be flexible when using points, as there are other factors that can bear on a game. A good rule of thumb is to divide the point difference by 3. Round up or down to find the goal differential. For example, 10 divided by 3 = 3.3. Rounding down we get a three-goal difference.

Using Sublords Effectively

Before you get too excited, understand that sublord scoring works best when there are few other indications in the chart. When there are other techniques in play, like cuspal strength or navamsha cuspal strength, sublord influence has to be contextualized. When no cusp is activated in either the rashi or the navamsha, or when other factors are balanced, sublord point totals become more indicative of the final outcome.

> **Sublord scoring works best when there are few other indications in the chart.**

To illustrate the rule that planets on cusps in the rashi (D1) or navamsha (D9) can supercede sublords, let's take another look at the baseball game between Chicago and Kansas City that we examined in chapter 4.

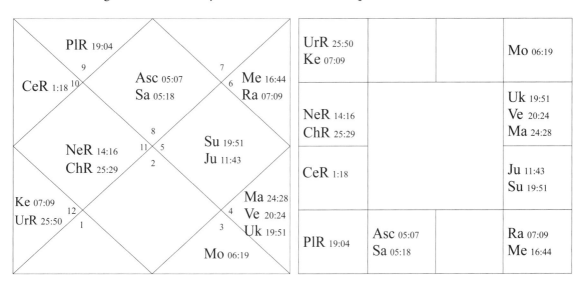

Bhava	Cusp	Lord/Sub/SS	D	C	B	A
1st h.	05:07:21 Sco	Sa/Sa/Ra	Sa, Ke	Sa	Mo	Ma
2nd h.	06:17:30 Sag	Ke/Ra/Sa				Ju
3rd h.	12:22:03 Cap	Mo/Ra/Ju			Sa, Ke	Sa
4th h.	18:42:55 Aqu	Ra/Mo/Sa	Ju	Ke	Sa, Ke	Sa
5th h.	19:41:29 Pis	Me/Ve/Ve				Ju
6th h.	14:27:51 Ari	Ve/Ve/Ju			Mo	Ma
7th h.	05:07:21 Tau	Su/Me/Me			Su	Ve
8th h.	06:17:30 Gem	Ma/Mo/Me	Me	Mo	Ma, Ve	Me
9th h.	12:22:03 Can	Sa/Ma/Ju	Mo, Su	Ma, Ju, Ve	Me	Mo
10th h.	18:42:55 Leo	Ve/Ra/Sa	Ra, Ma, Ve	Su, Me, Ra	Ra	Su
11th h.	19:41:29 Vir	Mo/Ke/Ke/			Ma, Ve	Me
12th h.	14:27:51 Lib	Ra/Ke/Ke			Su	Ve

Chicago White Sox (+179) vs. <u>Kansas City Royals (−217)</u>, 13:12:25 LT, Sept. 6, 2015, Kansas City, Missouri

In this game the Royals were heavily favored against the White Sox. Adding up the sublords, we get Saturn +10 vs. Mercury −2, a strong twelve-point difference in favor of the favorite. Nevertheless, they lost. The reason? Well, go back and review chapter 4.

Okay, fine, I'll tell you: the favorite had *two* powerful planets majorly cramping their style, Saturn and the Sun. A useful rule of thumb is to give nine points to a planet joining a rashi cusp—positive points if it is a good influence, negative if it is not. Yes, that means you can assign points to more than just the sublords; in fact, every technique in this book can be accorded points relative to its ability to influence outcomes. With Saturn and the Sun both afflicting the favorite, they get −18 points. Add to this the sublord strength of +12 and you're still left with −6 points for the favorite. Dividing by 3 we get a score differential of two runs. The underdog won 7 to 5.

A similar instance occured in another game mentioned in chapter 4, the Chicago Cubs vs. Cincinnati Reds:

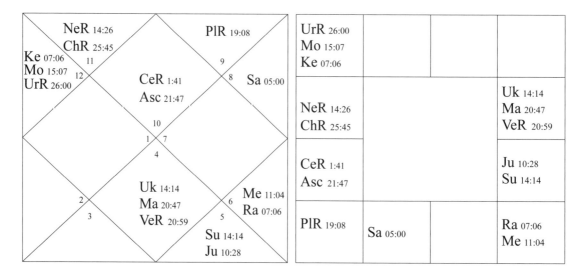

Bhava	Cusp	Lord/Sub/SS	D	C	B	A
1st h.	21:47:20 Cap	Mo / Ve / Ju	Ju	Ke	Mo, Sa, Ke	Sa
2nd h.	08:35:07 Pis	Sa / Ve / Su	Me	Mo		Ju
3rd h.	14:09:05 Ari	Ve / Ve / Ra				Ma
4th h.	09:49:38 Tau	Su / Ve / Me			Su	Ve
5th h.	01:23:21 Gem	Ma / Me / Ju			Ma, Ve	Me
6th h.	23:22:52 Gem	Ju / Sa / Ra	Su	Ma, Ve	Ma, Ve	Me
7th h.	21:47:20 Can	Me / Su / Ju	Ra	Su, Ju, Ra	Me	Mo
8th h.	08:35:07 Vir	Su / Ve / Ra	Ma, Ve	Me	Ma, Ve	Me
9th h.	14:09:05 Lib	Ra / Me / Sa	Mo, Sa, Ke	Sa	Su	Ve
10th h.	09:49:38 Sco	Sa / Ve / Sa				Ma
11th h.	01:23:21 Sag	Ke / Ve / Mo				Ju
12th h.	23:22:52 Sag	Ve / Sa / Ma				Ju

Chicago Cubs (−220) vs. Cincinnati Reds (+185), 19:07 LT, Aug. 31, 2015, Cincinnati, Ohio

Here, Mars and Venus on the 7th cusp add up to +18 for the underdog. The addition of three points gained from the sublord difference between lagna sublord Venus and 7th sublord Sun gives them a total of 21 points. Dividing this by 3 we get 7, which was the actual run differential. Underdog won 13 to 6.

Things don't always work out so neatly, but they do often enough to warrant attention.

Quantifying Influence According to Tiers of Strength

One way to accord yourself a quantum of solace when judging charts is to assign point values to various techniques according to tiers of strength. Third-tier strength is in the area of 14 to 18 points; second-tier strength may be worth about half that, 7 to 9 points; first-tier strength is between 2 and 4 points. This is, of course, a generalization. Strength increases or decreases depending on the tightness of an orb in cuspal strength or navamsha cuspal strength. It also depends on the strength of planets in the victory house and SKY and PKY techniques. Therefore, be wary of number systems that try to reduce reality to a simple equation. If Vedic astrology was that mechanically easy, computers could do all of a Jyotishi's work. They cannot.

In Buddhist psychology there are six realms of fixation illustrating how our minds become trapped. The *human realm* displays the misconception that if we only had enough data, technology, and understanding, we could figure out everything in the universe. That is an erroneous fixation on intellect and logic over grace and spirit, exercising one wing of the Jyotisha bird while leaving the other limp. Beware of falling into the human realm. The flip side is the *god realm*, in which one gives up logic entirely in the name of an otherworldly ideal. It is the New Age psychic fixation on divinity over everything else, an ultimately harmful mental construct that takes us away from reality and present-moment awareness. Both are to be avoided.

Having said that, this is a book on tools and techniques, and the more techniques we have to assess a sports chart, the more precise our predictions can become in the face of multiple influences.

The more techniques we have to assess a sports chart, the more precise our predictions can become in the face of multiple influences.

TABLE 6.5. POINTS VALUE TABLE

TIER	TECHNIQUE	AVERAGE POINTS
1	Victory house planets*	2–4 (each planet)
2	SKY/PKY	7–9
2	Cuspal strength†	7–9 (each planet)
3	Navamsha cuspal strength†	14–18 (each planet)
1	Navamsha combinations	5
2	Sublords	Points allotted as explained in table 6.3 on page 127
1	Sublord array	7–9

* In the victory house technique, planets get 2.5 points each. If they are exalted or otherwise powerful give them 3 points. Debilitated planets, on the other hand, get a little less, in the order of 2 points each.

† Invisible grahas get fewer points in cuspal strength and navamsha cuspal strength, in the order of 7 in the rashi and 12 to 15 in the navamsha.

You may have to adjust these values up or down according to the situation. For example, a heavily afflicted SKY may only be worth 3 or 4 points or less, well below the value of a full SKY. A planet on the outer edge of its orb, though still on a cusp, may exert a bit less influence than one in a tighter orb. This is where your intuition and experience will come in to nudge and adjust point values.

Let's now walk through our example chart from page 123 using sublords and point values to see if we can arrive at the final score.

TABLE 6.6. MILWAUKEE VS. CINCINNATI

TECHNIQUE	FAVE VS. DOG
Victory house	+4
SKY/PKY	none
Cuspal strength	+9
Navamsha cuspal strength	none
Navamsha combinations	none
Sublords	−19
TOTAL:	**−6**

In these calculations, all numbers apply to the favorite. Thus +4 means 4 points for the favorite, and −19 would mean 19 points subtracted from the favorite. The final total shows who is the likely winner: a plus sign (+) indicates the favorite, and by how many points; a minus sign (−) means the underdog.

Beginning with the victory house method, we have Saturn, Sun, and Rahu for the favorites, and Mars and Venus for the underdog. Saturn and Rahu each receive 2.5 points, while Sun will get 3, since he has extra strength in the form of dig bala. You can give extra-strong victory house planets an additional half point for every source of strength they display. For example, if the Sun in this chart were also exalted, he would receive 3.5 points. For the same reasons, Mars, a victory house graha for the underdog, would receive only 2 points, since he is debilitated.* The favorites also have the benefic Mercury on their side, who gets 2.5 points. His exaltation is enough to make him a victory house planet (if he had other strength like retrogression or dig bala, he would earn even more points). Likewise, Venus for the underdog also gets 2.5 points since his retrogression makes him a victory planet but does not give extra strength. Here is the final breakdown for the victory house planets:

> Saturn +2.5
> Rahu +2.5
> Mercury +2.5
> Sun +3
> Venus −2.5
> Mars −2
> ———————
> **Total +6**

"Wait, what about the Moon? It's exalted *and* in its own nakshatra! Surely it will have some say?" Well, you may be right. I normally do not use the Moon when figuring eligible benefics for the victory house method, but since you asked nicely . . . we can give the moon 2 points or so, in favor of the underdogs. Thus our final victory house total reads +4.

---

*If you do not have these sources of strength memorized, refer to the table of planetary strength and weakness on page 46.

Since there is no SKY/PKY we move to cuspal strength, which the favorite has in spades—a full 9 points for Jupiter.

In the navamsha we narrowly miss Venus on the 7th cusp, so nothing to report there.

Finally we arrive at the sublords, which we've already figured as −19. Totaling these factors, we get −6 points: a victory for the underdog. Dividing this total by 3 to arrive at a score differential, we get 2 runs or goals—the actual score difference. Even without fudging the victory house values for the Moon, we would still arrive at −4 total points and a score difference of 1.3 runs—close enough to predict our underdog victory.

I find this goal differential calculation (dividing by 3) to work well for soccer, and fairly well for baseball. Baseball has more dramatic margins of victory, so you may want to divide by 2.5 or 2.7 to arrive at the final run difference for that sport. For hockey, that figure is closer to 2. I am showing you this to illustrate that your logic and intuition are both necessary in order to soar in the heavens of accurate Jyotisha prediction.

Now let's take a look at another scenario—when both the 1st and 7th cuspal lords are the same planet. The chart on page 135 is the Germany-Portugal example from chapter 3.

Here we took our first stab at guessing the score using the victory house technique. Let's see if it still holds up after all we've learned thus far. Adding up the sublord values, we see Rahu +1 vs. Rahu +1. Uh-oh, what to do when the sublord for the 1st and 7th houses is the same? This is a bit of a pesky situation,* but here's one way to resolve it: count its score as the point differential for the favorite. In this case +1. If it had been Rahu −10, you would count −10 for the favorite. Rahu +10? You guessed it, +10 points for the favorite.

This is not the crushing difference you'd expect in a match where the favorite won 4 to 0. However, taking a look at the rest of the chart shows us the reason why they won. Beginning with the victory house technique, we get +8.5 for the German side, as Mercury and the Sun get 3 points each for being extra strong (Mercury is retrograde *and* in own sign, and the Sun has dig bala, i.e., directional strength, by

---

*When the 1st and 7th cusp sublords are the same planet, the sublord technique becomes much less reliable. In fact every technique in this book has cases where it does not apply. That is why it is important to have multiple techniques to draw on when necessary.

North Indian chart (left):
- Ra 02:34, SaR 23:35 (house 7/8)
- Ma 19:25, Asc 25:57 (houses 5/4)
- Ju 29:34, MeR 06:26, Su 01:28 (houses 6/9/3/12)
- Mo 19:58 (houses 10/11)
- Ve 27:54, Ke 02:34 (house 1)

South Indian chart (right):
- Ke 02:34, Ve 27:54
- Su 01:28, MeR 06:26, Ju 29:34
- Mo 19:58
- Ra 02:34, SaR 23:35
- Ma 19:25, Asc 25:57

Bhava	Cusp	Lord/Sub/SS	D	C	B	A
1st h.	25:57:09 Vir	Ma/Ra/Mo		Sa, Ra		Me
2nd h.	27:56:26 Lib	Ju/Ve/Ju				Ve
3rd h.	25:25:17 Sco	Me/Ra/Ve			Su, Me, Ra	Ma
4th h.	21:19:00 Sag	Ve/Ju/Su			Ju, Sa	Ju
5th h.	18:48:28 Cap	Mo/Me/Ma	Mo, Ma	Mo		Sa
6th h.	20:26:20 Aqu	Ju/Ju/Sa				Sa
7th h.	25:57:09 Pis	Me/Ra/Mo	Ke	Ve, Ke	Ju, Sa	Ju
8th h.	27:56:26 Ari	Su/Mo/Sa			Su, Me, Ra	Ma
9th h.	25:25:17 Tau	Ma/Ra/Ve	Ve	Su, Me		Ve
10th h.	21:19:00 Gem	Ju/Ju/Mo	Ju, Sa	Ju		Me
11th h.	18:48:28 Can	Me/Ke/Mo			Mo, Ma	Mo
12th h.	20:26:20 Leo	Ve/Ju/Sa	Su, Me, Ra	Ma	Ve	Su

<u>Germany (−110)</u> vs. Portugal (+260), 13:01 LT, June 16, 2014, Salvador, Brazil

being in the 10th house), while Mars gets 2.5 points. Jupiter tenanting his own star could count as a victory house planet, as introduced in chapter 3. But I find more and more that benefics need to be exaggerated if they are to truly behave like malefics for this technique. This means they should be either retrograde or exalted (refer to page 47 to see what gives a planet exaggerated condition). Remember that benefics count in the victory house technique when they are especially strong, and ones occupying their own nakshatra or sign could be eligible, but it's up to you to decide. Here, the Germans didn't need Jupiter's help.

Next, we look at the possibility of SKY/PKY in the chart. Since there is none, we can move to the following technique, cuspal strength. Here, the Germans have Ceres exactly on the lagna—an influence we didn't consider while doing this chart in chapter 3. Being direct, Ceres acts as a second-tier boost to the favorite in the order of +8 strength. (I give visible grahas +9 and invisible grahas +7, though in this case, with the orb being so tight, I accorded Ceres an extra point. As it turns out, the Germans didn't need it either.)

TABLE 6.7. GERMANY VS. PORTUGAL

TECHNIQUE	FAVE VS. DOG
Victory house	+8.5
SKY/PKY	none
Cuspal strength	+8
Navamsha cuspal strength	none
Navamsha combinations	none
Sublords	+1
TOTAL:	**+17.5**

There is nothing within orb of the navamsha lagna or 7th cusp, so adding up all the techniques we've studied so far, we arrive at a total of +17.5 points. This isn't the final total, as the underdogs have a nakshatra tara boost—a technique we haven't studied thus far—that drops the total down to about +11 points, but it's still a comfortable margin for the favorite (I know, it's unfair to include techniques we haven't studied yet, but there you go). This total, +11, can now help us find the final score, since dividing 11 by 3 we get 3.7, or 4 goals rounding up.

This looks nice and neat, but even if we didn't have the exact goal differential we could have arrived at a similar conclusion, as I did when judging this chart for the first time using only my victory house technique and SKY, which served me well enough to win hundreds of bets and thousands of dollars. Even without knowing about Ceres and Chiron, or cuspal and navamsha strength, it was clear that the favorite would win, and by more than one goal. Maybe I was just lucky that these other influences didn't get in the way. But the more you know, the less luck you need. For a blank table to help you allocate points using all the techniques in this book, see appendix 2.

You can also use sublords to help answer simple yes/no questions like the horary chart for the question posed in the previous chapter, "Will the Los Angeles Dodgers win the World Series?" As we said in that chapter, this could be any kind of yes/no question pitting one option against another. Here, the thing queried (the Dodgers and their chances of winning) takes the 1st house, and the 7th house represents the other option. Adding up the sublords, we get Mercury −3 vs. Saturn +6, a nine-point difference, making it not very likely. This, in addition to Jupiter on the D9 in 7th cusp, spells it out clearly: it's another early send-off for the boys in blue.

The Sublord Array

A case of sublord dominance occurs when the sublords from all twelve houses indicate victory for one side. This is called a *sublord array*. For example, if all twelve sublords occupy victory-house houses for the favorite, they give the favorite a second-tier boost. The same can also occur for the underdog. Treat the 2nd and 8th houses as neutral.

> Favorite houses: 1, 3, 6, 10, 11
> Underdog houses: 4, 5, 7, 9, 12

In the Aussie league soccer match charted on page 138, the reigning champion, Brisbane, was blown out by last-place Western Sydney, 4 to 1. Note that the sublords for every house except the 7th reside in victory houses for the underdog, with the 7th sublord Moon in the neutral 8th house. This complete sweep of the sublords by the underdog helped grant them a victory, which prompted the headline in the next day's *Sydney Morning Herald:* "Western Sydney Wanderers Stun Brisbane Roar in A-League." Not a stunner if you understand Jyotisha!

This technique becomes less powerful when only ten or eleven of the sublords are one-sided; all have to be there for the full sublord array to work, which, as in the example above, translates into a second-tier boost.

A weaker, first-tier effect is rendered when the sublords for the 1st, 7th, and 10th houses all point to the same team. For this version of the sublord array technique, give the 8th house to the favorite and the 2nd to the underdog. Thus, when all three sublords fall in houses 1, 3, 6, 8, 10, or 11 for the favorite or in houses 2, 4, 5, 7, 9, or 12 for the underdog, this gives a third-tier boost to the indicated team. This is a way to assess the three most important houses in the chart for a quick snapshot.

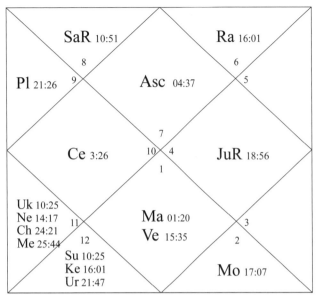

Ur 21:47 Ke 16:01 Su 10:25	Ma 01:20 Ve 15:35	Mo 17:07	
Me 25:44 Ch 24:21 Ne 14:17 Uk 10:25			JuR 18:56
Ce 3:26			
Pl 21:26	SaR 10:51	Asc 04:37	Ra 16:01

Bhava	Cusp	Lord/Sub/SS	D	C	B	A
1st h.	04:37:22 Lib	Ma / Ve / Me			Ve	Ve
2nd h.	06:20:27 Sco	Sa / Me / Mo	Su, Sa, Ke	Sa		Ma
3rd h.	01:32:20 Sag	Ke / Ve / Ma			Me	Ju
4th h.	25:13:18 Sag	Ve / Me / Ra			Me	Ju
5th h.	21:26:29 Cap	Mo / Ve / Ra			Su, Sa, Ke	Sa
6th h.	24:14:02 Aqu	Ju / Me / Ke	Ju, Ma	Su, Ma, Me, Ke	Su, Sa, Ke	Sa
7th h.	04:37:22 Ari	Ke / Mo / Ve	Ve	Ve		Ma
8th h.	06:20:27 Tau	Su / Me / Ra	Mo, Ra	Mo	Ve	Ve
9th h.	01:32:20 Gem	Ma / Me / Ju			Ju	Me
10th h.	25:13:18 Gem	Ju / Me / Ra	Me	Ju	Ju	Me
11th h.	21:26:29 Can	Me / Ve/ Ke			Mo, Ra	Mo
12th h.	24:14:02 Leo	Ve/ Me / Me		Ra		Su

Western Sydney Wanderers (+326) vs. Brisbane Roar (−119), 19:01 LT, March 25, 2015, Brisbane, Australia

Amma Always Brings the Rain

"Every time Amma comes to the desert, she brings rain," noted one of Ammachi's swamis upon her arrival. Every June, a caravan of trucks and buses rolls into New Mexico, carrying instruments, lights, food, and the irrepressible saint of Kerala, Ammachi, to hug her way into the hearts and minds of the eager masses—and perhaps by extension of that grace, to turn a bone-dry summer desert into a temporary oasis.

I'm no staunch devotee, but I do recognize Amma as an embodiment of Shakti, Divine Mother energy, and this presence is something everyone should experience at least once in their lives, if not more. I had been sports betting for only a week using the victory house technique, and after the first miraculous Costa Rica win over Uruguay (see page 43), I was emboldened to continue testing.

Knowing so little, I also sought divine guidance, which I found in Ammachi's portrait, a picture whose eyes followed you anywhere in the room, whose face would change according to what you were looking at, somehow responding to unarticulated questions—a twinkle in her eye when I was looking at an unlikely winner, a warning frown when it was a bad loser, and an indifferent shrug when the outcome would be a draw. But I didn't always listen. I made bets just to test out theories, often unsuccessfully. But for the main part I payed attention, and through that made wagers I couldn't have posted based only on techniques.

The next day was to be a crucial, deciding game. I had bet over a dozen six-team parlays,* and the five previous games had all won. I needed just one more to rake in a major win, something like ten to fifteen thousand dollars. Lying prone on the floor, unable to watch, I prayed in full prostration, not so much for the money we would win, which was significant, but to be right, to be so aligned with the universe that it sings your song—or more precisely, that you harmonize with it in such a way that out of cacophony emerges harmony, the sweetest sensation in creation. Feeling that in tune with nature is, I think, why people take drugs, gamble, and push the envelope of conformity—to feel the *twak* of the perfect golf shot or the *swish* of an impeccable three-pointer is to come close to perfection, and only God is perfect.

But on that day, they all came together, six games in a row—harmony in the universe, a feeling of oneness with creation. That's when then the floodgates opened. From somewhere inside a swell of tears, a wellspring, came flowing in bursts and sobs. I had prayed so hard, swallowed so many instances when our teams were down and seemingly out, only to come back and prove the experts wrong. It was too much. I crumpled to the floor and let the tears flow. And then, as if in concert, a symphonic *crash* forced me to my feet—it was the thunder signaling a massive storm that started to drench the thirsty desert. What minutes earlier had been a mostly clear sky with little hint of rain had clouded over and a deluge was ensuing. Amma always brings the rain. I was stunned, my tears rolling, and a summer storm outside. What were the odds?

---

*A parlay is a single bet that links together two or more individual wagers and is dependent on all of those wagers winning together.

Summary

- In this chapter we introduced the points system for quantifying likely outcomes. This is hugely important for arriving at accurate assessments. First-tier strength gives 2 to 4 points, the second tier 7 to 9, and the third tier 14 to 18 per instance per planet.
- The sublords of the 1st and 7th house cusp give us added insight into the spiritual force or luck of a team. Comparing the point difference between the two gives us an idea of who's going to be lucky that day.
- Adding the total positive and negative points arrived at through sublords and the other techniques in this book can give us an idea of the score differential. For soccer, divide this total by three. You will have to research what works for other sports.

7

The Name of the Game

Navamsha Syllables and the Importance of Sound

When people consult me, it's not that I'm reading the future; I am guessing at the future. The future belongs to God, and it is only he who reveals it, under extraordinary circumstances.

PAULO COELHO, *THE ALCHEMIST*

In 1976, the Swedish pop group ABBA had a hit with "The Name of the Game," a song about relationships. This book too is about relationships—specifically, the give-and-take between two teams. And who ends up taking more than giving is often the team with its name emblazoned on the marquee of the horoscope, the 10th house cusp, otherwise known as the MC, or *medium coeli*. The MC is the "glory of the chart," as the 10th house represents fame and victory, and the 10th cusp is the concentrated essence of that house. The same techniques used in India for selecting baby names and business slogans can also help us pick a match winner by looking at the MC. Let's take a look at how that's done.

To review, there are twelve signs of the zodiac with nine navamsha divisions each, making a total of 108 navamshas of 3°20'. The 108 navamshas of the zodiac each correspond to a syllable of the Sanskrit alphabet. Though some vary according to different experts, most are as indicated in table 7.1, shown on page 142. You may notice that the English letters *f, z,* and *w* appear unrepresented, while a whole array of sounds you'll never hear in English (like the aspirated or retroflex syllables, or worse, the aspirated retroflex, like *ḍha* and *ṭha*) seem

TABLE 7.1. THE 108 NAVAMSHA SYLLABLES OF THE SIGNS OF THE ZODIAC*

NAVAMSHA	ARIES	TAURUS	GEMINI	CANCER	LEO	VIRGO	LIBRA	SCORPIO	SAGITTARIUS	CAPRICORN	AQUARIUS	PISCES
1	cu	i	ka	hi	ma	ṭo	ra	to	ye	bo	gu	di
2	ce	u	ki	hu	mi	pa	ri	na	yo	ja/śa	ge	du
3	co	e	ku	he	mu	pi	ru	ni	ba	ji/śi	go	kha/jha
4	la	o	gha	ho	me	ṛu	re	nu	bi	ju/śu	sa	ṅa
5	li	va	ṅga/pha	ḍa	mo	ḍa	ro	ne	bu	je/śe	si	tha
6	lu	vi	cha	ḍi	ṭa	ṛa	ta	no	dha	jo/śo	su	de
7	le	vu	ke	ḍu	ṭi	ṭha	ti	ya	bha	jha/śa	se	do
8	lo	ve	ko	ḍe	ṭu	pe	tu	yi	ḍha	ga	so	ca
9	a	vo	ha	ḍo	ṭe	po	te	yu	be	gi	da	ci

*These are International Alphabet of Sanskrit Transliteration transliterations from the Devanagari script. Thus, *cu* sounds like *choo*, and *śa* like *sha* in English. For other approximations, refer to a good Sanskrit dictionary, or visit www.spokensanskrit.de.

to run amock. That is because this chart was built for Sanskrit speakers and needs to be updated for modern Western languages.

In the meantime, to use this chart, substitute *v* for *w, pha* or *pa* for *f,* and *jha* for *z*.

A Few Basics

The principle of naming according to the position of significant placements in the zodiac is called *nama pada* or *nama nakshatra*. Commonly, a person's Moon degree is used to find the first sound of their name, though other techniques exist. For example, if your Moon were at 28 degrees Cancer in the Vedic sidereal horoscope, your sound is *do,* so names like Dorothy or Domenico would be appropriate. (This is also the source of what in the West is called your primordial sound.) For our purpose, sports investing, we only use the position of the 10th house cusp—the MC—and its syllable, to see if it correlates with the first syllable of one of the teams playing that day.

Take a look at the chart on page 144. The chart shows Venus conjunct the D9 lagna, a bad sign for the favored Pirates, indicating laziness, entitlement, and a laissez-faire attitude on their part. Venus games also tend to be lower-scoring affairs, with the "under" being the better bet in the over/under (see chapter 3 for more on the over/under). With other factors washing out fairly evenly, it's easy to write off the favorite in this game. However, the 10th cusp is at 8°31' Virgo. The nama pada, or navamsha syllable, of that point (6°40' to 10° Virgo) is *pi* (pronounced *pih* or *pee*), exactly the sound of the Pittsburgh Pirates, which led me to predict a close victory for them. The result: Pittsburgh on top, 3 to 2. Always remember that vowels can be short or long in this technique; thus *pi* represents both the short vowel in the name Pittsburgh as well as the long one in *piano*. In Jyotisha, everything plays out. While the 10th cusp sound showed the likely winner, a Venus conjunction in the D9 lagna indicated it would not be an easy victory, and a bet on the underdog to not lose by more than one point (dog +1.5) was also a winner.

If you were to use the points method described in the last chapter, we would give third-tier points to *both* teams: to the favorite because they have the syllable *pi* on the 10th cusp, and to the underdog because Venus hugs the D9 lagna nice and tight. Note that these are the only third-tier techniques, and they both apply in this chart, each to its own team.

RASHI

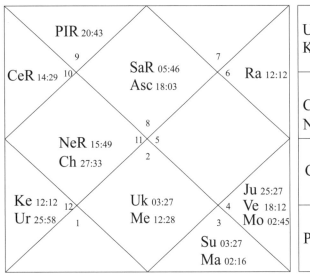

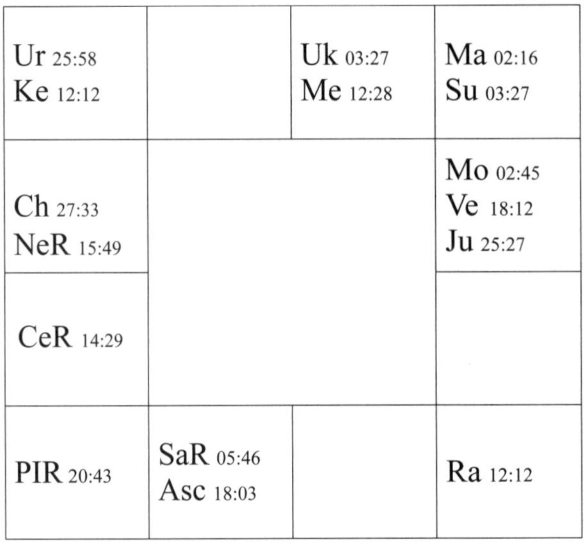

South Indian chart:

Ur 25:58 / Ke 12:12		Uk 03:27 / Me 12:28	Ma 02:16 / Su 03:27
Ch 27:33 / NeR 15:49			Mo 02:45 / Ve 18:12 / Ju 25:27
CeR 14:29			
PIR 20:43	SaR 05:46 / Asc 18:03		Ra 12:12

North Indian chart labels:
PIR 20:43; CeR 14:29; SaR 05:46; Asc 18:03; Ra 12:12; NeR 15:49; Ch 27:33; Ke 12:12; Ur 25:58; Uk 03:27; Me 12:28; Ju 25:27; Ve 18:12; Mo 02:45; Su 03:27; Ma 02:16

Bhava	Cusp	Lord/Sub/SS	D	C	B	A
1st h.	18:03:43 Sco	Me/Me/Ju			Su, Ma	Ma
2nd h.	22:11:00 Sag	Ve/Sa/Sa			Mo	Ju
3rd h.	01:49:57 Aqu	Ma/Me/Sa			Sa, Ke	Sa
4th h.	08:13:10 Pis	Sa/Ve/Ve		Ke	Mo	Ju
5th h.	06:35:55 Ari	Ke/Ra/Me			Su, Ma	Ma
6th h.	28:49:58 Ari	Su/Ma/Sa	Ju, Ve	Me	Su, Ma	Ma
7th h.	18:03:43 Tau	Mo/Me/Ke	Su, Ma	Su, Ma		Ve
8th h.	22:11:00 Gem	Ju/Sa/Me	Me, Ra, Mo	Mo, Ju, Ve	Ju, Ve	Me
9th h.	01:49:57 Leo	Ke/Ve/Ra				Su
10th h.	08:13:10 Vir	Su/Ve/Su		Ra	Ju, Ve	Me
11th h.	06:35:55 Lib	Ma/Mo/Ve				Ve
12th h.	28:49:58 Lib	Ju/Su/Mo	Sa, Ke	Sa		Ve

NAVAMSHA

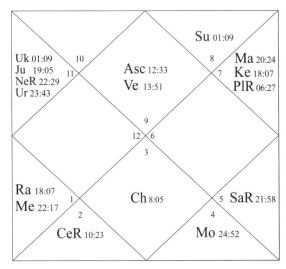

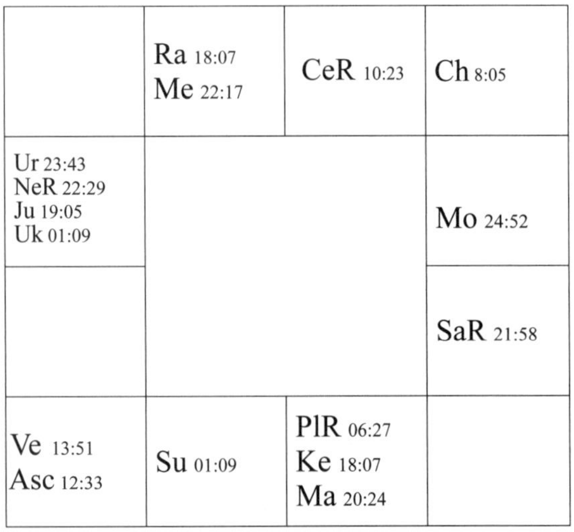

South Indian chart:

Ra 18:07 / Me 22:17	CeR 10:23	Ch 8:05	
Ur 23:43 / NeR 22:29 / Ju 19:05 / Uk 01:09			Mo 24:52
			SaR 21:58
Ve 13:51 / Asc 12:33	Su 01:09	PIR 06:27 / Ke 18:07 / Ma 20:24	

North Indian chart labels:
Uk 01:09; Ju 19:05; NeR 22:29; Ur 23:43; Asc 12:33; Ve 13:51; Su 01:09; Ma 20:24; Ke 18:07; PlR 06:27; Ra 18:07; Me 22:17; CeR 10:23; Ch 8:05; SaR 21:58; Mo 24:52

Pittsburgh Pirates (−135) vs. Chicago White Sox (+114), 19:11 LT, June 18, 2015, Chicago, Illinois

TABLE 7.2. PITTSBURGH PIRATES VS. CHICAGO WHITE SOX

TECHNIQUE	FAVE VS. DOG
Victory house	+0.5
SKY/PKY	none
Cuspal strength	none
Navamsha cuspal strength	−14
Navamsha combinations	none
Sublords	−1
Sublord array	none
Navamsha syllables	+18
TOTAL:	**+2.5**

In table 7.2, +2.5 normally indicates a draw (as does anything between 0 and 3), but since there are no ties in baseball, the favorite squeaks by with a close shave.

"Hold on! If navamsha cuspal strength and navamsha syllables are *both* third tier strength, shouldn't they get equal points? So why did you give more points to the syllable, 18, than you did to Venus in the navamsha, 14, eh?"

You've caught me again, my Canadian friend—and you're absolutely right. The point range for both navamsha cuspal strength and nama pada is 14 to 18 points. So why did I give Venus 14 and the *pi* syllable the full 18? Here's why: While Venus is a lazy influence, it is not as harmful as Saturn or Mars on the D9 cusp. Therefore I tend to err on the low side for Venus in the D9. In addition, the syllable *pi* applies not only to the first name of the team, but also to the *second*. This is extremely rare and only happens when teams are named after the first syllable of the city they're in. For that reason *pi* gets maximum exposure, and I gave it a full 18 points to emphasize the difference between its influence and that of Venus, even though both techniques are third-tier strength. Capisce?

It's not just the 10th house that can name a victor, however. The planets themselves can create a "buzz" around a team by occupying the syllables of that team's name. We can peek in on the conversations planets are having by looking at their nama padas, shown on page 146.

You'll note that here we've added a planetary information table listing, from left to right, the planet, degree, declination (useful for judging planetary war),

Mo 28:21 Ur 25:45 Ke 12:22	Uk 26:48	Me 10:35 Su 26:48 Ma 27:31	
Ch 27:30 Ne 15:50			Ve 12:03 Ju 24:18
Ce 15:00			
PlR 20:52 Asc 00:14	SaR 06:13		Ra 12:22

Bhava	Cusp	Lord/Sub/SS	D	C	B	A
1st h.	00:14:31 Sag	Ke / Ke / Mo				Ju
2nd h.	07:29:33 Cap	Sy / Ke / Ju			Ve, Sa, Ke	Sa
3rd h.	18:46:32 Aqu	Ra / Mo / Me		Ke	Ve, Sa, Ke	Sa
4th h.	23:29:55 Pis	Me / Ma / Ju	Me, Ra	Mo		Ju
5th h.	19:42:38 Ari	Ve / Re / Ve	Mo, Ju	Me	Su, Ma	Ma
6th h.	10:47:28 Tau	Mo / Mo / Me	Su, Ma	Su, Ma		Ve
7th h.	00:14:31 Gem	Ma / Me / Me			Mo, Ju	Me
8th h.	07:29:33 Can	Sa / Ke / Ve		Ju, Ve	Me, Ra	Mo
9th h.	18:46:32 Leo	Ve / Ra / Sa		Ra		Su
10th h.	23:29:55 Vir	Ma / Ma / Ju			Mo, Ju	Me
11th h.	19:42:38 Lib	Ra / Ma / Me	Ve, Sa, Ke	Sa		Ve
12th h.	10:47:28 Sco	Sa / Su / Me			Su, Ma	Ma

PLANETARY TABLE WITH SOUNDS

	Degree	Declination	Nakshatra	Sound	Lord/Sub/SS	Speed
As	00:14:31		Moola	Yay	Ke/Ke/Mo	
Su	26:48:51	23:07	Mrigashi	Vo	Ma/Ju/Me	00:57
Mo	28:21:12	07:28	Revati	Chee	Me/Sa/Me	14:06
Ma	27:31:45	23:46	Mrigashi	Vo	Ma/Ju/Ma	00:41
Me	10:35:25	16:56	Rohini	Oh	Mo/Mo/Sa	00:00
Ju	24:18:26	16:11	Ashlesha	Day	Me/Ra/Ra	00:10
Ve	12:03:32	20:54	Pushya	Hoh	Sa/Mo/Su	00:55
Sa	06:13:25	-18:05	Anuradha	Nah	Sa/Me/Su	-00:04
Ra	12:22:59	-02:52	Hasta	Poo	Mo/Ra/Ju	-00:02
Ke	12:22:59	02:52	U.Bhadra.	Jha	Sa/Ma/Sa	-00:02
Ur	25:45:03		Revati	Cha	Me/Ra/Su	00:02
Ne	15:50:40		Satabhi.	See	Ra/Ve/Mo	00:00
Pl	20:52:38		P.Shad.	Pah	Ve/Ju/Me	-00:01

Golden State Warriors (−182) vs. Cleveland Cavaliers (+158), 21:11 LT,
June 11, 2015, Cleveland, Ohio

nakshatra, nakshatra sound (our main focus in this chapter), the lord, sublord, and sub-sublord for that planet's degree position, and finally the planet's speed. Speed is an extremely useful indicator that allows us to see when planets go stationary. Parashara's Light (used for most illustrations in this book) and other quality software allow you to customize these tables to your needs.

Note that in the planetary information table, the fifth column shows the sounds for all of the planets, including the ascendant, in English approximation. Most Jyotisha software has tables like this, or you can memorize the Sanskrit alphabet or look up the syllables for the planets in table 7.1 on page 142, where they are presented in more accurate transliteration.

In this chart we see the favored Warriors facing the home team, Cleveland, in what turned out to be a 103 to 82 rout for Golden State. Notice that among the planets, both the Sun and Mars in the 6th house for the favorite also happen to occupy the nama pada *vo*. This is as close as you can come in Sanskrit to the first sound in the name Warriors, since Sanskrit doesn't have *w* (remember, substitute *v* for *w* and *p* or *pha* for *f*). Basically, think of the Sun and Mars speaking in a Russian accent, saying "Goolden Stet Vorriors," and you've got it. You may have to be flexible like this to see the possibilities offered by the navamsha syllables.

Also note that Mercury sits on the 6th house cusp, helping the favorite along. We don't use Mercury much, as his influence is difficult to gauge on the 1/7 and 4/10 cusps (at least for me), but on the 6th cusp he seems to show up well for his team. Finally, a look at the sublords shows a whopping twenty-point advantage again for the favorite. This is a clear case of fixed karma.

We'll never be royals . . .

unless we have the syllable *ro* in our names. On October 30, 2015, the Kansas City Royals lost to the New York Mets in game three of the World Series, which was reflected in a chart pitting two closely matched teams. The next day the horoscope remained much the same, save for the fact that the Sun moved from the 4th to the 5th navamsha of Libra, going from the sound *re* to *ro*, where it stayed for two games, both of which the Royals won, granting them the World Series championship. Coming from behind, as was their wont, the Royals proved that when fortune favors a person or a team, even the best efforts of mice and men cannot thwart their victory.

Here Comes the Sun

Tracking the Sun through the 108 navamsha syllables is a handy way to research winners without spending time or money on wagers and calculations. For example, when the Sun transits a *ti* navamsha, check to see if teams like the Minnesota Timberwolves or Timbuktu Timmies* prove to be winners. You may find that because the Sun rules victory and majesty, by highlighting these syllables he heightens the teams they represent. Of course, nothing operates in a vacuum, and you will still need to pay attention to the overall chart to see if other influences counter this. If you're counting points, you might consider this technique a first- or even second-tier influence. There you go, another free technique for you. You're welcome.

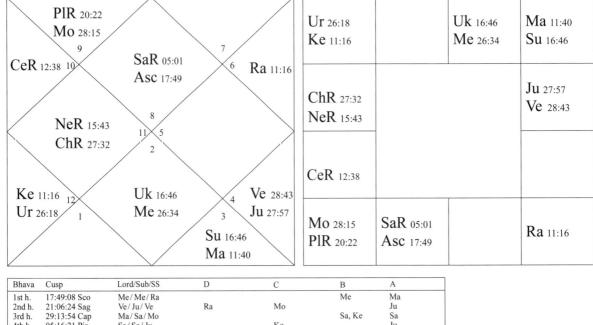

Bhava	Cusp	Lord/Sub/SS	D	C	B	A
1st h.	17:49:08 Sco	Me/Me/Ra			Me	Ma
2nd h.	21:06:24 Sag	Ve/Ju/Ve	Ra	Mo		Ju
3rd h.	29:13:54 Cap	Ma/Sa/Mo			Sa, Ke	Sa
4th h.	05:16:21 Pis	Sa/Sa/Ju		Ke		Ju
5th h.	04:23:55 Ari	Ke/Mo/Me			Me	Ma
6th h.	27:37:33 Ari	Su/Mo/Ra			Me	Ma
7th h.	17:49:08 Tau	Mo/Me/Me	Mo, Me, Ju, Ve	Su, Ma, Me		Ve
8th h.	21:06:24 Gem	Ju/Ju/Ve		Ju, Ve	Ju, Ve	Me
9th h.	29:13:54 Can	Me/Sa/Mo			Ra	Mo
10th h.	05:16:21 Vir	Su/Me/Me	Su, Ma	Ra	Ju, Ve	Me
11th h.	04:23:55 Lib	Ma/Ve/Sa				Ve
12th h.	27:37:33 Lib	Ju/Ve/Ra	Sa, Ke	Sa		Ve

San Diego Padres (+100) vs. <u>St. Louis Cardinals (−118)</u>, 18:50:20 LT, July 2, 2015, St. Louis, Missouri

*The Timbuktu Timmies play in a special triple A league in my imagination.

In most respects the chart on page 148 shows a victory for the favored Cardinals. The game was close, going to extra innings before San Diego pulled ahead to win 5 to 3. The sound on the 10th cusp? *Pa,* as in the San Diego Padres. Note that the cuspal sound can reflect any of the initial syllables of a team's name, in this case *sa, di,* and *pa* (therefore it makes sense to have long, compound names if you want to have more chances to win). I saw this work several times over the season, with the Padres winning games they shouldn't have, only because their *pa* sound resonated on the marquee of the sky. What God has written in the heavens, in the script of signs and planets, is hard, indeed, to overwrite!

Sanskrit Lesson Part 1: Dipthongs

Dipthongs are not just something you wear at the beach. The definition of *diphthong* is "a vowel sound, occupying a single syllable, during the articulation of which the tongue moves from one position to another, causing a continual change in vowel quality, as in the pronunciation of *a* in English *late,* during which the tongue moves from the position of (e) towards (I)."*

Yeah, I know, easy, right? A diphthong is a vowel that makes two sounds, like the *i* in *tiger.* What starts off as *aah* becomes an *ee*—that's a diphthong, and Sanskrit has definite rules about how they are used. For example, you may have noticed that in the navamsha syllable table (table 7.1), the Sanskrit sounds *ai* and *au* are unrepresented, even though they are important letters of the alphabet. Hmmm, a bias against diphthongs? I think not.

Implied in this alphabet is the understanding that any *eh* sound also stands for *ai* (as in "aye-aye, Captain!") and any *oh* sound also stands for *au* (as in *powwow*). For example, as you can see in the navamsha syllable table, *to* is the first sound of the sign Scorpio; it can represent the Toronto Blue Jays as well as the Tower of London Dungeon Masters. Okay, that last one was a stretch. But the chart shown on page 150 is not.

The 10th cusp in this chart gets the sound *te,* the ninth sound of Leo, which doesn't sound like the words of either team, except maybe the *de* in *Detroit.*

---

*www.dictionary.com.

RASHI

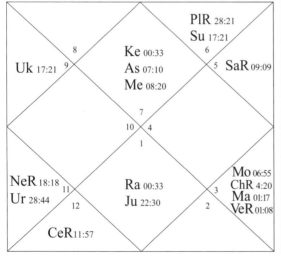

Ur 26:31 Ke 10:03			Uk 08:35 Ma 26:48
ChR 27:08 NeR 15:22			Su 08:35 Me 10:55
CeR 8:00			Ju 02:30 VeR 06:47
PlR 19:49	SaR 04:21 Asc 10:47	Mo 27:26	Ra 10:03

Bhava	Cusp	Lord/Sub/SS	D	C	B	A
1st h.	10:47:49 Sco	Sa/ Su/ Me				Ma
2nd h.	13:24:47 Sag	Ve/ Ve/ Ve			Mo, Ma	Ju
3rd h.	21:53:28 Cap	Mo/ Ve/ Sa			Su, Me, Sa, Ke	Sa
4th h.	28:50:33 Aqu	Ju/ Su/ Mo	Ju, Ve	Ke	Su, Me, Sa, Ke	Sa
5th h.	28:26:06 Pis	Me/ Sa/ Me			Mo, Ma	Ju
6th h.	21:28:20 Ari	Ve/ Ju/ Mo				Ma
7th h.	10:47:49 Tau	Mo/ Mo/ Me				Ve
8th h.	13:24:47 Gem	Ra/ Me/ Mo		Su, Ma, Me		Me
9th h.	21:53:28 Can	Me/ Su/ Sa	Mo, Ma	Ju, Ve	Ra	Mo
10th h.	28:50:33 Leo	Su/ Ma/ Me		Ra		Su
11th h.	28:26:06 Vir	Ma/ Sa/ Me				Me
12th h.	21:28:20 Lib	Ju/ Ju/ Ma	Ra, Su, Me, Sa, Ke	Mo, Sa		Ve

NAVAMSHA

CeR 11:57	Ra 00:33 Ju 22:30		VeR 01:08 Ma 01:17 ChR 4:20 Mo 06:55
Ur 28:44 NeR 18:18			
			SaR 09:09
Uk 17:21		Ke 00:33 As 07:10 Me 08:20	Su 17:21 PlR 28:21

Detroit Tigers (+106) vs. <u>Boston Red Sox (−127)</u>, 16:06 LT, July 25, 2015,
Boston, Massachusetts

However, the diphthong rule says that the English dipthongs *eh* and *ai* are inter-changeable in Sanskrit, which means we now have the clear sound for the Detroit *Tigers*. And just like Johnny B. Goode, whose name was meant to be in lights, teams with this kind of marquee purchase are born to win—in this case, despite a chart stacked against them.

Sanskrit Lesson Part 2: Nasals

Though English has only two nasals in its alphabet, *m* and *n,* Sanskrit identifies five such sounds: guttural, palatal, cerebral, dental, and labial. Spanish makes use of the palatal nasal *ñ* in words like *año,* but few languages have given nasals their due like Sanskrit has. Confusion between nasal sounds can lead to awkward situations, and not just in Sanskrit. Consider the phrase *Feliz Año Nuevo,* which takes on a puzzling connotation if you fail to pronounce the tilde on the *ñ.* With the tilde, *año,* it means "Happy New Year!" Without it, *ano,* it is the more direct "Congratulations on your new anus"—perhaps appropriate in medical circles, but not at a New Year's Eve party.

So how do you tell the difference? Pronounce these words:

incomplete inch international indentured impractical illegal

Note that the first three words all have the letter *n* standing in for the nasal. But you will notice when pronouncing them that in the first, *incomplete,* the *n* sounds like it's coming from the back of your throat, the same place that the letters *g* and *k* come from. This is what's known as a guttural nasal, and it is written like this in Sanskrit: ङ, or *ṅa* in transliteration.

In the next example, *inch,* that same *n* stands for a sound coming from the palate, more forward from the guttural sound. It is the same sound as in the Spanish *año* ("year," not *ano,* "anus"), and is known as a palatal nasal. It looks like this: ञ, or *ña* in transliteration.

The *n* in *international* is even more forward than the previous two, with the tongue touching the roof of the mouth in a retroflex position. This is what's known as a cerebral or retroflex nasal, and it is the typical "Indian" sound Westerners imitate when we doing Indian accents. It looks like this: ण, or *ṇa* in transliteration.

The next *n* is a dental nasal, with the tongue coming slightly more forward than the previous sound. It is written like this: न, or simply *na* in transliteration.

Finally, we have the labial nasal, which becomes an *m* as the tongue cannot travel any further forward. Thus the prefix *in* (meaning "not") turns into *im*, though English has no rule to account for why this happens. Sanskrit does, however.

Okay, on to our final word. *Illegal* is actually a combination of the same prefix *in* (meaning "not") and *legal*. Why did the *n* turn into an *l*? English has few answers, though in Sanskrit this is a standard rule that accounts for the way the human apparatus articulates sounds. Try saying *inlegal* ten times fast. You'll see what happens naturally, and why this rule was invented.

Sanskrit is called the perfect language partly because its grammar is consistent; it has few surprises or exceptions, unlike English, which has many. Consider the *a* sound in the following words: *father, bather, lather.* Why does the *a* sound change so dramatically in English, though only the first letter of each word is different? English grammar, again, is silent on this. In Sanskrit a vowel is a vowel, pronounced the same regardless of where it is found and in what combination of sounds.

And now, back to our regularly scheduled programming.

How to Build a Winning Franchise

Hey, sports team owners, meet me at camera three.

One of the easiest things you can do to create a winning franchise, skyrocket profits, and ensure a lasting legacy is to name your team according to astrological principles. Giving a team the right name is not only aesthetically pleasing, it creates real results. In this chapter I've shown you a few examples of the power of the 10th cusp and its syllable. Imagine if your team *always* played with its name on the 10th, or on a sensitive point that guarantees profits as well as pennants. It's easy enough to do: hire a Vedic astrologer to research the team's horoscope and suggest the best sounds for its name. Done. If the team's chart can't be found, you can do a prashna, a horary chart, or do the reverse: reincorporate the team at a moment that lines it up for victory. What's that, you want an example?

Say you are the owner of the Milwaukee Bucks, and the sounds of their name, *mi* and *buh,* happen to fall in the chart's 8th or 12th houses. You might as well buy them a plot in the graveyard of the league, for suffering and loss will be themes associated with this franchise. If, on the other hand, you can anchor those syllables to key planets or points like the yogi point, a money-producing point in the chart, or the MC, then the opposite would become your reality. Words have power. The most powerful words are names; use them wisely.

Words have power. The most powerful words are names; use them wisely.

Had the owners of this basketball franchise decided to reincorporate, renewing their vows, as it were, and traveling down to Florida to sign the papers, they would have found in the chart on page 154 a remarkable case for victory. First, the rashi lagna is conjunct Mars, which additionally forms a classic *ruchaka yoga*—one of the five great planetary yogas—conferring both victory house and cuspal strength. That Mars also avoids conjoining the D9 lagna, thus preventing problems there. Second, the lagna is hemmed in by benefics, adding a SKY to make sure the team stays healthy and blessed by the angels. Third, the MC contains both the royal star Regulus (covered in the next chapter) and the desired sound *mi* as in *Milwaukee.* Take a look yourself. Next, if we weren't greedy enough, the sublord of the ascendant, also Mars, gets +9 points (counting the 2nd house). This powerful Mars makes another appearance as the lord of the day that is ruled by Mars, Tuesday. This and other minor factors, like the incorporation date (11/11) matching the rashi lagna degree (1°11'), the D9 degree (11°), and the D9 Moon degree (11°), add an element of fatedness. Add to these the coral red team color (a change from their previous green team color), and you have the makings of a winning franchise for any owner willing to fly to Miami, sign the papers, and start collecting championships.

It took about twenty minutes to find a chart suitable for this team, though not all charts will be this clear. This chart also could have worked for any team

RASHI

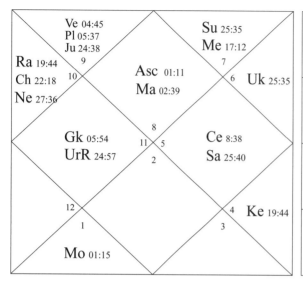

Bhava	Cusp	Lord/Sub/SS	D	C	B	A
1st h.	01:11:23 Sco	Ju / Ma / Ve		Ma		Ma
2nd h.	00:52:59 Sag	Ke / Ve / Ve	Su, Ma, Ju, Sa	Ju, Ve	Su, Ma	Ju
3rd h.	02:52:24 Cap	Su / Ju / Ra	Me	Ra		Sa
4th h.	06:21:06 Aqu	Ma / Mo / Me				Sa
5th h.	08:28:26 Pis	Sa / Ve / Ve	Ra	Mo	Su, Ma	Ju
6th h.	06:43:32 Ari	Ke / Ra / Ke				Ma
7th h.	01:11:23 Tau	Su / Ra / Ma			Ju, Sa	Ve
8th h.	00:52:59 Gem	Ma / Me / Mo			Ke	Me
9th h.	02:52:24 Can	Ju / Ra / Ve	Mo, Ve	Ke	Ra	Mo
10th h.	06:21:06 Leo	Ke / Ra / Sa		Sa		Su
11th h.	08:28:26 Vir	Su / Ve / Ma			Ke	Me
12th h.	06:43:32 Lib	Ra / Ra / Ra	Ke	Su, Me	Ju, Sa	Ve

NAVAMSHA

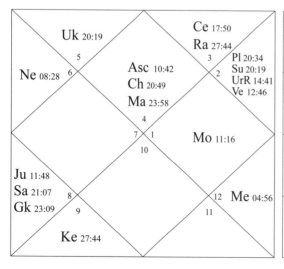

Milwaukee Bucks possible team chart, 7:06 LT, Nov. 11, 2008, Miami, Florida

with the first syllable *Mi* in its name. The possibilities are endless if you apply the techniques in this book to your muhurtas, or electional astrology charts. You could end up making some team or business owner—or yourself—very rich and happy.

Summary

- Find the sound on the 10th cusp of any game chart. If it matches the first syllable of one of the competing teams' names, it is a third-tier influence denoting victory.

8

The Fault, Dear Brutus, Is Not in Our Stars

Using Nakshatra Taras

The essence of a country is the city; the essence of a city is the home; the essence of the home is the living room; the essence of the living room is the couch, whereon a noble and radiant woman adorned with jewels sits. This is the pith of a kingdom.

ADAPTED FROM VARAHAMIHIRA'S *BRIHAD SAMHITA*

"If you look up at the night sky, what do you see?"

Street lights.

"True, modern-day skywatching is difficult, especially from urban centers. Let's try this: if you look up at the clear night sky, with no other lights around, what do you see?"

A bunch of points in the sky.

"Correct! And which of those points are stars and which are planets?"

Uh, I don't know. Most of them are stars, I guess.

"Exactly, which brings us to the point of this lesson: the fault, dear Brutus, is not in our stars, but in that we do not use them. The fixed stars, some of which shine as bright as planets, can be as effective at influencing outcomes as the planets themselves."

This is my conversation with an imaginary student (apparently named Brutus), to impress on him, and you, the importance of using the nakshatras and

156

their yogataras or specific marker stars when judging competitive outcomes. The word *tara,* which translates as "star," is often used interchangeably with *nakshatra* (which also means "star"), though a nakshatra in Jyotisha is technically an asterism, a mini constellation usually composed of a number of stars. Among these there is often a main or "marker" star that stands out. For example, the Pleiades are a group of six (or seven) visible stars, but Alcyone gets top billing as the marker star of this asterism, called Krittika in Sanskrit.*

In ancient times, Western astrologers differentiated between fixed and movable stars. "Fixed" stars refer to actual stars; "movable" stars refer to planets, comets, asteroids, and other grahas that appear to move. Modern Western astrology has moved away from using fixed stars in chart interpretation, though in Vedic astrology marker stars were given specific attributes and placed as centerpieces of their "mansions," i.e., the nakshatras. Recall from previous chapters that the number of nakshatras reflects the number of days in a sidereal month and that the width of a nakshatra is traversed by the Moon in about one day—which is why nakshatras are also called *lunar mansions.* Think of them as beautiful pieces of real estate, each housing an important star, or tara, that marks the mansion and gives it its identity. When we say "that's Madonna's house," it's not the house so much that matters but the fact that Madonna lives in it. The tara is all-important, and when planets or cusps come close to one of these taras, they become imbued with their star power. Most nakshatras have one or more such stars, or taras, and when these taras conjoin sensitive points in the horoscope, they produce effects otherwise unknowable in a chart. In game charts, they can be invaluable.

But wait, there are so many fixed stars, won't it get confusing?

Absolutely, which is why we exclude a huge chunk of the sky and mainly focus on the stars along the ecliptic,† and among them, mostly those that make up the twenty-eight Vedic nakshatras. Yes, that's right, I said twenty-eight. In older Vedic

---

Nakshatra literally means "that which doesn't fade" or perhaps "that which doesn't cross space," pertaining to the stars' apparent fixity and permanence in the sky, as opposed to the planets and other heavenly bodies that travel. Both Vedic and Western astrologers too often take the fixed stars for granted, missing out on critical information communicated by these bright sentinels of the sky.

†The ecliptic forms the center of the band about 20 degrees wide called the zodiac, on which the Sun, Moon, and planets are seen always to move. This region is divided into the twelve signs of the zodiac, each of which approximates the Sun's motion through about one month.

times twenty-eight nakshatras were used. Later these were reduced to twenty-seven since there are nine planets, and nine divides nicely into twenty-seven, each planet ruling three nakshatras. Twenty-seven also divides nicely into 360, the span of the zodiac, thereby creating nakshatras' 13 degrees and 20 minutes of arc for each nakshtra; dividing by 28 yields the harder-to-handle 12 degrees, 51 minutes, 26 seconds. For these and additional reasons, the twenty-eighth nakshatra, Abhijit, is left out of most modern astrological applications. We are bringing it back, however, since Abhijit in Sanskrit means "victorious" or "undefeatable" and more importantly since Vega, Abhijit's marker star, works well for contest prediction.

Abhijit: "Victorious"

The ancient rishis were in a quandary. Should we keep Abhijit and its bright star Vega, or should we let it go in favor of greater symmetry in the zodiac? Perhaps realizing that baseball wouldn't be invented for another few millennia, they agreed to abandon it in favor of easier mathematics. After all, it's a lot simpler to divide 360 degrees by twenty-seven nakshatras than by twenty-eight. In the era before solar-powered calculators—Vedic mathematics notwithstanding—this must have made their lives easier. Still, they knew that Abhijit's power would one day come back into favor. To help us remember, they assigned the brightest part of the day to it—Abhijit muhurta—the approximately forty-eight-minute span during which the Sun transits the MC, the highest point along the ecliptic, and the 10th house cusp.

The rishis, of course, were not wrong. Abhijit—specifically its bright star Vega—acts like a graha on any cusp it conjoins to give victory, save that instead of 2°30' its orb must be not much over a single degree. Abhijit also confers victory to people who have it prominent in their horoscopes. Dennis Rodman, who won five basketball championships with two different teams, has this rising. And like the surplus twenty-eighth nakshatra, he was the powerful sixth man who helped them to victory.

We will use these taras in two ways: (1) in conjunctions with planets, specifically the lords of houses 1 and 10 for the favorite and houses 7 and 4 for the underdog; and (2) in conjunctions with *the cusps of these houses.* You can also use yogataras in natal, horary, or mundane astrology. In natal charts, a planet or cusp within 2°30' of a nakshatra tara strongly evokes the meaning of that nakshatra, whether for good or ill. For example, Krittika nakshatra (the Pleiades in Western astronomy) is said to confer a critical nature to a person (*Krittika* in fact means "cutter" and is related to the English word *critical*). Having your Moon or lagna in this nakshatra at birth may give you an incisive, cutting personality. But focus this Moon or lagna at 6 degrees Taurus, and this may well bring your cutting ability to a trenchant point.*

For sports prediction, we narrow the orb of stars to 1 degree, and even here, the closer the conjunction the better, with 1 degree being the outside limit. When tight, these stars can influence cusps the way planets do, but with more flair. A good conjunction can exert a second-tier effect, just the way cuspal strength influences outcomes. However, that influence drops off dramatically as the orb increases.

A Sky Full of Stars:
The Twenty-Eight Nakshatras and Their Taras

In table 8.1 you'll see a summary of the twenty-eight nakshatras, the position of their marker stars, and their effects on sports outcomes. Degrees are sometimes rounded up or down for ease of expression. Where no effect is noted, the space has been left blank. Where an effect not directly pertaining to victory or defeat is expressed, such as "violence" in the case of Bharani's marker star, that is noted in parentheses. For this technique we will mainly consider the bolded stars and their effects exclusively in the rashi chart. We do not look at taras in the navamsha. Let's take a look at how they work.

---

*For more about the fixed stars independent of Vedic astrology, I recommend Elsbeth Ebertin and Georg Hoffman's concise and insightful book *Fixed Stars and Their Interpretation,* published by the American Federation of Astrologers (1971). Other good books include *The Fixed Stars and Constellations in Astrology,* by Vivian Robson, first published in 1923 and reissued in 2005. Finally, Bernadette Brady's *Brady's Book of Fixed Stars,* published in 1998, is a worthy and well-researched reference. Though these books speak to a Western astrology audience, the fixed stars depend less on such distinctions than do other factors, making them relatively accessible to Vedic astrologers.

TABLE 8.1. TWENTY-EIGHT NAKSHATRAS*

NAKSHATRA	YOGATARA POSITION	NAKSHATRA QUALITY	EFFECT ON GAMES
Ashvini	10° Aries, 13°45' Aries	Light, swift	(Gives speed)
Bharani	24°20' Aries	Fierce	(Violence, injury)
Krittika	6° Taurus	Soft and sharp	Mildly positive
Rohini	16° Taurus	Fixed	
Mrigashira	29°45' Taurus	Soft	Mildly positive
Ardra	**5° Gemini**	**Sharp, dreadful**	**Negative**
Punarvasu	**29°30' Gemini**	**Movable**	**Positive**
Pushya	13°30' Cancer, 15° Cancer	Light, swift	
Ashlesha	18° Cancer, 20°40' Cancer	Sharp, dreadful	(Paralyzes)
Magha	**6° Leo**	**Fierce**	**Positive**
Purva Phalguni	17°30' Leo	Fierce	Mildly negative
Uttara Phalguni	27°45' Leo	Fixed	Mildly negative
Hasta	10° Virgo, 20° Virgo	Light, swift	
Chitra	**29°55' Virgo**	**Soft**	**Negative**
Svati	0° Libra	Movable	
Vishakha	**21° Libra**	**Soft and sharp**	**Positive**
Anuradha	8° Scorpio, 10° Scorpio	Soft	
Jyeshtha	16° Scorpio	Sharp, dreadful	
Mula	28°30' Scorpio, 0°45' Sagittarius, 3° Sagittarius	Sharp, dreadful	
Purva Ashadha	10°40' Sagittarius	Fierce	
Uttara Ashadha	18°30' Sagittarius, 19°40' Sagittarius	Fixed	
Abhijit	**21°30' Sagittarius**	**Light, Swift**	**Positive**
Shravana	8° Capricorn	Movable	(Speed)

*Where no quality or effect has been noted, the space has been left blank.

NAKSHATRA	YOGATARA POSITION	NAKSHATRA QUALITY	EFFECT ON GAMES
Dhanishta	22°30' Capricorn, 24° Capricorn	Movable	
Shatabhisha	17°45' Aquarius	Movable	Mildly positive
Purva Bhadrapada	29°30' Aquarius	Fierce	
Uttara Bhadrapada	15° Pisces	Fixed	
Revati	26° Pisces	Soft	

Additional stars and constellations

Algol	2° Taurus		(Lose your head)
The Hyades	11°–13° Taurus		Mildly positive
Wasat	25° Gemini		(Like Saturn)

Judging Power

Use table 8.1 to see where the stars are as you are examining the following charts. For example, 6 Leo is always 6 Leo—you simply look at the game chart to see where 6 Leo is. If there is a planet or cusp there, you've got a connection.

A victory house and sublord advantage gives the underdog, Philadelphia, hope in the chart on page 162. But is that enough to put them ahead? Perhaps. Remember kala, desha, and patra—an underdog has to play significantly better than expected to vanquish a heavy favorite. The question in this chart is answered by the bright star Pollux, main tara of Punarvasu nakshatra, at 29°30' Gemini, which exactly conjoins the 7th house cusp (look at the cusp column in the box to see that Gemini is 29°29'40" and at table 8.1 to see that this matches the Punarvasu nakshatra). The Phillies managed an unexpected win over their rivals, 6 to 2. Pollux, here in a tight orb, acted like a positive graha on the cusp, giving them a turbo boost past their opponents.

Note that the ruler of the 1st house, Jupiter, is 1°23' away from another important star, Regulus, the royal star of Magha nakshatra. This could have given the favorite strength had the conjunction been tighter, but the rule of 1-degree maximum orb for taras is not a joke. Honor it and it will give you results; abandon it at your peril. Whereas in natal astrology you can widen the orb of stars to 2 degrees or more, for specific event charts like this, be strict and keep it to 1 degree or less.

North Indian Chart (left):

- CeR 5:50
- Sa 04:18
- NeR 15:08 — 10
- 11
- ChR 26:50
- PlR 19:35 / Asc 29:29
- 8
- 7
- Ke 09:31 / Mo 20:21 / UrR 26:29
- 9
- 12 — 6
- 3
- Ra 09:31
- 1
- 2
- Uk 18:16
- 5 / Ju 04:37 / VeR 04:35 / Me 00:53
- 4
- Su 18:16 / Ma 03:25

South Indian Chart (right):

UrR 26:29 / Mo 20:21 / Ke 09:31			Uk 18:16
ChR 26:50 / NeR 15:08			Ma 03:25 / Su 18:16
CeR 5:50			Me 00:53 / VeR 04:35 / Ju 04:37
Asc 29:29 / PlR 19:35	Sa 04:18		Ra 09:31

Bhava	Cusp	Lord/Sub/SS	D	C	B	A
1st h.	29:29:40 Sag	Su/Ra/Ra				Ju
2nd h.	14:00:51 Aqu	Ra/Me/Ju	Me, Ju, Ve	Mo, Ke	Ma, Sa, Ke	Sa
3rd h.	23:52:09 Pis	Me/Ma/Ke				Ju
4th h.	22:58:37 Ari	Ve/Sa/Ve				Ma
5th h.	15:37:16 Tau	Mo/Ju/Ra				Ve
6th h.	06:17:32 Gem	Ma/Mo/Me			Su, Mo	Me
7th h.	29:29:40 Gem	Ju/Mo/Mo	Ra, Su, Mo	Su, Ma, Me, Ju, Ve	Su, Mo	Me
8th h.	14:00:51 Leo	Ve/Ve/Ma		Ra	Ra	Su
9th h.	23:52:09 Vir	Ma/Ma/Ke			Su, Mo	Me
10th h.	22:58:37 Lib	Ju/Sa/Su	Ma, Sa, Ke	Sa		Ve
11th h.	15:37:16 Sco	Sa/Ju/Me				Ma
12th h.	06:17:32 Sag	Ke/Ra/Sa				Ju

<u>Los Angeles Dodgers (−227)</u> vs. Philadelphia Phillies (+188), 19:05:50 LT, Aug. 4, 2015, Philadelphia, Pennsylvania

> **The rule of 1-degree maximum orb for taras is not a joke. Honor it and it will give you results; abandon it at your peril.**

Another note: when the 1st lord is also the 4th lord, which happens for Gemini or Sagittarius ascendants, there is a potential conflict of interest, as the significator for one team also represents the significator for the opposing team's 10th house. In such cases, take the lord of the 1st house as the primary significator and do not use the lord of the 4th. When choosing between one team's 10th lord and the other team's lagna lord, always prefer the lagna lord; the ruler of the ascendant is always primary, since it represents the team itself. Tenth lords are secondary players, since they represent a team's *honor*.

Let's take a look at an example:

Bhava	Cusp	Lord/Sub/SS	D	C	B	A
1st h.	05:25:33 Cap	Su/Me/Ke			Sa, Ke	Sa
2nd h.	24:19:15 Aqu	Ju/Me/Ve	Mo, Ve	Ke	Sa, Ke	Sa
3rd h.	03:37:28 Ari	Ke/Su/Ve				Ma
4th h.	00:34:35 Tau	Su/Ra/Ve			Ma, Ju	Ve
5th h.	21:37:32 Tau	Mo/Ve/Ju			Ma, Ju	Ve
6th h.	11:31:58 Gem	Ra/Sa/Ve				Me
7th h.	05:25:33 Can	Sa/Sa/Ju	Su, Ma, Ju	Mo, Ma, Ju, Ve	Sa	Mo
8th h.	24:19:15 Leo	Ve/Me/Ke	Me, Ra	Su, Me, Ra	Me, Ra	Su
9th h.	03:37:28 Lib	Ma/Ve/Ra			Ma, Ju	Ve
10th h.	00:34:35 Sco	Ju/Ma/Ma	Sa, Ke	Sa		Ma
11th h.	21:37:32 Sco	Me/Su/Mo				Ma
12th h.	11:31:58 Sag	Ke/Me/Me				Ju

Texas Rangers (+200) vs. <u>Toronto Blue Jays (−244)</u>, 15:37:50 LT, Oct. 8, 2015, Toronto, Canada

In this chart's 8th house we have two key conjunctions: the Moon and Venus with Magha's yogatara, Regulus, at 6 degrees Leo. In table 8.1 you can see that the celestial longitude of Magha is 6 Leo and that these are very tight conjunctions indeed.

So why did the underdog win? In a contest between lagna lord and 10th house lord, the lagna usually wins. In this case the Moon as the lagna lord of the underdog is more important than Venus, which is the lord of the 10th house for the favorite. Read that again and let it sink in.

Of course, the near 20-point difference in sublords didn't hurt. Check it out and see for yourself—this is fixed karma galore, all pointing to an underdog victory.

"What if both the 1st house lord and the 7th house lord conjunct the same star?" Somehow I knew you'd ask. Feast your eyes on this example:

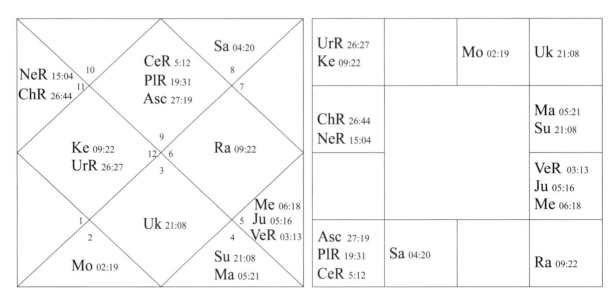

<u>**Los Angeles Dodgers (−147)**</u> **vs. Pittsburgh Pirates (+121), 19:07 LT, Aug. 7, 2015,** Pittsburgh, Pennsylvania

Here the 1st house lord is Jupiter and the 7th house lord is Mercury. Note that both Jupiter and Mercury are within 1 degree of the star Regulus, but that Mercury is closer. When it comes to determining the influence of two significators, the one that's closer usually wins. This game went into extra innings, highlighting how evenly matched the two teams were, but the underdog, represented by Mercury, eventually pulled it off, winning 5 to 4.

> **When it comes to determining the influence of two significators, the one that's closer usually wins.**

It is said that regal Regulus, in conjunction with Venus and Jupiter, was the star the three magi followed from the East to find Jesus. This conjunction, particularly when tight, signals the birth of a king. And if it can signal a king, someone who conquers people and countries, it should also indicate victory when configured with vital cusps or planets.

Judging Star Strength

In our three-tier system of assessing strength, nakshatra taras are accorded second-tier strength. This can be a bit misleading since taras can be quantified in a number of ways. For example, a lot depends on how close they are in orb to a cusp or planet. Also, certain stars like Krittika's Alcyone are not as powerful in giving results as, say, Pollux or Regulus. As well, keep in mind the nature of the star you're dealing with; they can't all be royals. That's why the main players in the nakshatra table (table 8.1) are bolded. Below is a further breakdown of the twenty-eight nakshatras, their marker stars, and a summary of their effects.

Nakshatra Tara Effects on Cusps

Ashvini: Ashvini has two marker stars: Beta Arietis (a.k.a. Sheratan) at 10° Aries and Alpha Arietis (a.k.a. Hamal) at 13°45' Aries. Since Ashvini rules twins, it makes sense that there are two marker stars, which give speed and efficiency, though I haven't seen them translate into victory in one-on-one competitions. Perhaps in auto, horse, or dog races—competitions that rely on speed—they could portend better outcomes. For sporting events such as I've described in this book I don't use them much.

Bharani: At 24°20' Aries, Bharani's stars form a downward triangle and are said to represent the female sex organs. They are also associated with violence and bloodshed. Like birth and death, which Bharani rules, there can be trauma associated with cusps located here, though I haven't seen that it translates necessarily into victory or defeat. In mundane astrology applications, do not plan potentially dangerous events like running with the bulls—or even marriage, for that matter—with this nakshatra's taras prominent.

Krittika: At 6° Taurus, the main star of this nakshatra, Alcyone, gives a boost to the cusps it touches. But perhaps because Krittika is both a sharp and soft nakshatra this boost is not as strong as that of other unconflicted taras like Regulus or Pollux. In 2015, when Saturn transited 6° Scorpio opposite Krittika, his placement usually trumped Krittika's on a cusp, though it was close. This means that cusps placed here get a first-tier strength boost, unlike the second-tier strength bolded nakshatras confer.

The Hyades: Between 11° and 13° Taurus, this is not actually a nakshatra but a constellation that is connected to libido, power, and ambition, giving a first-tier boost to the cusp it touches.

Rohini: At 16° Taurus, the red star Aldebaran (Alpha Tauri) sits exactly opposite Jyeshtha's red star Antares at 16° Scorpio. In my experience, when they both sit on cusps they more or less nullify each other. Some astrologers are big on Antares; I haven't yet seen enough evidence to agree. Mind you, I mainly focus on cusps. When the lords of the 1st and 10th houses or the lords of the 7th and 4th houses are placed on these points, the results may be positive for Rohini and destructive for Antares, though more research is needed.

Mṛigashira: At 29°45' Taurus, this is another soft star with warrior connotations. Because of its hunting symbolism it can be useful for sports like tennis and archery, and I find it gives a mild boost like Krittika does, in the order of first-tier strength.

Ardra: At 5° Gemini, the bright star Betelgeuse is the main tara of Ardra nakshatra, which gives tears, suffering, and lament against injustice. Upon creating the universe, Brahma smugly showed off his creation to the god Rudra, whereupon Rudra began to cry. Feeling he was being a wet blanket, Brahma inquired, "Why are you crying? Don't you see the wonder of what I've created?" Rudra, through his third eye, had indeed glimpsed all, including the suffering and karma of his creation, and he felt a flood of sorrow that transcended space and time. Unable to bear it all, Rudra ran away to the woods, to live with and tend to the creatures of the forest. Betelgeuse on the ascendant or 10th cusp in a natal chart can indicate working with leftovers—people or things society has left behind, such as the dead and dying, inmates, the chronically ill, and ascetics. In a match, it is a negative placement. There can be perceived unfairness against the team indicated by Ardra, though how this plays out ultimately depends on that team's resilience. Betelgeuse presents serious obstacles, but with the option for the team it indicates to overcome those hurdles and win a hard victory.

Wasat: In Arabic this translates as "middle." Wasat (Delta Geminorum) is a triple-star system that sits between the Gemini twins at 25° Gemini. Though it is not a nakshatra tara, I have found this star to behave very much like Saturn on a cusp: good on the 6th and 12th and on the 4th and 10th house cusps, and terrible on the 1st and 7th houses. Treat it like Saturn, with perhaps a touch less effect than the grim ring-bearer, and you'll have yet another influence by which to judge charts. Noteworthy is that Pluto was discovered very near this star in 1930, and the radiant point of the Geminids meteor shower (visible in early October) is also just north of Wasat.

Punarvasu: At 29°30′ Gemini, Punarvasu's bright star Pollux is the first big victory tara, as it is rife with triumphal symbolism: the quiver of arrows that is always full, and the Mother Goddess Aditi, who presides over eternity (a victory over time and space, the ultimate limiting factors in the universe). If you see Pollux within 1 degree of a cusp, think victory for that team, unless other factors conspire against it. For most mundane events Punarvasu is a good nakshatra to have prominent, especially if you want eternal (Aditi) repeated (full quiver) enjoyment of whatever your event symbolizes.

Pushya: This asterism sits at either 13°30′ or 15° Cancer. I haven't seen much evidence either way to make a judgment about it, perhaps because it has no bright star, or perhaps because, as it rules care and nourishment, there is little place for its symbolism in the arena of fierce sports competition. The cluster of stars at 15° Cancer looks like a flower or an udder, both Pushya symbols.

Ashlesha: At either 18° or 20°40′ Cancer, these stars are neither bright nor close to the ecliptic, so they have less influence over games, at least as far as I've observed. One would imagine that cusps caught in the clutches of these lurker taras would be frozen or suffocated, unable to move, in accord with their serpent symbolism. For speed events like auto, horse, or dog racing, they may be potentially harmful, the opposite of Ashwini.

Magha: The next big influencer is the regal star Regulus, which at 6° Leo confers victory to the cusps it conjoins. We've discussed Regulus's effects in the examples earlier in this chapter, though that does not mean it is the only player among the taras. In fact (don't tell this to your Leo friends), Pollux seems to produce better results for teams than Regulus does, at least on the cusps. Nonetheless, it still warrants its status as a first-class (but generally second-tier) star of influence.

Purva Phalguni: Also known by the name of its marker star, Zosma, which is at 17°30′ Leo, this nakshatra sits opposite the marker star of the nakshatra

Shatabhisha's marker star in Aquarius. In one-on-one contests, Shatabhisha proves a winner, though neither nakshatra really warrants significant status. In the order of first-tier strength, Purva Phalguni proves a mildly negative, lazy influence to planets and cusps placed on it.

Uttara Phalguni: At 27°45' Leo, this nakshatra's marker star, Denebola, exerts a lazy influence both on cusps and on planets.

Hasta: Though different taras are proposed for this nakshatra, I find it active at 16° Virgo, corresponding to the star Vindemiatrix (Epsilon Virginis), also known as the Widow Maker in Western astrology, for its tendency to create relationship loss, often tragically. Hasta in Vedic astrology is a swift nakshatra, giving speed, mastery of words, skill with the hands (*hasta* means "hand"), and an association with the Gayatri mantra, which is particularly important for Hasta-borns. For sports charts, I haven't seen enough evidence to pronounce its usefulness. For relationship questions, like choosing when to go on a date, I would avoid placements at 16° Virgo, unless you're my kind of astrologer, who likes to learn the hard way.

Chitra: This artistic softie is a major pain for teams who have it on their cusps. Its illustrious marker star, Spica, at 29°55' Virgo, has produced nothing but loss when placed on the cusps. Too bad, since it's my birth star. No wonder I never excelled at sports! More research is needed to see Spica's effects on the lords of 1, 10, 7, and 4.

Svati: At 0°15' Libra, the bright star Arcturus is at practically the same celestial longitude as Spica, so it is difficult to differentiate between their influences. Even so, these stars are very far apart in the sky, as their declinations (positions north or south in the sky) are radically different (11S08 for Spica and 19N13 for Arcturus).

Vishakha: The victory-oriented star Zuben Elgenubi, representing the South Scale at 21° Libra, is symbolized by Indra, chief of the gods, and Agni, god of fire, the main honchos in heaven who have conquests galore on their walls. A good second-tier boost to any cusp it touches.

Anuradha: I have not observed the stars of this nakshatra, at either 8° or 10° Scorpio, enough to comment on their effects.

Jyeshtha: I've already discussed the star Antares in Rohini above. At 16° Scorpio, Jyeshta's marker star makes a big ruckus, but it is more or less nullified when it sits on a cusp by his celestial opposite, Aldebaran, 180 degrees away in Taurus.

Mula: Mula nakshatra houses the Milky Way and the galactic center, whose longitude is currently at 3° Sagittarius. This is where the black hole in the center of the galaxy is said to reside, and perhaps what the Mayans referred to as Xibalba—the dark rift and gateway to the underworld.* Accordingly, Mula natives can be quite deep, or otherworldly, with interests in drugs and medicine, research, and profound subjects such as dharma. With no clear yogatara for this nakshatra, you can use 28°30' Scorpio (the star Ras Alhaque or alpha Ophiuchus), 0°45' Sagittarius (the star Shaula or the Scorpion's sting), or even 3° Sagittarius for the galactic center as hotspots. Because of this confusion, more research needs to be done, and Mula's stars haven't produced discernable effects on games that I've noticed. Except that Mula nakshatra is associated with ups and downs in the field of finance, so maybe it's not a great idea to wager when Moon is in Mula, especially if it is in a negative house for you. Mula is bad for moolah.

Purva Ashadha: At 10°40' Sagittarius, Delta Sagittari or Kaus Medius marks the center of Sagittarius's bow. There is some disagreement about which stars make up the Purva and Uttara pair of Ashadhas. In experimenting with this degree, I don't find Purva to have much influence—perhaps a mild benefic, first-tier strength at best.

Uttara Ashadha: Represented by a tusk, a symbol of penetration and removal of obstacles (because of its association with Ganesha), and because of its name, which means "undefeated one," this nakshatra should be auspicious for victory. I have not found this to be the case when its marker star is placed on the cusps, though more research is needed. Part of the difficulty in determining its effects is the discrepancy about the main tara of Uttara. Pelagus (Sigma Sagittarii), at 18°30', or Ascella (Zeta Sagittarii), at 19°40', are both candidates. Being close together, some of their orbs interact, making judgment more difficult. Adding to the mix is the presence of Vega next door, at 21°30' Sagittarius. Because Vega does exert an effect, I usually leave both the Ashadhas and focus on Abhijit when it comes to prediction.

---

*The Milky Way crosses the ecliptic at about 6° Sagittarius, while the galactic center, at a declination of -29° sits just south of the ecliptic, which corresponds to 3° Sagittarius. Since the Milky Way only crosses the ecliptic in Mula and its opposite nakshatra, Ardra, it makes sense that the Vedic tradition termed these both as "sharp" and "dreadful" asterisms to be handled with care

Abhijit: The bright star Vega, marker star of Abhijit, at 21°30' Sagittarius, is a major player, even though it sits way north of the ecliptic at almost 40° N declination. As a result, no graha ever transits this star, though it can still predict victory. As an aside, Vega sits almost exactly opposite the star Canopus by longitude (Canopus is at 21° Gemini), which means that when Abhijit is on a cusp, it could be Canopus creating a loss for the opposing team rather than Vega conferring victory. However, since the rishis didn't appoint a nakshatra to Canopus, particularly one named "Unto Victory!" it's safe to assume that Abhijit is doing the heavy lifting.

Shravana: Altair, at 8° Capricorn, is the alpha star of the constellation Aquila, the eagle, and the main tara of Shravana nakshatra. It relates to flight and transcendence. In Vedic mythology Altair is associated with the god Vishnu and his three steps with which he covers all three worlds, transcending limitation. Shravana's symbol is an ear, but its related words *shroni,* "pelvis," and *shrona,* "crippled," indicate limping if this nakshatra is afflicted. I have found Altair to produce results in the order of first-tier strength. It gives swiftness and surprise, the ability to perform beyond expectations, much as Vishnu, disguised as the avatar Vamana, was underestimated by King Bali. In the match between the Houston Astros and New York Yankees in chapter 5, Shravana sat exactly on the 10th cusp, giving a 3 to 0 victory for the favorite, relating its triune symbolism directly to the outcome of the game. Allow your flights of inspiration to lift you into making such associations with the nakshatras. Could we predict high-scoring games for Punarvasu, which rules an *endless* quiver of arrows (points), or imagine a player or team losing with Purva Phalguni due to excess cavorting and bed pleasures the night before? I think yes, which is why it's important to learn the mythology of each nakshatra.

Dhanishta: At about 22°30' and 24° Capricorn, Dhanishta's marker taras Beta and Alpha Delphini don't seem to affect charts much, though I have not studied them extensively. I have noticed that 24° Cancer is an active point; perhaps Dhanishta's stars are the reason. More research is needed.

Shatabhisha: At 17°45' Aquarius, Shatabhisha's star sits opposite Zosma, Purva Phalguni's main star. As noted above, I find teams with Shatabhisha do better on their cusp than those with Phalguni's star.

Purva and Uttara Bhadrapada: Whereas the Phalguni pair in Leo mark the feet of the marital bed (or sometimes the hospital recovery bed), the Bhadrapadas mark the feet of the funeral cot or burial bed. At 29°30' degrees Aquarius, Alpha

Pegasii, PB's main marker star, doesn't have an appreciable effect on sports cusps, nor does Uttara Bhadrapada's star Algenib (Gamma Pegasi), at 15° Pisces, at least as far as I've been able to ascertain.

Revati: This nakshatra's marker star or stars, at around 26° Pisces, do not portend great influence on the cusps.

More on Stars . . .
and the Ones That Got Away

I really like it when you talk about taras and nakshatras. Can you tell me more about how to use them?

Ah, Brutus, sure. It's like this: We can use taras to help determine victory or defeat in a match, or to give color commentary and details, as the Shravana example illustrates. In a business horosocope, Rohini is auspicious, since the Sanskrit root *ruh,* where *Rohini* comes from, means "to grow" or "to turn red" (to invigorate with blood). Rohini is also a nakshatra of creation and rules the upward direction, all useful for growing a business or a marriage, or even a love affair, for that matter.

Consider also its opposite, Jyeshtha nakshatra and its star Antares, which rules dissolution and is attributed a fierce quality, as useful for matters like corporate take-overs, where one party dissolves and is subsumed by another. For sports matches, the lords of the 1st, 10th, 7th, and 4th on this star does not bode well for that team.

In a nativity, planets representing people in your life, like the lord of the 5th house for children, the 7th lord for spouse, or the 4th lord for mother, can take on qualities of a nakshatra especially strongly if they conjoin its tara. The 5th lord in Chitra nakshatra could make your child artistic, but this 5th lord within 1 degree of Spica, Chitra's marker star, could very well signal a person who needs artistic expression like they need air and water. The lord of the 7th house in Ardra nakshatra may mean that your partner is fiercely independent, has issues with their name, and doesn't get along with their parents. But with the 7th lord exactly on Betelgeuse, Ardra's marker star, those issues may very well become explosive. Similarly, your 4th lord in Ashvini could mean that your mother has a prominent nose or teeth (Ashvini means "female horse"), that she married someone from a different caste or social order, and that she has a penchant for speed. But at 10 degrees Aries, exactly conjunct Ashvini's marker star, Sheratan, that penchant for speed may well turn her into a race-car driver.

Add the meaning of the planet and the houses it rules to the nakshatra qualities when assessing the effects of stars. You can do this in sporting events, and you don't have to just use the stars I've given above. There are many stars that didn't make it onto my list. That doesn't mean they don't work; it merely means I didn't have the time to research them. If you find some that work especially well, do let me know.

For instance, consider Italy's match versus Costa Rica in the World Cup. In the game chart below, the lord of the 1st house sits at 2°38′ Taurus in the 8th house, within 1 degree of the ghoulish star Algol, one of the most sinister taras, presiding over such things as beheadings and mass murder. Even though Italy didn't lose its head, it found itself without a *head coach* soon after this match, when the team

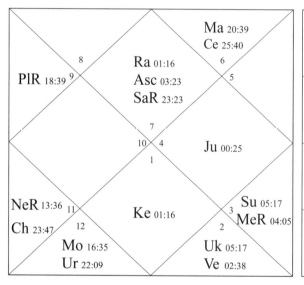

Bhava	Cusp	Lord/Sub/SS	D	C	B	A
1st h.	03:23:45 Lib	Ma/Ve/Ma	Mo	Sa		Ve
2nd h.	04:07:09 Sco	Sa/Sa/Ve			Su, Me, Ra	Ma
3rd h.	01:29:59 Sag	Ke/Ve/Ma			Ju, Sa	Ju
4th h.	28:09:09 Sag	Su/Mo/Ke			Ju, Sa	Ju
5th h.	26:49:53 Cap	Ma/Ju/Me			Mo	Sa
6th h.	29:05:55 Aqu	Ju/Su/Sa	Ma, Ke	Mo, Ke	Mo	Sa
7th h.	03:23:45 Ari	Ke/Su/Sa		Ve	Su, Me, Ra	Ma
8th h.	04:07:09 Tau	Su/Sa/Su				Ve
9th h.	01:29:59 Gem	Ma/Me/Ju	Ve	Su, Me		Me
10th h.	28:09:09 Gem	Ju/Ve/Sa	Ju, Sa	Ju		Me
11th h.	26:49:53 Can	Me/Ju/Me			Ma	Mo
12th h.	29:05:55 Leo	Su/Ma/Ve	Su, Me, Ra	Ma, Ra	Ve	Su

Italy (−169) vs. Costa Rica (+549), 13:00 LT, June 20, 2015, Recife, Brazil—World Cup game to demonstrate using Algol

failed to advance in the World Cup. A star's meaning doesn't have to be literal to apply to a chart, though sometimes it's pretty close!

Algol isn't on the list because it's one of those stars that provides event commentary but probably doesn't influence outcomes the way Regulus and the other taras do. You can put it on the list, especially if you do your own research to back it up. You may find that Algol also relates to artificial teeth, alcohol, and spirit possession:

> [Algol is the] Head of Gorgo Medusa. This name is derived from the Arabic "Al Ghoul" meaning "demon," "evil spirit" or "devil." Derived from the same root is "Golem" of Prague and "alcohol." Algol is part of a double star system. Its darker brother circles the brighter star in about 69 hours, in such a manner that an occultation for 9 hours appears as viewed from Earth, and this gives a periodical change in brightness. . . . Dr. Lomer wrote in "Kosmobiologie," August 1950, Page 302: "Arabic commanders in chief, in times of conquest, made it a point that no important battles were begun when the light of Algol was weak."*

Dancing with the Stars

When I first began exploring nakshatra taras, I thought Spica, Chitra's marker star, to be good for victory. I was disappointed. Out of the many examples of its treachery, here are two.

In the game charted on page 174, the favorite has Spica on the 10th house cusp, softening them up. The underdog won, 7 to 4.

The chart on page 175 shows an example of when a Chitra lagna won, barely. Mercury on the D9 in the 1st house helped push them across the victory line, but not without trouble—they won 8 to 6. This should emphasize the need to evaluate a chart using different techniques. Note the other placements in this complex chart: Sun on the 10th cusp and Ceres retrograde on the 4th. Just for fun, I've filled out the points table (table 8.2, page 174), which tallies with the winner and the final score; see if you agree.

---

*Elsbeth Ebertin and Georg Hoffman, *Fixed Stars and Their Interpretation,* translated by Irmgard Banks (Tempe, Ariz.: American Federation of Astrologers, 1971), 24.

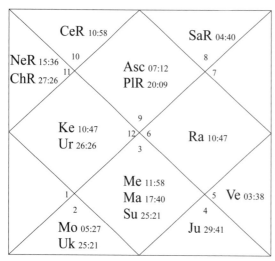

Bhava	Cusp	Lord/Sub/SS	D	C	B	A
1st h.	07:12:25 Sag	Ke/Ra/Su			Su	Ju
2nd h.	15:25:51 Cap	Mo/Ju/Ra			Sa, Ke	Sa
3rd h.	26:13:39 Aqu	Ju/Ke/Ju	Ve	Ke	Sa, Ke	Sa
4th h.	29:51:11 Pis	Me/Sa/Ju			Su	Ju
5th h.	25:31:03 Ari	Ve/Me/Ju	Ra	Mo		Ma
6th h.	16:45:56 Tau	Mo/Sa/Ve				Ve
7th h.	07:12:25 Gem	Ra/Ra/Ju	Mo, Ju	Su, Ma, Me	Ju	Me
8th h.	15:25:51 Can	Sa/Ju/Me	Su	Ju, Ve	Ra	Mo
9th h.	26:13:39 Leo	Ve/Ke/Ra	Ma, Me	Ra	Mo	Su
10th h.	29:51:11 Vir	Ma/Sa/Ju			Ju	Me
11th h.	25:31:03 Lib	Ju/Me/Sa	Sa, Ke	Sa		Ve
12th h.	16:45:56 Sco	Me/Me/Me				Ma

Washington Nationals (+108) vs. <u>Baltimore Orioles (−127)</u>, 19:16:30 LT,
July 11, 2015, Baltimore, Maryland

TABLE 8.2. TORONTO BLUE JAYS VS. SEATTLE MARINERS

TECHNIQUE	POINTS
Victory house	+3
SKY/PKY	none
Cuspal strength	−2 (Sun −9, CeresR +7)
Navamsha cuspal strength	+18
Navamsha combinations	none
Sublords	−13
Sublord array	+7
Navamsha syllables	none
Nakshatra tara	−7 (orb is not tight)
TOTAL:	**+6**

RASHI

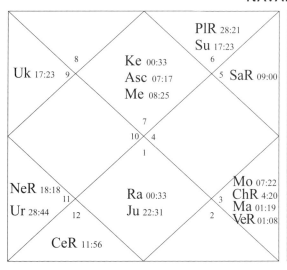

North Indian chart (left):
- SaR 04:21 (house 8)
- PlR 19:49 (house 9)
- Asc 00:48, Mo 27:29
- Ra 10:03 (house 6)
- VeR 06:47, Ju 02:30 (house 5)
- CeR 8:00
- Me 10:56, Su 08:35
- NeR 15:22, ChR 27:08 (house 11)
- Ma 26:48, Uk 08:35 (house 3)
- Ke 10:03, Ur 26:31 (house 12)
- Houses labeled: 7, 10, 4, 1, 2

South Indian chart (right):
Ur 26:31, Ke 10:03			Uk 08:35, Ma 26:48
NeR 15:22, ChR 27:08			Su 08:35, Me 10:56
CeR 8:00			Ju 02:30, VeR 06:47
PlR 19:49	SaR 04:21	Asc 00:48, Mo 27:29	Ra 10:03

Bhava	Cusp	Lord / Sub / SS	D	C	B	A
1st h.	00:48:39 Lib	Ma / Me / Mo	Ra	Mo		Ve
2nd h.	27:57:44 Lib	Ju / Ve / Ju	Su, Me, Sa, Ke	Sa		Ve
3rd h.	00:44:08 Sag	Ke / Ke / Me			Mo, Ma	Ju
4th h.	07:25:32 Cap	Su / Ke / Ra			Su, Me, Sa, Ke	Sa
5th h.	11:22:57 Aqu	Ra / Sa / Ve			Su, Me, Sa, Ke	Sa
6th h.	09:02:06 Pis	Sa / Ve / Ra	Ju, Ve	Ke	Mo, Ma	Ju
7th h.	00:48:39 Ari	Ke / Ve / Ve				Ma
8th h.	27:57:44 Ari	Su / Mo / Sa				Ma
9th h.	00:44:08 Gem	Ma / Me / Su		Ma		Me
10th h.	07:25:32 Can	Sa / Ke / Ve	Mo, Ma	Su, Me, Ju, Ve	Ra	Mo
11th h.	11:22:57 Leo	Ke / Sa / Ju				Su
12th h.	09:02:06 Vir	Su / Ve / Ju		Ra		Me

NAVAMSHA

North Indian chart (left):
- PlR 28:21, Su 17:23 (house 6)
- Ke 00:33, Asc 07:17, Me 08:25 (house 5)
- SaR 09:00
- Uk 17:23 (house 9)
- NeR 18:18, Ur 28:44 (house 11)
- Ra 00:33, Ju 22:31
- CeR 11:56
- Mo 07:22, ChR 4:20, Ma 01:19, VeR 01:08 (house 3)
- Houses labeled: 8, 7, 10, 4, 1, 2, 12

South Indian chart (right):
CeR 11:56	Ra 00:33, Ju 22:31		VeR 01:08, Ma 01:19, ChR 4:20, Mo 07:22
Ur 28:44, NeR 18:18			
			SaR 09:09
Uk 17:23		Ke 00:33, Asc 07:17, Me 08:25	Su 17:23, PlR 28:21

Toronto Blue Jays (−133) vs. Seattle Mariners (+112), 13:11 LT, July 25, 2015, Seattle, Washington

Brutus piped up: *But what about when, instead of working together in a prediction, the stars fight one another?*

In that case, closer analysis is required. Take a gander at the delicate situation charted below.

The heavily favored Chicago Cubs barely escaped with a victory in this tightly wound thriller. The reason? Both teams had their rulers on powerful taras: the lord of the 1st house on Regulus (Magha) at 6°25' Leo, and the lord

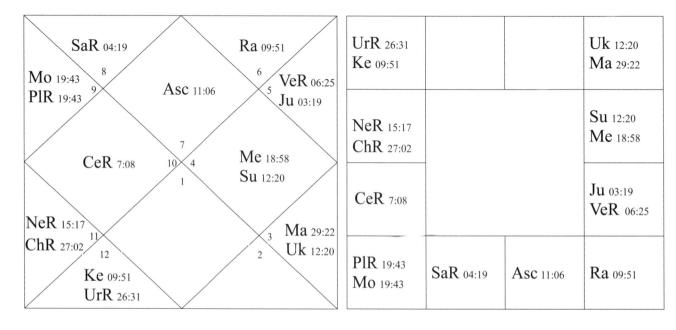

Bhava	Cusp	Lord/Sub/SS	D	C	B	A
1st h.	11:06:13 Lib	Ra/Sa/Ke	Su, Sa, Ke	Sa	Mo	Ve
2nd h.	09:39:24 Sco	Sa/Ve/Sa				Ma
3rd h.	12:48:25 Sag	Ke/Me/Ju		Mo	Ma	Ju
4th h.	18:29:46 Cap	Mo/Me/Su			Su, Sa, Ke	Sa
5th h.	21:31:21 Aqu	Ju/Ju/Ra	Ju, Ve	Ke	Su, Sa, Ke	Sa
6th h.	18:56:14 Pis	Me/Ke/Ra			Ma	Ju
7th h.	11:06:13 Ari	Ke/Sa/Ra				Ma
8th h.	09:39:24 Tau	Su/Ve/Me			Mo	Ve
9th h.	12:48:25 Gem	Ra/Me/Me	Ra	Su, Ma	Me	Me
10th h.	18:29:46 Can	Me/Me/Sa	Me, Ma, Mo	Me, Ju, Ve		Mo
11th h.	21:31:21 Leo	Ve/Ju/Ma		Ra	Ra	Su
12th h.	18:56:14 Vir	Mo/Me/Ra			Me	Me

Colorado Rockies (+200) vs. <u>Chicago Cubs (−244)</u>, 13:22 LT, July 29, 2015, Chicago, Illinois

of the 7th on Pollux (Punarvasu) at 29°22' Gemini. The verdict? When a chart looks even, give it to the favorite. Chicago won 3 to 2.

There's nothing like a good blowout to really drive home the effectiveness of a technique. Though all taras have the potential to help bring about victory, especially when in a tight orb, the king of giant victories is Regulus, the heart of the lion who not only likes to win, but win big.

In the chart below, Magha's bright star, Regulus, sits exactly on the lagna,

South Indian / North Indian chart:

Su 28:36 Ur 22:50 Ke 15:34 Ce 5:19	Me 01:32 Ma 14:57	Ve 07:23	
Ch 28:57 Uk 28:36 Ne 14:53			Ju 18:38
Mo 07:07			Asc 06:11
Pl 21:34	SaR 10:16		Ra 15:34

Bhava	Cusp	Lord/Sub/SS	D	C	B	A
1st h.	06:11:09 Leo	Ke/Ra/Sa			Mo, Ve	Su
2nd h.	28:49:09 Leo	Su/Ma/Sa		Ra	Mo, Ve	Su
3rd h.	26:46:05 Vir	Ma/Ju/Me			Su, Ju	Me
4th h.	00:02:36 Sco	Ju/Mo/Sa	Sa, Ke	Sa		Ma
5th h.	05:28:18 Sag	Ke/Ma/Su	Ra	Mo		Ju
6th h.	08:05:52 Cap	Su/Ve/Ve			Sa, Ke	Sa
7th h.	06:11:09 Aqu	Ma/Mo/Sa			Sa, Ke	Sa
8th h.	28:49:09 Aqu	Ju/Su/Mo	Me	Ke	Sa, Ke	Sa
9th h.	26:46:05 Pis	Me/Ju/Me	Mo, Ve, Su, Ju	Su, Ma, Me		Ju
10th h.	00:02:36 Tau	Su/Ra/Sa	Ma	Ve	Ma	Ve
11th h.	05:28:18 Gem	Ma/Su/Ve			Su, Ju	Me
12th h.	08:05:52 Can	Sa/Ke/Me		Ju	Ra	Mo

Charlotte Hornets (+296) vs. Detroit Pistons (−385), 15:36 LT, April 12, 2015, Detroit, Michigan

ensuring lasting glory for the space-time event it represents. True, Detroit was a heavy favorite. Its winning margin, however, was not expected. Rarely do NBA teams get blown out by thirty-nine points, but that's what Charlotte got with Magha nakshatra pitted against them. The final score? 116 to 77.

Lost for Words

So, why did you stop betting? Brutus asked me as we promenaded down a street with manicured lawns and a made-up city sky, whose inner beauty lay hidden behind the glitz of artificial light.

"Because I realized a deeper meaning of what it is to be an astrologer. And also because I started losing . . . and actually, not in that order."

What do you mean?

"In Sanskrit, one of the words for astrologer is *daivajna,* a knower of fate. On a deeper level it also means a knower of light, and even more profoundly, a knower of the mind of God."

And why *did that make you stop betting?*

"When you realize how many variables go into predicting an event and the seconds that make a difference one way or the other, you understand that only God knows the precise timing of things. I began to realize that I can't outthink the universe, stats and software notwithstanding. I began to realize that the true daivajna is sometimes an ordinary person with an extraordinary feeling, a *knowing* deep down in their bones about a thing. That knowing cannot be outwitted by a spreadsheet. That knowing is the real astrology. And to invite it, you have to let yourself be open to grace."

How do you invite grace?

"The best way I know is to do your dharma. Earlier I told you that it is not the dharma of Educators or Warriors to work exclusively for money. Only Merchants get to frolic in the speculation game, and even then it's a tightrope. Ultimately the Educator's aim is *enlightenment*, not *emolument*. It is our role to communicate and teach."

But what about meee? Brutus interupted, perhaps sensing one of my Educator lectures coming on.

"For you, dear Brutus, it is acceptable to play for a while, as you are in a

Merchant life cycle, a period that, though you are not a Merchant type, allows you to wear its mask in service to your dharma."

Is that what makes us unique? The fact that, whatever our dharma type, we can be in any life cycle, any period, based on our specific dasha and bhukti?

"That's right, Brutus. Now tell everyone to buy my book *The 5 Dharma Types: Vedic Wisdom for Discovering Your Purpose and Destiny,* so that they too can learn about their dharma."

Um, what people . . . and who are you talking to? You know I'm just a voice in your head, right?

And so ends my final conversation with Brutus. I really should get out more often.

This Is the End, My Only Friend

July 18, 2015. Having wrapped up my research, it was time to start writing in earnest. No more wagering, no more pulling charts. Deadlines were looming. A few short months from now a finished manuscript was due on the editor's desk or else! Every author has their rituals to keep them on track. Mine is simple: stop doing everything else.

But just as this sense of completion settled, an innocent thought floated to the surface: *How about one more day? Just one more day of pulling charts, mister . . . you know, for old time's sake?*

Sure, why not? Who am I to refuse innocent thoughts bubbling to the surface?

A quick check of the schedule showed the only sport worth considering was baseball, and as I began to pull horoscopes a pattern emerged: one by one, the matches unfurled the complement of techniques enumerated in this book—all the methods, displayed in one day's games, often combining together in a single match to indicate a winner. Perhaps this was my good-bye present from the world of sports prediction.

Like many authors, I am a couch adventurer, a pilgrim for truth poring through research from the comfort of my home. After months of late nights and early mornings, I had arrived at some semblance of this truth, a personal pilgrimage on behalf of an idea that had pushed me to find its original face and describe it for posterity. During such voyages a relationship forms; like sharing a long bus ride with a stranger, you begin to understand things about them perhaps their own family doesn't even know. A bond is made with the subject, one cemented by the elation of sometimes getting it right, and more often tested by the frustration of being wrong, but a bond that I would think remains for life. Perhaps today's farewell is an acknowledgment of that friendship.

My Jyotisha mentor repeatedly emphasized that every *vidya*, or body of knowledge, is a living being. Cultivating a relationship with the Jyotir Vidya is tantamount to sharing yourself with sincerity and assiduous application. Being your friend, she can rouse you in the middle of the night—and she often does.

"You can observe a lot by watching."

This quote is from the legendary baseball guru Yogi Berra, who also noted that "baseball is 80 percent mental; the other half is physical," and that "in theory, there is no difference between theory and practice; in practice there is." This, of course, is true, especially in Jyotisha. The only way to confirm these techniques for yourself is in the crucible of your own experience.

The subject is exhaustive but this text isn't. As many principles as we've shared in this book, there are dozens more that also exist or that are there to be found by further research. For example, we have not covered classic Jyotisha techniques such as *ashtakavarga* or *shad bala,* or used other systems of interpretation such as Jaimini, or fully fleshed out Krishnamurti Paddhati (though we have borrowed from it). In addition, Western techniques such as midpoints, Arabic parts, and antiscia, none of which have made it into our study, may well be candidates to help us make greater sense out of the messages of the sky.

9

The Spiritual Side of Betting

Avoiding the Pitfalls of Gambling

Pleasure may come from illusion, but happiness can come only of reality.

NICOLAS DE CHAMFORT

Can there be a spiritual benefit to building wealth by investing in sports? Can gambling have a spiritual side? Maybe. Investment in stocks is no different than investment in sports, and it is the dharma of some entrepreneurs to gamble with their savings in order to build wealth.

Entrepreneurship and gambling straddle a fine line that religious and spiritual circles traditionally eschew because of how easily the mind can become prey to greed, despair, false pride, and the swarm of egoic fixation that attends the speculative arts. But in tantra there is a saying: "Push yourself up by the ground that makes you stumble," meaning that if you can digest the powerful cocktail of hormones and chemicals produced by the body as a result of speculation, then you can handle almost any situation.

Digesting the hormone cocktail means positively harnessing the emotional and physical states triggered by the up-and-down nature of speculation. Natural emotions like infatuation do it. Synthetic chemicals like cocaine do it. And gambling does it. Winning, like being in love or high on drugs, jacks up dopamine production to make us feel elated. Losing, like breaking up a relationship or coming down from a high, can make us feel haggard, useless, and depressed.

As dopamine shoots up in our bodies, elation and ego inflation also attend. When dopamine and serotonin crash, as they do when our teams lose, the depths of despair the mind can entertain are almost limitless. We are literally awash with the hormones of joy and sorrow, which sometimes play us like puppets.

These bodily juices are called *rasa* in Sanskrit, and they affect how we see the world. Knowing this long ago, the Vedic sages taught that we have the power, through spiritual discipline, to control these rasas. Today, masters of neurolinguistics programming like Tony Robbins have a similar take on this: harness the waves of your emotions and surf them to success. This is modern tantra, without the history or spirituality.

Gambling as a spiritual path is a precarious road, and to navigate it requires a mentor. Gurus or teachers are invaluable in the spiritual process because you can bounce good and bad ideas off them, even if they are not in the physical body. Like a rudder, they give direction when we're awash in the stormy sea of chemical forces. And while the guru is the rudder, our anchor is Jyotisha itself, by having the kind of faith in which we can face the tides of the mind and its attendant rasas with quiet perseverance, a faith born of experience that Jyotisha works. It works not only for predicting sports outcomes, for this is but a tiny subset of a giant equation that comprises the totality of human endeavor. In other ages it was Jyotisha's ability to predict the weather, crop health, and how and where to find water that sustained humankind. It could predict natural disasters as well as wars and famine, and this is how it earned its reputation, surviving all the way up to today, after five thousand years of constant testing.

Through my own testing my faith has grown. The techniques in this book are an extension of that testing, a rudimentary and imperfect expression of the independent spirit all Jyotishis harness to further the capacities of their art. Every Jyotishi, in their own way, adds a drop to the bucket. The greats of old like Parashara, Varahamihira, and Satyacharya and modern-age rishis like Krishnamurti, Iyer, and Raman have poured gallons of their own sweat and inspiration therein.

For those who wish to use Jyotisha to guide their investments, great care is needed, as discussed in chapter 2. Here are some additional considerations and explanations to build on the material from that chapter.

Seeing in 3-D

If you're planning to predict or even bet on matches with any regularity, it's best to give yourself time to sit with the charts you pull in order to see them with 3-D vision. This means pulling horoscopes for the events the night before they happen to see if anything stands out. This is your first look. The second happens while you're sleeping. Allowing the information to marinate in your subconscious mind lets your intuition give you the benefit of its wisdom. Finally, after sleeping on it, return to the charts the next morning for a final look, well before the games are scheduled to start.

You don't want to feel pressured before making predictions or big decisions. This 3-D approach improves your chances of correct prediction by getting you in touch with your inner knowing self, the third eye of your intuition. It also helps correct for mistakes by giving you a chance to physically see the charts at least twice before making a decision.

Oftentimes astrologers feel pressured to give predictions for clients on the spot, and these may end up being wrong or incomplete because of errors of omission or comission. With sports investing, especially if you do it for yourself, you should give yourself the time and space to really see a chart in 3-D before venturing forth. I know when I do, it works.

Charity, the Merchant's Antidote

The United States consumes over 80 percent of the world's prescription opiates.* That's because the United States is a Merchant nation. Countries, like people, have dharma types. Merchants can harbor feelings of emptiness, missing that sense of *self* that they try to hide by filling up on *stuff*, or by numbing themselves to the world. But these are only temporary fixes. The permanent remedy for Merchant types is charity—giving what you have in abundance to those who don't.

---

*Jim Avila, "Prescription Painkiller Use at Record High for Americans," ABC News, http://abcnews.go.com/US/prescription-painkillers-record-number-americans-pain-medication/story?id=13421828.

The concept of *upaya,* "skillful means" or "remedial methods," is as well known in Jyotisha as it is in Buddhism. Charity, especially for Merchants, is the best upaya. Charity does not mean only giving money; it can take the form of a sincere compliment or a smile, which can change a person's day. Merchants have tremendous Shakti—personal energy and magnetism—which can influence others positively when they choose to access it. Sharing this is a gift, and for Merchant countries, like Merchant people, it is the strongest drug available, building goodwill and positive karma, acting as an antidote to loneliness, hurt, and depression. If you engage in gambling/investing, which is a Merchant game, you must devote a portion of your winnings and time to charity. This will promote not only continued investment success but health and happiness as well.

The Healing Power of Charity

An ayurvedic therapist once approached me with a story about her stubborn client. For months she had tried everything to help her—herbs, therapies, and yoga—with no success. Finally, she considered going outside the box. Knowing her client to be a Merchant type, as a homework assignment after their weekly session she recommended finding a charitable cause to become involved in, something dear to her client's heart. The woman balked at this, remonstrating that she had enough problems of her own without taking on someone else's. But her therapist insisted it was a mandatory part of her treatment.

The following week the woman returned and reported that she was pleasantly surprised to find that she felt better—not completely well, but better, after donating an hour or so helping out at a local charity. The therapist doubled down and pushed her to do more the following week. Over the next several weeks, my therapist friend noted that the herbs began to work, as did the yoga and other therapies; her client was responding not only emotionally but physically as well, losing those extra stubborn pounds and shedding the grief and depression along with them.

Charity can be a catalyst to major life change. Our bodies hold on to fat and waste as a buffer, a defense against loneliness and pain. When we become engaged in helping others, the need for that buffer lessens, and we are given permission to let go. If you choose to play, remember to pay; paying it forward is an insurance policy on your continued success.

> **If you choose to play, remember to pay;**
> **paying it forward is an insurance policy on**
> **your continued success.**

Feed Others
and Nature Will Feed You

One late summer morning, after playing a particularly difficult underdog parlay, I heard a knock on my door. I opened to find two sweet women, Jehovah's Witnesses, smiling at me, out of breath from climbing the stairs and perspiring in the dry and pungent heat of a New Mexico summer. Preoccupied with my games, I made some excuse about working and that yes, I would take their literature. I had closed the door and slumped into the couch when Vyasa's words from the Mahabharata hit me: "Charity is the hardest penance of all."

Stupid boy, I thought. *Here you are playing a Merchant game and you don't even know how to invite grace into your home.* Having written the book on what each dharma type must do as a spiritual practice, I realized that feeding others and charity had to be part of my life as long as I was living a Merchant lifestyle.

Rushing to my kitchen, I flung open the freezer, which I had just stacked with three quarts of premium ice cream. Plastic spoons in tow, I sped down the stairs, Häagen-Dazs vanilla in one hand and McConnell's San Francisco peppermint stick in the other. I caught them at the gate just as they were about to leave. Smiling gratefully, they accepted my better-late-than-never treats, the more so because it was almost 100 degrees outside, and they had been walking up and down the neighborhood for a while.

Later that day I too was walking on air—my parlays had won, and I remembered an important teaching: feed a hungry soul, and nature in turn will feed you a thousand times over. The ten dollars I spent on ice cream was well worth the thousands I won betting that day. Sometimes we have to start with selfish motives to get to real selflessness. I was a long way away, but I had at least taken one step.

The Brahmasthana
in Jyotisha, Vastu,
Ayurveda, and Yoga

In vastu shastra, the Vedic science of placement, the *brahmasthana* holds a special place of importance. *Brahmasthana* means "place of spirit." The rule says that the center of any lot, house, room, or artistic composition should be free, open, and uncluttered in order to invite in prosperity, love, and divine inspiration. That means no staircases or furnaces in the middle of your house unless you want a heart attack or a good dose of depression. The center of your home is like your heart, and heavy objects there literally press down on it, leading to all kinds of relationship and health problems.

Ayurveda, vastu's big sister, like any older sibling, co-opted this principle for herself, saying the center of our own vastu-dwelling, the human body, should also remain empty, free, and uncluttered in order to beckon prosperity in the form of health and longevity. Human beings come with a brahmasthana—our GI tract—and this is marked externally by the depression of our belly button. Accordingly, ayurveda requires at least four to six hours between meals to allow our tummy to rest and rebuild. It also prescribes regular fasting, cleansing, herbal protocols, and other procedures to keep the brahmasthana spic and span.

Now of course yoga, vastu, and ayurveda's first cousin also took a shine to this principle, so much so that she defined it: *Yogash chitta vritti nirodhah,* "Yoga is cessation of the fluctuations of the mind stuff." This mind stuff isn't just the gray matter between your ears but also the stuff between your heart and pelvis, the entire digestive system. In modern science we know that the gut has a brain of its own and is responsible for up to 95 percent of serotonin production and 70 percent of our entire immune system.

Our digestive organs, including the villi and microvilli in our intestines, work in a wavelike manner to process and push food through the system. These waves are called *vrittis,* and the cessation of all vrittis is the purported goal of yoga. As a result, yogis made fasting into an art, and fasting is a staple of practically every religion on the planet. Jesus fasted, Buddha fasted, Mohammed fasted, Moses fasted. Fasting is a core religious ritual because it brings us closer to God, which is none other than our own brahmasthana, or sacred space. Even the wise Benjamin Franklin said, "The best of all medicines is resting and fasting." Keep your space uncluttered and its center empty, and you will invite God into your body and home.

So, how is this relevant to Jyotisha? Glad you asked. The principle of the brahmasthana in Jyotisha is the principle of sandhi. As discussed in chapter 2, Jyotisha honors sandhis as portals to different realities and advises against predicting during such periods. Sunday is a sandhi because it's the day God rested. Sandhis should also be times of rest for Jyotishis, in order to honor their own brahmasthana.

The spirit of Jyotisha aims with dogged dedication to understand phenomenal creation, and by understanding, to predict events in time and space. With thousands of possible techniques aimed at grokking every aspect of the time-space continuum, it is tireless in its quest to know truth. However, it too must rest. And the best time to take a rest from the quest is during a sandhi. Therefore, don't predict on an eclipse, at sunrise or sunset, or at other times when nature is on break, such as when planets are stationary or close to it. If you reach out to feel it, there is a stillness in the world during such times, a hush that is almost palpable, as if God were napping. And if you grow really still, you can almost hear God's breath, softly wheezing, coming from your own brahmasthana.

> **Mondays are fine,**
> **just don't bet on sandhis.**

Mondays are fine, just don't bet on sandhis. Major sandhis to avoid for sports prediction include:

- Eclipses: Give three days on either side of a major eclipse. Instead of prediction, do research or charity work, or consider using Jyotisha for your own and your clients' inner growth.
- Solar *sankranti,* the ingress of the sidereal Sun into a new sign: When the Sun is at the very end or beginning of a sign it is caught between two

worlds, and as a result it may be difficult to judge which house it is affecting in whole-sign Parashari Jyotisha. A Sun at 29°35' Leo may have more to do with Virgo than with Leo, and this can make it difficult to predict its effects. A rule of thumb: when the Sun is 29 degrees or higher, consider it equally affecting the next sign as well.

- Stationary planets: When a planet's motion goes from retrograde to direct, or from direct to retrograde, there is a period of one to up to seven days (for faster- to slower-moving planets) during which it is stationary, i.e., apparently motionless in the sky. Stationary planets have a heavy, dead quality and can flip your predictions on their heads. The day that a planet goes stationary is especially to be avoided for worldly activities. Treat such days like eclipses, especially as concerns the planet Jupiter, or if the stationary planet rules your ascendant or dasha/bhukti period. Trust me on this; I paid dearly for this knowledge.

From astronomy we know that Jupiter is essentially a failed sun, a planet that couldn't gather enough mass to become a star. Just as the Sun and the Moon are vital to astrology, so too is Jupiter because like these luminaries he is humanity's grand protector. Life on Earth would not be possible without Jupiter's help, because with its gravity, this massive giant pulls asteroids and comets away from Earth, allowing for a relatively peaceful environment here in which life can flourish. The guru likewise does this for us on a personal level by shielding us from the slings and arrows of our own outrageous karma. Because of the Sun, Moon, and Jupiter's importance to Jyotisha, we especially want to avoid major sandhis involving these players.

The Trouble with Eclipses

Eclipses skewer results and can produce contrary predictions. For the purposes of counseling and evolutionary astrology, eclipse timings can be helpful in producing inner breakthroughs and understanding. But because Rahu and Ketu are underdogs who usurp the status quo, even if you make the correct prediction at this time, it may not ultimately be the right one as reflected by the outcome. Because Jyotisha is the "study of light," when the light is eclipsed, the science of Jyotisha itself becomes eclipsed and more difficult to practice objectively.

The legend of Rahu/Ketu states that this clever and visionary titan's heart burned to become immortal, even though it was not his dharma. Nonetheless, with great skill and courage born of ambition, he disguised himself and succeeded in wheedling his way to the nectar of immortality, earning a drink of the storied liquid just before he was discovered and beheaded. Because he had become immortal, he remained severed but alive, and though he achieved his outcome, it was tainted with failure: he had become a headless body, a severed but immortal corpse.

This legend tells us that results obtained during eclipse periods may be less than satisfactory. It also implies that underdogs are more favored at such times, as the shadow lurkers Rahu/Ketu get their day in the sun, so to speak. This is the time when Outsiders and those betting against the market do well, as Rahu/Ketu are the consummate Outsider underdogs who hoisted their trophy, the cup of nectar, in victory.

Consider Facebook's IPO, which happened a couple of days before a total solar eclipse and was summarily called the worst flop in history.* Most investors do not know that a few secretive, top-level investment groups that bet against it scored billions of dollars on the backs of everyday John and Jane Does who invested thinking they would quickly double their money. Such is the fate of events around eclipses: favorites tend to tank while underdogs and shadow groups leave through the back door with the pot of gold. In practical terms, eclipses are a time to rest and refine your techniques through meditation, research, and reflection, not active prediction.

---

*Khadeeja Safdar, "Facebook, One Year Later: What Really Happened in the Biggest IPO Flop Ever," *Atlantic,* www.theatlantic.com/business/archive/2013/05/facebook-one-year-later-what-really-happened-in-the-biggest-ipo-flop-ever/275987/.

What's Wrong
with Being Right?

The perils of gambling await both losers and winners. When you win, there is a sense of being one with God, with nature, and with the divine flow of things. This is called *dharma,* and it's a real high. However, this feeling is based on temporal events, not on spiritual evolution. Take away the win and you lose the emotion; therefore it is ultimately as unreal as it is fleeting. The ego, however, is not worried about such niceties and can take credit for being one with the divine to such a degree as to develop a superiority complex. Surprisingly, this complex doesn't always go away when you lose, instead believing *if I only made a slight change I could get it right next time.* This is the slippery slope to addiction, which is a perverted desire for dharma, the sense of feeling alright with the universe.

The perils of losing are similar, save that they batter the ego into believing it is unworthy of being in the universal flow. There's an ugly duckling sense that overwhelms you when you lose, begging the question *What did I do wrong*? It is also illusory since it's based on transient events and the hormones they trigger.

One of the aims of tantra is *svatantrya*—independence, freedom, and self-reliance. According to tantra, our bodies, thoughts, and emotions constantly vie to take us over, removing our freedom, making us reactive. Somebody cuts you off, and you get mad and give them the finger. You are trapped by the anger and the reaction it produces. But a split second before the anger rises up there is a moment during which you have a choice. That is the gap, and spiritual traditions seek to make us one with this gap, widening it until it becomes our ultimate reality. One way to do this is to practice svatantrya in everyday situations.

The first step is practicing calmness and presence during *neutral* situations, like driving or washing the dishes. Cultivating awareness while doing routine activities turns these into opportunities for spiritual growth.

The next step is doing this during *pleasurable* situations, like sex, or winning with Jyotisha. This is exponentially more difficult since it pits you against a flood of emotions seeking to take over your body and mind.

The final step is to practice equanimity and self-awareness during *painful* circumstances. For many people this is the most difficult step, which is why traditions like tantra put practitioners in uncomfortable situations to help them move past pain and pleasure into serenity.

You can flip steps two and three, around pain and pleasure, if maintaining equipoise during pain is easier for you than during pleasure. Either way, handling these is easier to say than to do, as related in the cautionary tale about Jesse Livermore, one of the great speculators on Wall Street, as reported in *Forbes* magazine:

A week after Thanksgiving 1940, Jesse walked into the Sherry-Netherland Hotel in New York, had two drinks at the bar while scribbling something in his notebook, then proceeded to the cloakroom, where he sat on a stool and shot himself in the head. He was sixty-two and left behind $5 million, down from the $100 million fortune he had amassed just ten years earlier.

And the note he had scribbled?

"My dear Nina: Can't help it. Things have been bad with me. I am tired of fighting. Can't carry on any longer. This is the only way out. I am unworthy of your love. I am a failure. I am truly sorry, but this is the only way out for me. Love, Laurie"*

A multimillionaire in an era when millions were scarcer than today, Livermore nonetheless considered himself a failure.

As summarized by *Forbes,* there are three major lessons we can take away from this parable:

1. Those who are on top now are not certain to finish in that position and are not guaranteed everlasting success or happiness.
2. Be careful whom you choose to idolize.
3. The life of a professional speculator is an unpleasant one, filled with highs and lows but ultimately unsatisfying and, in all probability, mentally ruinous.

The goal of Jyotisha is to help you find your dharma. Jyotisha is a *darpana,* a mirror, a tool for self-knowledge, not self-deception. In the words of one Jyotishi, "We'd like to put ourselves out of business" by teaching people, including the

---

*Joshua Brown, "The Nine Financiers, a Parable about Power," *Forbes,* www.forbes.com /sites/joshuabrown/2012/07/25/the-nine-financiers-a-parable-about-power/.

astrologer him- or herself, to flow with their dharma. As incredible as it may seem, even a book on using Jyotisha as a predictive tool for speculation can serve that purpose. At least that is my hope. Helping you to hone and use your intuition, build self-awareness, and become an ambassador of dharma is the aim of any worthy astrologer. Hari Om!

APPENDIX 1

Sublords Table

This table shows the sublords for the entire zodiac, a total of 249 divisions. Krishnamurti used these 249 divisions masterfully for reading and rectifying natal horoscopes, as well as with prashna (horary charts). After a question was posed he would ask the querent to choose a number between 1 and 249. Assigning this subdivision to fix the ascendant for the question asked, he would then divide the chart into houses, using Placidus house cusps for his locality. He would then predict based on the current planetary position and placement of the cuspal sublords.*

TABLE A.1. SUBLORDS

NO.	SIGN	FROM (DEG/MIN/SEC)	TO (DEG/MIN/SEC)	SIGN LORD	STAR LORD	SUBLORD
1	Aries	00°00'00"	00°46'40"	Mars	Ketu	Ketu
2	Aries	00°46'40"	03°00'00"	Mars	Ketu	Venus
3	Aries	03°00'00"	03°40'00"	Mars	Ketu	Sun
4	Aries	03°40'00"	04°46'40"	Mars	Ketu	Moon
5	Aries	04°46'40"	05°33'20"	Mars	Ketu	Mars

---

*For more information on Krishnamurti's methodology, refer to his excellent KP Readers. Though many authors have written about KP (Krishnamurti Paddhati, or Krishnamurti Method), the KP Readers remain the most authentic source for this information. They are available online at www.scribd.com.

NO.	SIGN	FROM (DEG/MIN/SEC)	TO (DEG/MIN/SEC)	SIGN LORD	STAR LORD	SUBLORD
6	Aries	05°33'20"	07°33'20"	Mars	Ketu	Rahu
7	Aries	07°33'20"	09°20'00"	Mars	Ketu	Jupiter
8	Aries	09°20'00"	11°26'40"	Mars	Ketu	Saturn
9	Aries	11°26'40"	13°20'00"	Mars	Ketu	Mercury
10	Aries	13°20'00"	15°33'20"	Mars	Venus	Venus
11	Aries	15°33'20"	16°13'20"	Mars	Venus	Sun
12	Aries	16°13'20"	17°20'00"	Mars	Venus	Moon
13	Aries	17°20'00"	18°06'40"	Mars	Venus	Mars
14	Aries	18°06'40"	20°06'40"	Mars	Venus	Rahu
15	Aries	20°06'40"	21°53'20"	Mars	Venus	Jupiter
16	Aries	21°53'20"	24°00'00"	Mars	Venus	Saturn
17	Aries	24°00'00"	25°53'20"	Mars	Venus	Mercury
18	Aries	25°53'20"	26°40'00"	Mars	Venus	Ketu
19	Aries	26°40'00"	27°20'00"	Mars	Sun	Sun
20	Aries	27°20'00"	28°26'40"	Mars	Sun	Moon
21	Aries	28°26'40"	29°13'20"	Mars	Sun	Mars
22	Aries	29°13'20"	30°00'00"	Mars	Sun	Rahu
23	Taurus	00°00'00"	01°13'20"	Venus	Sun	Rahu
24	Taurus	01°13'20"	03°00'00"	Venus	Sun	Jupiter
25	Taurus	03°00'00"	05°06'40"	Venus	Sun	Saturn
26	Taurus	05°06'40"	07°00'00"	Venus	Sun	Mercury
27	Taurus	07°00'00"	07°46'40"	Venus	Sun	Ketu
28	Taurus	07°46'40"	10°00'00"	Venus	Sun	Venus

NO.	SIGN	FROM (DEG/MIN/SEC)	TO (DEG/MIN/SEC)	SIGN LORD	STAR LORD	SUBLORD
29	Taurus	10°00'00"	11°06'40"	Venus	Moon	Moon
30	Taurus	11°06'40"	11°53'20"	Venus	Moon	Mars
31	Taurus	11°53'20"	13°53'20"	Venus	Moon	Rahu
32	Taurus	13°53'20"	15°40'00"	Venus	Moon	Jupiter
33	Taurus	15°40'00"	17°46'40"	Venus	Moon	Saturn
34	Taurus	17°46'40"	19°40'00"	Venus	Moon	Mercury
35	Taurus	19°40'00"	20°26'40"	Venus	Moon	Ketu
36	Taurus	20°26'40"	22°40'00"	Venus	Moon	Venus
37	Taurus	22°40'00"	23°20'00"	Venus	Moon	Sun
38	Taurus	23°20'00"	24°06'40"	Venus	Mars	Mars
39	Taurus	24°06'40"	26°06'40"	Venus	Mars	Rahu
40	Taurus	26°06'40"	27°53'20"	Venus	Mars	Jupiter
41	Taurus	27°53'20"	30°00'00"	Venus	Mars	Saturn
42	Gemini	00°00'00"	01°53'20"	Mercury	Mars	Mercury
43	Gemini	01°53'20"	02°40'00"	Mercury	Mars	Ketu
44	Gemini	02°40'00"	04°53'20"	Mercury	Mars	Venus
45	Gemini	04°53'20"	05°33'20"	Mercury	Mars	Sun
46	Gemini	05°33'20"	06°40'00"	Mercury	Mars	Moon
47	Gemini	06°40'00"	08°40'00"	Mercury	Rahu	Rahu
48	Gemini	08°40'00"	10°26'40"	Mercury	Rahu	Jupiter
49	Gemini	10°26'40"	12°33'20"	Mercury	Rahu	Saturn
50	Gemini	12°33'20"	14°26'40"	Mercury	Rahu	Mercury
51	Gemini	14°26'40"	15°13'20"	Mercury	Rahu	Ketu

NO.	SIGN	FROM (DEG/MIN/SEC)	TO (DEG/MIN/SEC)	SIGN LORD	STAR LORD	SUBLORD
52	Gemini	15°13'20"	17°26'40"	Mercury	Rahu	Venus
53	Gemini	17°26'40"	18°06'40"	Mercury	Rahu	Sun
54	Gemini	18°06'40"	19°13'20"	Mercury	Rahu	Moon
55	Gemini	19°13'20"	20°00'00"	Mercury	Rahu	Mars
56	Gemini	20°00'00"	21°46'40"	Mercury	Jupiter	Jupiter
57	Gemini	21°46'40"	23°53'20"	Mercury	Jupiter	Saturn
58	Gemini	23°53'20"	25°46'40"	Mercury	Jupiter	Mercury
59	Gemini	25°46'40"	26°33'20"	Mercury	Jupiter	Ketu
60	Gemini	26°33'20"	28°46'40"	Mercury	Jupiter	Venus
61	Gemini	28°46'40"	29°26'40"	Mercury	Jupiter	Sun
62	Gemini	29°26'40"	30°00'00"	Mercury	Jupiter	Moon
63	Cancer	00°00'00"	00°33'20"	Moon	Jupiter	Moon
64	Cancer	00°33'20"	01°20'00"	Moon	Jupiter	Mars
65	Cancer	01°20'00"	03°20'00"	Moon	Jupiter	Rahu
66	Cancer	03°20'00"	05°26'40"	Moon	Saturn	Saturn
67	Cancer	05°26'40"	07°20'00"	Moon	Saturn	Mercury
68	Cancer	07°20'00"	08°06'40"	Moon	Saturn	Ketu
69	Cancer	08°06'40"	10°20'00"	Moon	Saturn	Venus
70	Cancer	10°20'00"	11°00'00"	Moon	Saturn	Sun
71	Cancer	11°00'00"	12°06'40"	Moon	Saturn	Moon
72	Cancer	12°06'40"	12°53'20"	Moon	Saturn	Mars
73	Cancer	12°53'20"	14°53'20"	Moon	Saturn	Rahu
74	Cancer	14°53'20"	16°40'00"	Moon	Saturn	Jupiter

NO.	SIGN	FROM (DEG/MIN/SEC)	TO (DEG/MIN/SEC)	SIGN LORD	STAR LORD	SUBLORD
75	Cancer	16°40'00"	18°33'21"	Moon	Mercury	Mercury
76	Cancer	18°33'21"	19°20'00"	Moon	Mercury	Ketu
77	Cancer	19°20'00"	21°33'20"	Moon	Mercury	Venus
78	Cancer	21°33'20"	22°13'20"	Moon	Mercury	Sun
79	Cancer	22°13'20"	23°20'00"	Moon	Mercury	Moon
80	Cancer	23°20'00"	24°06'40"	Moon	Mercury	Mars
81	Cancer	24°06'40"	26°06'40"	Moon	Mercury	Rahu
82	Cancer	26°06'40"	27°53'20"	Moon	Mercury	Jupiter
83	Cancer	27°53'20"	30°00'00"	Moon	Mercury	Saturn
84	Leo	00°00'00"	00°46'40"	Sun	Ketu	Ketu
85	Leo	00°46'40"	03°00'00"	Sun	Ketu	Venus
86	Leo	03°00'00"	03°40'00"	Sun	Ketu	Sun
87	Leo	03°40'00"	04°46'40"	Sun	Ketu	Moon
88	Leo	04°46'40"	05°33'20"	Sun	Ketu	Mars
89	Leo	05°33'20"	07°33'20"	Sun	Ketu	Rahu
90	Leo	07°33'20"	09°20'00"	Sun	Ketu	Jupiter
91	Leo	09°20'00"	11°26'40"	Sun	Ketu	Saturn
92	Leo	11°26'40"	13°20'00"	Sun	Ketu	Mercury
93	Leo	13°20'00"	15°33'20"	Sun	Venus	Venus
94	Leo	15°33'20"	16°13'20"	Sun	Venus	Sun
95	Leo	16°13'20"	17°20'00"	Sun	Venus	Moon
96	Leo	17°20'00"	18°06'40"	Sun	Venus	Mars
97	Leo	18°06'40"	20°06'40"	Sun	Venus	Rahu

NO.	SIGN	FROM (DEG/MIN/SEC)	TO (DEG/MIN/SEC)	SIGN LORD	STAR LORD	SUBLORD
98	Leo	20°06'40"	21°53'20"	Sun	Venus	Jupiter
99	Leo	21°53'20"	24°00'00"	Sun	Venus	Saturn
100	Leo	24°00'00"	25°53'20"	Sun	Venus	Mercury
101	Leo	25°53'20"	26°40'00"	Sun	Venus	Ketu
102	Leo	26°40'00"	27°20'00"	Sun	Sun	Sun
103	Leo	27°20'00"	28°26'40"	Sun	Sun	Moon
104	Leo	28°26'40"	29°13'20"	Sun	Sun	Mars
105	Leo	29°13'20"	30°00'00"	Sun	Sun	Rahu
106	Virgo	00°00'00"	01°13'20"	Mercury	Sun	Rahu
107	Virgo	01°13'20"	03°00'00"	Mercury	Sun	Jupiter
108	Virgo	03°00'00"	05°06'40"	Mercury	Sun	Saturn
109	Virgo	05°06'40"	07°00'00"	Mercury	Sun	Mercury
110	Virgo	07°00'00"	07°46'40"	Mercury	Sun	Ketu
111	Virgo	07°46'40"	10°00'00"	Mercury	Sun	Venus
112	Virgo	10°00'00"	11°06'40"	Mercury	Moon	Moon
113	Virgo	11°06'40"	11°53'20"	Mercury	Moon	Mars
114	Virgo	11°53'20"	13°53'20"	Mercury	Moon	Rahu
115	Virgo	13°53'20"	15°40'00"	Mercury	Moon	Jupiter
116	Virgo	15°40'00"	17°46'40"	Mercury	Moon	Saturn
117	Virgo	17°46'40"	19°40'00"	Mercury	Moon	Mercury
118	Virgo	19°40'00"	20°26'40"	Mercury	Moon	Ketu
119	Virgo	20°26'40"	22°40'00"	Mercury	Moon	Venus
120	Virgo	22°40'00"	23°20'00"	Mercury	Moon	Sun

NO.	SIGN	FROM (DEG/MIN/SEC)	TO (DEG/MIN/SEC)	SIGN LORD	STAR LORD	SUBLORD
121	Virgo	23°20'00"	24°06'40"	Mercury	Mars	Mars
122	Virgo	24°06'40"	26°06'40"	Mercury	Mars	Rahu
123	Virgo	26°06'40"	27°53'20"	Mercury	Mars	Jupiter
124	Virgo	27°53'20"	30°00'00"	Mercury	Mars	Saturn
125	Libra	00°00'00"	01°53'20"	Venus	Mars	Mercury
126	Libra	01°53'20"	02°40'00"	Venus	Mars	Ketu
127	Libra	02°40'00"	04°53'20"	Venus	Mars	Venus
128	Libra	04°53'20"	05°33'20"	Venus	Mars	Sun
129	Libra	05°33'20"	06°40'00"	Venus	Mars	Moon
130	Libra	06°40'00"	08°40'00"	Venus	Rahu	Rahu
131	Libra	08°40'00"	10°26'40"	Venus	Rahu	Jupiter
132	Libra	10°26'40"	12°33'20"	Venus	Rahu	Saturn
133	Libra	12°33'20"	14°26'40"	Venus	Rahu	Mercury
134	Libra	14°26'40"	15°13'20"	Venus	Rahu	Ketu
135	Libra	15°13'20"	17°26'40"	Venus	Rahu	Venus
136	Libra	17°26'40"	18°06'40"	Venus	Rahu	Sun
137	Libra	18°06'40"	19°13'20"	Venus	Rahu	Moon
138	Libra	19°13'20"	20°00'00"	Venus	Rahu	Mars
139	Libra	20°00'00"	21°46'40"	Venus	Jupiter	Jupiter
140	Libra	21°46'40"	23°53'20"	Venus	Jupiter	Saturn
141	Libra	23°53'20"	25°46'40"	Venus	Jupiter	Mercury
142	Libra	25°46'40"	26°33'20"	Venus	Jupiter	Ketu
143	Libra	26°33'20"	28°46'40"	Venus	Jupiter	Venus

NO.	SIGN	FROM (DEG/MIN/SEC)	TO (DEG/MIN/SEC)	SIGN LORD	STAR LORD	SUBLORD
144	Libra	28°46'40"	29°26'40"	Venus	Jupiter	Sun
145	Libra	29°26'40"	30°00'00"	Venus	Jupiter	Moon
146	Scorpio	00°00'00"	00°33'20"	Mars	Jupiter	Moon
147	Scorpio	00°33'20"	01°20'00"	Mars	Jupiter	Mars
148	Scorpio	01°20'00"	03°20'00"	Mars	Jupiter	Rahu
149	Scorpio	03°20'00"	05°26'40"	Mars	Saturn	Saturn
150	Scorpio	05°26'40"	07°20'00"	Mars	Saturn	Mercury
151	Scorpio	07°20'00"	08°06'40"	Mars	Saturn	Ketu
152	Scorpio	08°06'40"	10°20'00"	Mars	Saturn	Venus
153	Scorpio	10°20'00"	11°00'00"	Mars	Saturn	Sun
154	Scorpio	11°00'00"	12°06'40"	Mars	Saturn	Moon
155	Scorpio	12°06'40"	12°53'20"	Mars	Saturn	Mars
156	Scorpio	12°53'20"	14°53'20"	Mars	Saturn	Rahu
157	Scorpio	14°53'20"	16°40'00"	Mars	Saturn	Jupiter
158	Scorpio	16°40'00"	18°33'20"	Mars	Mercury	Mercury
159	Scorpio	18°33'20"	19°20'00"	Mars	Mercury	Ketu
160	Scorpio	19°20'00"	21°33'20"	Mars	Mercury	Venus
161	Scorpio	21°33'20"	22°13'20"	Mars	Mercury	Sun
162	Scorpio	22°13'20"	23°20'00"	Mars	Mercury	Moon
163	Scorpio	23°20'00"	24°06'40"	Mars	Mercury	Mars
164	Scorpio	24°06'40"	26°06'40"	Mars	Mercury	Rahu
165	Scorpio	26°06'40"	27°53'20"	Mars	Mercury	Jupiter
166	Scorpio	27°53'20"	30°00'00"	Mars	Mercury	Saturn

NO.	SIGN	FROM (DEG/MIN/SEC)	TO (DEG/MIN/SEC)	SIGN LORD	STAR LORD	SUBLORD
167	Sagittarius	00°00'00"	00°46'40"	Jupiter	Ketu	Ketu
168	Sagittarius	00°46'40"	03°00'00"	Jupiter	Ketu	Venus
169	Sagittarius	03°00'00"	03°40'00"	Jupiter	Ketu	Sun
170	Sagittarius	03°40'00"	04°46'40"	Jupiter	Ketu	Moon
171	Sagittarius	04°46'40"	05°53'20"	Jupiter	Ketu	Mars
172	Sagittarius	05°53'20"	07°33'20"	Jupiter	Ketu	Rahu
173	Sagittarius	07°33'20"	09°20'00"	Jupiter	Ketu	Jupiter
174	Sagittarius	09°20'00"	11°26'40"	Jupiter	Ketu	Saturn
175	Sagittarius	11°26'40"	13°20'00"	Jupiter	Ketu	Mercury
176	Sagittarius	13°20'00"	15°33'20"	Jupiter	Venus	Venus
177	Sagittarius	15°33'20"	16°13'20"	Jupiter	Venus	Sun
178	Sagittarius	16°13'20"	17°20'00"	Jupiter	Venus	Moon
179	Sagittarius	17°20'00"	18°06'40"	Jupiter	Venus	Mars
180	Sagittarius	18°06'40"	20°06'40"	Jupiter	Venus	Rahu
181	Sagittarius	20°06'40"	21°53'20"	Jupiter	Venus	Jupiter
182	Sagittarius	21°53'20"	24°00'00"	Jupiter	Venus	Saturn
183	Sagittarius	24°00'00"	25°53'20"	Jupiter	Venus	Mercury
184	Sagittarius	25°53'20"	26°40'00"	Jupiter	Venus	Ketu
185	Sagittarius	26°40'00"	27°20'00"	Jupiter	Sun	Sun
186	Sagittarius	27°20'00"	28°26'40"	Jupiter	Sun	Moon
187	Sagittarius	28°26'40"	29°13'20"	Jupiter	Sun	Mars
188	Sagittarius	29°13'20"	30°00'00"	Jupiter	Sun	Rahu
189	Capricorn	00°00'00"	01°13'20"	Saturn	Sun	Rahu

NO.	SIGN	FROM (DEG/MIN/SEC)	TO (DEG/MIN/SEC)	SIGN LORD	STAR LORD	SUBLORD
190	Capricorn	01°13'20"	03°00'00"	Saturn	Sun	Jupiter
191	Capricorn	03°00'00"	05°06'40"	Saturn	Sun	Saturn
192	Capricorn	05°06'40"	07°00'00"	Saturn	Sun	Mercury
193	Capricorn	07°00'00"	07°46'40"	Saturn	Sun	Ketu
194	Capricorn	07°46'40"	10°00'00"	Saturn	Sun	Venus
195	Capricorn	10°00'00"	11°06'40"	Saturn	Moon	Moon
196	Capricorn	11°06'40"	11°53'20"	Saturn	Moon	Mars
197	Capricorn	11°53'20"	13°53'20"	Saturn	Moon	Rahu
198	Capricorn	13°53'20"	15°40'00"	Saturn	Moon	Jupiter
199	Capricorn	15°40'00"	17°46'40"	Saturn	Moon	Saturn
200	Capricorn	17°46'40"	19°40'00"	Saturn	Moon	Mercury
201	Capricorn	19°40'00"	20°46'40"	Saturn	Moon	Ketu
202	Capricorn	20°46'40"	22°40'00"	Saturn	Moon	Venus
203	Capricorn	22°40'00"	23°20'00"	Saturn	Moon	Sun
204	Capricorn	23°20'00"	24°06'40"	Saturn	Mars	Mars
205	Capricorn	24°06'40"	26°06'40"	Saturn	Mars	Rahu
206	Capricorn	26°06'40"	27°53'20"	Saturn	Mars	Jupiter
207	Capricorn	27°53'20"	30°00'00"	Saturn	Mars	Saturn
208	Aquarius	00°00'00"	01°53'20"	Saturn	Mars	Mercury
209	Aquarius	01°53'20"	02°40'00"	Saturn	Mars	Ketu
210	Aquarius	02°40'00"	04°53'20"	Saturn	Mars	Venus
211	Aquarius	04°53'20"	05°33'20"	Saturn	Mars	Sun
212	Aquarius	05°33'20"	06°40'20"	Saturn	Mars	Moon

NO.	SIGN	FROM (DEG/MIN/SEC)	TO (DEG/MIN/SEC)	SIGN LORD	STAR LORD	SUBLORD
213	Aquarius	06°40'20"	08°40'00"	Saturn	Rahu	Rahu
214	Aquarius	08°40'00"	10°26'40"	Saturn	Rahu	Jupiter
215	Aquarius	10°26'40"	12°33'20"	Saturn	Rahu	Saturn
216	Aquarius	12°33'20"	14°26'40"	Saturn	Rahu	Mercury
217	Aquarius	14°26'40"	15°13'20"	Saturn	Rahu	Ketu
218	Aquarius	15°13'20"	17°26'40"	Saturn	Rahu	Venus
219	Aquarius	17°26'40"	18°06'40"	Saturn	Rahu	Sun
220	Aquarius	18°06'40"	19°13'20"	Saturn	Rahu	Moon
221	Aquarius	19°13'20"	20°00'00"	Saturn	Rahu	Mars
222	Aquarius	20°00'00"	21°46'40"	Saturn	Jupiter	Jupiter
223	Aquarius	21°46'40"	23°53'20"	Saturn	Jupiter	Saturn
224	Aquarius	23°53'20"	25°46'40"	Saturn	Jupiter	Mercury
225	Aquarius	25°46'40"	26°33'20"	Saturn	Jupiter	Ketu
226	Aquarius	26°33'20"	28°46'40"	Saturn	Jupiter	Venus
227	Aquarius	28°46'40"	29°26'40"	Saturn	Jupiter	Sun
228	Aquarius	29°26'40"	30°00'00"	Saturn	Jupiter	Moon
229	Pisces	00°00'00"	00°33'20"	Jupiter	Jupiter	Moon
230	Pisces	00°33'20"	01°20'00"	Jupiter	Jupiter	Mars
231	Pisces	01°20'00"	03°20'00"	Jupiter	Jupiter	Rahu
232	Pisces	03°20'00"	05°26'40"	Jupiter	Saturn	Saturn
233	Pisces	05°26'40"	07°20'00"	Jupiter	Saturn	Mercury
234	Pisces	07°20'00"	08°06'40"	Jupiter	Saturn	Ketu
235	Pisces	08°06'40"	10°20'00"	Jupiter	Saturn	Venus

NO.	SIGN	FROM (DEG/MIN/SEC)	TO (DEG/MIN/SEC)	SIGN LORD	STAR LORD	SUBLORD
236	Pisces	10°20'00"	11°00'00"	Jupiter	Saturn	Sun
237	Pisces	11°00'00"	12°06'40"	Jupiter	Saturn	Moon
238	Pisces	12°06'40"	12°53'20"	Jupiter	Saturn	Mars
239	Pisces	12°53'20"	14°53'20"	Jupiter	Saturn	Rahu
240	Pisces	14°53'20"	16°40'00"	Jupiter	Saturn	Jupiter
241	Pisces	16°40'00"	18°33'20"	Jupiter	Mercury	Mercury
242	Pisces	18°33'20"	19°20'00"	Jupiter	Mercury	Ketu
243	Pisces	19°20'00"	21°33'20"	Jupiter	Mercury	Venus
244	Pisces	21°33'20"	22°13'20"	Jupiter	Mercury	Sun
245	Pisces	22°13'20"	23°20'00"	Jupiter	Mercury	Moon
246	Pisces	23°20'00"	24°06'40"	Jupiter	Mercury	Mars
247	Pisces	24°06'40"	26°06'40"	Jupiter	Mercury	Rahu
248	Pisces	26°06'40"	27°53'20"	Jupiter	Mercury	Jupiter
249	Pisces	27°53'20",	30°00'00"	Jupiter	Mercury	Saturn

APPENDIX 2

Points Template

Here is a copy of the points template to help you make sense of the different influences on a contest chart, arriving at a + or − point value for the total, and thereby determining if the favorite (+) is going to win or the underdog (−). Feel free to photocopy this page and use it for your matches, or make your own custom version.

POINTS TEMPLATE

TECHNIQUE	POINTS
Victory house	
SKY/PKY	
Cuspal strength	
Navamsha cuspal strength	
Navamsha combinations	
Sublords	
Sublord array	
Navamsha syllables	
Nakshatra tara	
TOTAL:	

Tara Balam

The sixteenth-century astrologer Satyacharya had a brilliant method of assessing good and bad days based on the nakshatra of the Moon. When the Moon transits the 3rd, 5th, or 7th star from your Moon's birth nakshatra, those days are losing days. They are named accordingly. Here's the full list:

1st Janma: Birth Star
2nd Sampat: Wealth
3rd Vipat: Calamity
4th Kshema: Comfort
5th Pratyari: Enemy
6th Sadhana: Accomplishment
7th Vadha: Death
8th Mitra: Friend
9th Parama Mitra: Great Friend

This means that if you were born in Punarvasu Moon, whenever in the sky the Moon transits nakshatras ruled by Mercury (Ashlesha, Jyeshtha, Revati), Venus (Bharani, Purva Phalguni, Purva Ashadha), and the Moon (Rohini, Hasta, Shravana) it is better to stay away from wagering, starting a business, or other auspicious events. This is especially so if these stars happen to fall in negative houses like the 6th, 8th, or 12th in your horoscope, or if those planets (Mercury, Venus, and Moon) also happen to indicate loss and poverty by, say, being involved in daridra yogas, or being the avayogi of your chart.

On the flip side, for this example, it's good to play when the Moon transits the stars ruled by Saturn, Ketu, the Sun, Mars, and Rahu since these indicate wealth and success. This is especially so if these planets are also involved in positive, wealth-producing yogas in your horoscope.

The birth star's ruler (Jupiter, in this example) is considered mildly malefic and is also avoided for most undertakings, including wagering. As you can see, these are general rules of muhurta used for more than wagering, including planning everything from weddings to business openings.

Another way to gauge when to wager is provided by Jyotishi K. S. Krishnamurti, using his powerful sublord theory. Basically, it's good to invest on days when the Moon is in a star and sublord that is a strong significator for houses 2, 5, and 11, and *not* a significator of houses 1, 4, and 10. For finer timing it is also desirable for the ascendant to be in a star and sublord that signifies these houses as well. For more on this, refer to Krishnamurti's excellent KP Readers.

Glossary

adhi yoga: benefics occupying the 6th, 7th, and 8th houses from the Moon or lagna; in practice, even if two of these houses are occupied by benefics, adhi yoga is still said to exist

ascendant: the 1st house or rising sign, known in Vedic astrology as the *lagna*

ayanamsha: the offset between the sidereal and the tropical zodiacs

bhava: a state of being more commonly referred to as a *house* in Western astrology

bhukti: from the root *bhuj,* "to eat, enjoy, or experience," referring specifically to a dasha subperiod

combustion: when a planet gets too close to the Sun, especially less than 6 degrees

cusp: the concentrated essence of a house; also, in most systems, the point where a house begins

daridra yoga: poverty-inducing planetary combinations, such as when the lord of the 1st house occupies the 12th, and the 12th lord occupies the 1st while aspected by a maraka lord (ruler of house 2 or 7)

dasha: from the root *damsh,* "to bite," referring to one of the major planetary periods totaling 120 years; also called the vimshottari dasha

descendant: the 7th house cusp, exactly 180 degrees away from the ascendant, or lagna

desha: country, place, or space where an event happens

dharma: the right path, or your rightful purpose

dig bala: directional strength, conferred when the visible planets occupy one of the four angular houses: 1, 4, 7, or 10

graha: grabber or planet; a celestial seizer that *grabs* on to us and influences how we express

graha yuddha: planetary war, when two planets fall within 1 degree celestial longitude of each other

house: any one of the twelve divisions of the zodiac that rules an aspect of life; also called a *bhava* in Sanskrit

IC: *imum coeli,* literally "bottom of the sky," representing the nadir, or 4th house cusp

ishta devata: the muse, i.e., the external manifestation of a body of knowledge or an inspirational deity that gives access to this knowledge

jataka: natal astrology

Jyotir Vidya: the muse or goddess of Vedic astrology

Jyotisha: the lore of light, or Vedic astrology

kala: time

kosha: "bodies" or layers of influence

Krishnamurti Paddhati: Krishnamurti's method, the system of sublords innovated by Vedic astrology master K. S. Krishnamurti

kutila: stationary

lagna: the ascendant, or the zodiacal sign and degree rising on the eastern horizon at the specific time and place of an event. The word *lagna* comes from the Sanskrit root *lag,* which means "to tie down." The ascendant of any horoscope *ties down* the heavens to a specific time and locality, making it possible for us to interpret. Celestial phenomena reflect or determine human activity on the esoteric principle of *as above, so below.* Thus the ascendant signifies a person's—or an event's—awakening consciousness, in the same way that the Sun's appearance on the eastern horizon signifies the dawn of a new day.

MC: *medium coeli,* literally "middle of the sky," or 10th house cusp

muhurta: a division of time equal to forty-eight minutes in the Hindu calendar; also, the branch of astrology devoted to selecting the optimum time for a future event

mutual reception: see PY

nakshatra: an asterism or mini constellation, with a span of 13°20', sometimes also called a lunar mansion—these lunar mansions are said to be (or at least to house) the consorts of the Moon, as the Moon spends one night in each nakshatra before moving on to the next; accordingly, there are 27 days in the lunar month, and twenty-seven nakshatras. In Vedic astrology the nakshatras are personified as feminine, while all the planets are masculine.

nastikas: nonbelievers; people who are not in line with the spirit of dharma

natal chart: the chart for the birth (or nativity) of any event, including humans, animals, and sporting events. In humans it is taken as the moment a baby draws its first breath. For games, it is based on the exact moment the game begins, i.e., tipoff, kickoff, or the first pitch.

navamsha: a harmonic subdivision of the main chart, the navamsha is the ninth division, also used to assess relationships; also known as the D9

patra: vessel; the capacity of a team or person

PKY: papa katari yoga, formed when the ascendant is hemmed in on both sides by malefic planets

prashna: a horary chart; a question chart cast for the moment the question is asked, or the moment the astrologer sits to analyze it

PY: parivartana yoga, or mutual reception, occurs when two planets occupy each other's signs, strengthening both planets in turn

raja yoga: a horoscope combination for success

rashi: heap, an astrological sign; used to refer to the main chart, or D1, as opposed to the divisional charts, which number from D2 to D150

sandhis: junctures in time and space; transitions from one state (*bhava*) to another

sankranti: the sidereal solar ingress, roughly around the fifteenth of every month

Shakti: primordial Divine Mother energy; the creative force

significator: a planet signifying a particular matter or influence in a chart

SKY: shubbha kartari yoga, when the lagna is hemmed in by benefic planets, providing a person or team good health and protection.

tantra: in the Indian traditions, any systematic, broadly applicable text, theory, system, method, instrument, technique, or practice

tara: the main star of a specific nakshatra

upachaya: the best house placements for the natural malefic planets

upagraha: shadow or subplanet that is actually a mathematical point

vastu shastra: the traditional Indian science of architecture

Vedanta: one of the six orthodox schools of Indian philosophy

victory house: referring to a technique wherein planets occupy houses 1, 3, 6, 10, or 11 from their respective ascendant

Suggested Resources

Recommended Astrological Software

Parashara's Light

www.parashara.com

Most of the charts in this book were created in Parashara's Light software, which I use almost exclusively and recommend to students. The following are other good programs I also recommend.

Shri Jyoti Star

vedicsoftware.com

This is excellent Jyotisha software, though complex and somewhat more difficult to learn than Parashara's Light.

Solar Fire

www.esotech.com.au or www.solarfire.info

One of the gold standards of Western astrological software, this program calculates all major fixed-star positions in addition to a myriad of other minor points, including dwarf planets, asteroids, midpoints, and such. I use it to find the minor planet positions (such as Chiron and Ceres) since as of this writing no Vedic astrology software calculates this yet. It also has a nice Vedic astrology feature.

Junior Jyotisha

www.jyotishtools.com

This free software program is made for beginners. Its developers also offer a low-cost app for smartphones. It's useful in a pinch, and I really like their ephemeris.

Beginner Resources for Vedic Astrology

James Kelleher

www.jameskelleher.com

His *Path of Light* books, volume 1, *Introduction to Vedic Astrology,* and volume 2, *The Domains of Life,* were written with the beginner in mind, but can enlighten even advanced practitioners. Kelleher makes simple concepts profound and complex subjects easy to understand. His section on Drekkanas is worth the price of the books itself. A must-have on the shelf of any Jyotisha student or practitioner.

Hart de Fouw and Robert Svoboda

www.vedicvidyainstitute.com and www.drsvoboda.com

Their coauthored *Light on Life: An Introduction to the Astrology of India* is, in my mind, the gold standard for authentic Jyotisha instruction. Like a jungle of Vedic wisdom, it is sometimes difficult to penetrate, but contains deep medicine for the stalwart student.

De Fouw is a living, breathing embodiment of the art and science of Vedic astrology. He is the first Westerner to authentically imbibe and carry on a Vedic tradition normally inaccessible to Western students. His books and classes on jyotisha make for tough reading but set the standard in authentic instruction.

The original ayurvedic Westerner, Svoboda holds the distinction of truly honoring India's spiritual traditions in his books as well as in his life.

Other Resources from the Author

All of the resources listed below and more as well as information about the author's services, seminars, and workshops can be found at **www.spirittype.com**.

Decoding Your Life Map With Vedic Astrology DVD Series

This is my beginner program for people who want to know what their chart says about them. Dive into discovering the secrets of Vedic astrology using your own horoscope as a guide.

The Dharma Types

My website contains both basic information about and a test to determine your dharma type. Further information about the dharma types can be found in my books *The Five Dharma Types: Vedic Wisdom for Discovering Your Purpose and Destiny* and *Sex, Love, and Dharma: Ancient Wisdom for Modern Relationships.*

Index

Books of Related Interest

The Five Dharma Types
Vedic Wisdom for Disovering Your Purpose and Destiny
by Simon Chokoisky

Sex, Love, and Dharma
Ancient Wisdom for Modern Relationships
by Simon Chokoisky

The Science of Getting Rich
Attracting Financial Success through Creative Thought
by Wallace D. Wattles

The DNA Field and the Law of Resonance
Creating Reality through Conscious Thought
by Pierre Franckh

Numerology
With Tantra, Ayurveda, and Astrology
by Harish Johari

The Complete I Ching—10th Anniversary Edition
The Definitive Translation by Taoist Master Alfred Huang
by Taoist Master Alfred Huang

Aspects in Astrology
A Guide to Understanding Planetary Relationships in the Horoscope
by Sue Tompkins

How to Practice Vedic Astrology
A Beginner's Guide to Casting Your Horoscope and Predicting Your Future
by Andrew Bloomfield

INNER TRADITIONS • BEAR & COMPANY
P.O. Box 388
Rochester, VT 05767
1-800-246-8648
www.InnerTraditions.com

Or contact your local bookseller